Imagination and Meaning

Edited by
Norman J. Girardot
and
Mac Linscott Ricketts

Imagination and Meaning

The Scholarly
and Literary Worlds
of Mircea Eliade

The Seabury Press / New York

1982
The Seabury Press
815 Second Avenue
New York, N.Y. 10017

Printed in the United States of America

Library of Congress Cataloging in Publication Data

Main entry under title:
Imagination and meaning.

Includes index.
1. Eliade, Mircea, 1907–   . I. Girardot,
N.J. II. Ricketts, Mac L.
BL43.E414   291'.092'4   81–13535
ISBN 0–8164–2371–7   AACR2

*The editors gratefully acknowledge the permission of Harcourt Brace Jovanovich, Inc. and Faber
& Faber Ltd. in reprinting selections of T. S. Eliot's "Little Gidding" from* Four Quartets,
copyright, 1943, by T. S. Eliot, copyright, 1971, by Esme Valerie Eliot.

To Mircea Eliade on his seventy–fifth anniversary of birth

When a writer leaves monuments on the different steps of his life, it is chiefly important that he should have an innate foundation and good-will; that he should, at each step, have seen and felt clearly, and that, without any secondary aims, he should have said distinctly and truly what has passed in his mind. Then will his writings, if they were right at the step where they originated, remain always right, however the writer may develop or alter himself in after times.

Goethe

from *Conversations of Goethe with Eckermann and Soret*, trans. by John Oxenfourd (London: George Bell and Sons, 1874), p. 510

Contents

Preface ix

Norman J. Girardot
Introduction
Imagining Eliade: A Fondness for Squirrels 1

Part I Meaning and the Scholarly World
Adrian Marino
Mircea Eliade's Hermeneutics 19

Douglas Allen
Phenomenological Method and the Dialectic of the Sacred 70

Mircea Eliade
The Fact (from *Fragmentarium*) 82

**Part II Coincidentia Oppositorum:
Reflections on Parallel Worlds**
Seymour Cain
Poetry and Truth: The Double Vocation in Eliade's Journals
and Other Autobiographical Writings 87

Mac Linscott Ricketts
Mircea Eliade and the Writing of *The Forbidden Forest* 104

Mircea Eliade
Autobiographical Fragment 113

Part III Meaning and the Literary World
Eugen Simion
The Mythical Dignity of Narration 131

Matei Calinescu
The Function of the Unreal: Reflections on Mircea
Eliade's Short Fiction 138

Mircea Eliade
Good-bye! 162

Part IV Oceanographic Fragments
About Miracle and Event (from *Oceanografie*) 181

Concerning the "Unseen God" and Other Fragments
(from *Soliloquies*) 184

Inferior Forms of Mysticism (from *Fragmentarium*) 189

A Detail from Parsifal (from *Insula lui Euthanasius*) 191

Notes about Genius
(from *Fragmentarium*) 196

A Great Man (from *Oceanografie*) 199

The Detective Novel (from *Oceanografie*) 201

About a Certain "Sacrifice" (from *Fragmentarium*) 205

Contributors 208

Index 210

Preface

Some of the story of the conception and prolonged gestation of this volume needs to be told. Its almost mythical origins go back now several years and are related to the University of Notre Dame Press publication of Mircea Eliade's novel, *The Forbidden Forest*, and the decision of Professor Norman Girardot to mark that event with a conference devoted to the twin scholarly and literary passions of Eliade's career. With funding provided by the Notre Dame Theology Department, a three-day conference entitled "Coincidentia Oppositorum: The Scholarly and Literary Worlds of Mircea Eliade," was convened in April, 1978, which attracted scholars representing such disciplines as the history of religions, anthropology, theology, philosophy, and comparative literature. To those who either gave or responded to papers (Professors Douglas Allen, Jay Kim, John Saliba, Charles Long, Reginald Ray, Frank Podgorski, Hans Penner, Mac Ricketts, Virgil Nemioanu, Matei Calinescu, Thomas Munson, Gilford Dudley, and James Hart), and to all others who participated in that stimulating and happy affair, we take this opportunity to express again our appreciation.

We would also like to note that on the last evening of the conference, with Professor Eliade in attendance, a unique dramatic reading of Eliade's play, "The Endless Column," which concerns the famous Romanian sculptor Constantin Brâncuşi, was staged under the direction of Professor Miles Coiner and students from the Notre Dame-St. Mary's Speech and Drama Department. This proved to be an especially memorable moment—a time when one of the stories told so tirelessly by Eliade truly recaptured some of the expressive and haunting power of a myth unbroken from its ritual dramatization. We can only reiterate our special gratitude to Professor Coiner who, in addition to directing, portrayed a particularly impassioned and convincing Brancusi, to his students, and also to Mary Park Stevenson who provided the English translation of the Romanian text and to Professor Florence Hetzler who introduced the production.

The success of the conference naturally led to the idea of a book which would expand on the discussion of the nature and significance of Eliade's scholarly and literary enterprise. With this in mind, the editors felt that a meaningful analysis and appreciation of Eliade's *opus* could best be served by a work that was more than just a proceedings of the conference. Regretfully, therefore, a number of the original conference presentations are not included; while a few papers published here were first delivered at Notre Dame (i.e., those by Allen and Calinescu), the others were selected, translated, or commissioned especially for this volume. Most significant in this regard was the decision to include selections by Eliade, heretofore unpublished in English translation, which illustrated each of the thematic divisions of the book. One of the editors, Professor Mac Ricketts, translated all of the articles which were originally published in Romanian by Eliade, Marino, and Simion.

It is impossible to note all those who deserve thanks for their advice, help, and encouragement during the protracted production of this book. We would, however, like to acknowledge the understanding and generosity of Oberlin College in providing a special grant for the completion of the editorial work. Finally, we want to mention the special help and support, in all sorts of ways both important and trivial, rendered by Douglas Allen and Seymour Cain.

N. J. Girardot
Lehigh University

M. L. Ricketts
Louisburg College

The concept of *imaginatio* is perhaps the most important key to the understanding of the *opus*.

C. G. Jung
Psychology and Alchemy

Norman J. Girardot

Introduction Imagining Eliade: A Fondness for Squirrels

I

Because man does not imagine perfectly at all times, arts and sciences are uncertain, though, in fact, they are certain and, by means of imagination can give true results. Imagination takes precedence over all. Resolute imagination can accomplish all things.

Paracelsus[1]

From the beginning, it was Mircea Eliade's personal myth that he was fated to live and work reciprocally in the two worlds of reason and imagination, fact and fiction. While he is primarily renowned for his numerous scholarly works in the history of world religions, the recent publication in English of some of his major literary creations, as well as the reflections found in his journals and autobiographical writings, serve to dramatize the interrelated importance of both scholarly and literary activities throughout Eliade's career. As E. M. Cioran tells us, Eliade was always "drawn, with equal attraction, to essence and accident."[2]

1

This "deep-seated duality" in Eliade's character and work makes the decipherment of his significance all the more difficult since his scholarship and fiction dialectically overlap in method and intention.[3] In fact Eliade more than once suggests that his historical and literary works episodically constitute a single grand opus. It is, however, a work that is without closure, always in process and waiting to be finished "by someone else."[4] For many of his critics such an epic creativity and confluence of methods and interests is romantically naive, superannuated, or simply "pathetic and ludicrous."[5] Aside from the polar extremes of a cloying acceptance by initiates or an indignant damnation by some professional academics, the shifting interplay between the concrete and the ideal, history and fiction, reason and imagination in Eliade's work has, at the very least, led to critical bewilderment. In this sense, for example, Northrop Frye once found his scholarship intriguing but insensitive to literature while, more recently, and armed with the confessions of Eliade's journals, a reviewer for the *Times Literary Supplement* found him essentially a literary artist who is only accidentally and reluctantly masquerading as a critical scholar.[6]

The real paradox of Eliade is yet to be imagined fully by his devotees or critics. As the articles in this book cumulatively suggest, it is precisely the mystery of the accidental nature of essence in the human experience of the world that has meaning for Eliade and prevents his work from being merely schizophrenic. Thus in an early essay Eliade remarked that if he had to choose between a "truth and a paradox" he would "choose the paradox."[7] The difference is that "truths change, but paradox is of such a nature that it remains always full, real, and justified."[8] Characteristically this statement is itself paradoxically enigmatic and, at the same time, an essential truth for and about Eliade. Above all else, an "absence of curiosity" about the overwhelming and swarming vitality of life is "a proof of impotence and mediocrity."[9] To discover the meaning of human experience as paradox requires, therefore, a method for understanding and interpretation that is also paradoxical, full, imaginative, vital, and remains always open to the hidden and partial disclosure of essence in "what William James called life's 'buzzing, blooming confusion.' "[10]

Eliade's idea of truth is not that there is essence—or, for that matter, the "Sacred"—as the really real, with accident as its unreal shadow or veil. In keeping with his *Māyā*-like metaphysics, what he does suggest is that the ideal *becomes* real and is known only accidentally.[11] Reality depends on the accident of creation. What is imaginary is *made* a fact in time. What is real and has meaning is by virtue of the creation of the world as the temporal embodiment of the imaginary, the fact that the ideal came into historical existence. In this way, essence is the source of reality but becomes meaningful only because of the creation and reality of the concrete world of things, facts, events—only because of the consciousness and historicity of man, the experience of temporality where something actually happened, is happening, and will happen. The felt tension of human life is that, like language, life has tense. Understanding from this perspective requires a method that is alive. It calls for, as Eliade frequently reminds us, a "creative hermeneutics" which is capable of finding a hidden coherence, grammar, or narrativity in human history.[12]

This methodological perspective indicates Eliade's particular indebtedness to the German tradition of historiography and metaphysical idealism from Herder and Goethe through Dilthey. German idealism generally represented a rejection of the Enlightenment concern for a wholly rational or abstract understanding of man in favor of a more romantic affirmation that "within natural human experience one can find the clue to an understanding of the ultimate nature of reality, and this clue is revealed through those traits which distinguish man as a spiritual being."[13] Finding the inner spiritual unity of man, nature, and culture calls for a kind of romantic empiricism, a confluence of reason and imagination, or, in Diltheyan terms, a combination of realism and idealism.[14] This entails an historical approach to understanding which respects the concrete diversity and constant transformation of lived experience and, at the same time, seeks an imaginative reconstruction of the inner spiritual meaning of historical forms.

In sympathy with these convictions coming from German tradition, and in consideration of the fact that Eliade has claimed Goethe, along with Balzac, as his most important scientific and literary model ("as always I see Goethe's destiny as my own"),[15] the concern for essence or essential meanings—ideal systems, patterns, archetypes, structures—is not identical with a concern for the Platonic *eidos*—"something separate in existence or even in thought" from the particular or accidental.[16] Paradoxically, essence "exists only in and through the particular and can be known only by opening our eyes and hearts to the sensuous living world."[17]

It is in this way that Eliade tells us that he follows a "structuralist" methodology in the mode of Dumézil, Propp, and especially Goethe. Thus Goethe, in his morphological study of plants, felt that "one could relate all vegetable forms" to that which he called the essential, original, or "primordial plant" (*Ürpflanze*).[18] In the Goethean sense, an authentic structural or "morphological enterprise is 'to recognize living forms as such, to see in context their visible and tangible parts, to perceive them as manifestations of something within and thus to master them to a certain extent in their wholeness through a concrete vision (*An-*

schauung).' "[19] Moreover, Propp's structuralism draws upon this same idea and is indicated by the fact that "in the Russian edition of the *Morphology of Fairy Tales* each chapter epigraphically carries a long passage from the work of Goethe."[20] Applying this to his own work, Eliade says that "in order to see clearly into the ocean of facts, forms, rites, the historian of religions must in his own domain search for 'the primordial plant,' the primordial image."[21] For Eliade the kind of "structuralism" that seems "to be fruitful is that which consists of an examination into the essence of an ensemble of phenomena, into the primordial order which is the foundation of meaning."[22]

Eliade's embracing of a Goethean morphological method clearly sets his structuralism apart from that of the Lévi-Straussian variety since, for Eliade, structure, while by definition atemporal, is indissolubly linked with historical experience. Meaning depends not just on the discovery of a single paradigmatic binary form or code but on accidental content—what was created and experienced in history. This idea of structure recalls Dilthey's notion of an *erworbener Zusammenhang,* a "structure of the mind," which is linked to "concrete, real, dynamic systems."[23] Rather than a totally abstract structuralism, Eliade like Dilthey, as well as Goethe and Propp, emphasizes the importance of the "contents of the structure and the relationships of those contents."[24] Thus in seeking to understand the meaning of a myth, Eliade's structural method is both morphological and syntagmatic to the extent that it depends, in varying degrees, on an appreciation of the particular existential form or content of the symbols employed (e.g., a tree rather than a snake) and on the narrative order of the elements in the myth. Moreover, as Ricoeur notes in his review of the first volume of Eliade's *History of Religious Ideas,* the meaning of religion is not only to be found in the repetition of archaisms, but in the fact that, for example, the "great myths of origins come to light in history as bearers of *irreducible difference.*"[25] It is the "inexhaustible capacity for *reinterpretation*" that insures that religion has a history and "is not absorbed into the morphology of the sacred."[26] In other words, structure, or the "fundamental unity" of religion, is ultimately nonhistorical but meaning depends on the real, though hidden, relation that exists between structure and history.

Meaning can only be understood cosmogonically, as a creation which is made possible by temporal experience. Meaning depends on the act of interpretation as a re-creation or discovery of a relation between both historical content and ideal form, accident and essence. Eliade is consequently Lévi-Strauss' "binary opposite" since Eliade fundamentally affirms the phenomemological principle that there is a necessary continuity between experience and reality. Lévi-Strauss, on the contrary, states that while experience and reality obviously envelop and explain each other, "there is no continuity in the passage between the two and that to reach reality we must first repudiate experience, even though we may later reintegrate it into an objective synthesis in which sentimentality plays no part."[27] As Clifford Geertz remarks, this is really to preach the sentiments of the "universal rationalism of the French Enlightenment."[28] For Eliade and Goethe, as in the phenomenological hermeneutics of Merleau-Ponty, a coherent theory of structuralism should include historical and subjective experience: "structural analysis must take place within phenomenology in that its goal must be that of explicating and formalizing what is phenomenally given in the subject's relation to his cultural objects."[29] To reach the structure of reality we must see with experience to see through it.

Given to this kind of phenomenological sentiment, if not sentimentality, and never in danger of being accused of a lapidary style or crisp enunciation of principle, Eliade's scholarly writings in the history of religions remain delphic exactly to the extent that they have said so much, eternally returning to the same essential themes yet constantly uncovering a new historical content. There is finally an inexhaustible number of more myths and stories to be told and retold. Eliade's scholarship is paradoxical because his "history" of religions is so creatively imaginative, so impossibly repetitious, so essentially unverifiable, so apparently fictitious. As one commentator has put it, "Eliade's weakness is that he is all too prone to bend his sources, however recalcitrant, to the exigencies of his creative imagination."[30] As this critic goes on to say, " 'creative spontaneity' is one thing, accurate scholarship is quite another. Can the two be combined? This is the dilemma between the horns of which Professor Eliade has uneasily perched for some forty years."[31] Only compounding this dilemma is Eliade's production of literary universes where he tells "made-up" or unreal stories, where imaginative creation is totally free yet, as he claims, accidentally discloses meanings discovered, or *still to be discovered*, by his historical research.[32] In other words, Eliade must finally be seen as the leading "anti-historian of religions,"[33] for, after all, as he seems to admit in his journals, he imagines meanings "even when they aren't there."[34]

II

Could we not say that by opening us to the different, history opens us to the possible, while fiction, by opening us to the unreal, brings us back to the essential?

Paul Ricoeur

Eliade certainly would espouse the dictum that historical and literary understanding, philosophy and romance, "take their origin in the Prin-

ciple of Wonder."[35] But while historical interpretation and literary creation can both partake of a general similarity of narrative form, they
draw upon the constructive power of the imagination in varying degrees and with an important referential difference. Historical interpretation depends on its meaningful ordering of culturally shared facts,
documents, texts. Historical insight is bound to the reality of what was
already made, done, imagined, or created in the remembered and
verifiable past. Historical sources, however, are not just facts pure and
simple but were once created, imagined, or "made-up" ("facts are *facta,*
things made") as symbols, stories, rites, texts, or intrepretations which
cultures preserve because they have said and continue to "say something of something."[36] As Eliade notes, it is finally not facts that are
important for human knowledge—but *"the fact"* that something was
created and experienced by men in history.[37]

Literary fabulation, on the other hand, depends on the free act of
imagining a parallel or metaphorical reality. History imaginatively reas-
sembles the real to discover the meaning of past creations; fiction imaginatively orders the unreal to create meaning. Thus history refers to
the meaning of what was created and fiction tells of the meaning of
the act of creation. Both represent *interpretations* of human experience
and both, in their own way, require the use of the interpretive faculty,
the imagination, to make understanding possible.

The critical question is not whether history and imagination can ever
be combined, but whether they can ever be really separated? This is
not to suggest that Eliade's hermeneutic for the history of religions
magically absolves itself of sins committed in the name of history.
Indeed, there is no doubt that Eliade sometimes seems to manipulate
his historical details to fit with a predetermined synthetic pattern.
Eliade, however, does not consider his scholarly work to be immune
from all canons of historical integrity or verification.[38] As emphasized
in his "Autobiographical Fragment," he has always abhorred the di-
lettante who consciously disregards or distorts historical sources in
favor of a completely personal vision.[39]

While recognizing the need for the history of religions to be grounded
firmly in specialized philological and historical scholarship, Eliade
would maintain that the capitulation to a concern for only specialized
analysis results in a dehumanization of the act of understanding since
it ignores the universal human meaning, the interpretive quality, of
the very texts and facts it studies. It fails precisely because it neglects
the creative element which links the subject and object of research.
Since any interpretation is not just a determination of facts but a rec-
reation of the fact and meaning of creation itself, all interpretations are
fated to be provisional. For Eliade, as with Goethe, it is finally the case

that a poor or incomplete synthesis is better than none at all. At least with an interpretive synthesis there is something that means something; at the very least there is something to be revised. In fact, the real issue concerning the merit of Eliade's scholarship is not so much that it has given rise to fawning admiration by disciples or outright dismissal by specialists, but that there has been so little critically sensitive and intelligent revision of his work from either a theoretical or factual standpoint. In line with his own methodological premises, Eliade's interpretations seek systematic reinterpretation and constructive correction.[40]

Given these considerations it must be said that Eliade's previously mentioned confession that he finds meanings "even when they aren't there" refers only to his personal interpretation of his accidental history as a wandering exile. Viewing his personal life as a story with initiatory meanings—"even if they aren't there"—does not, therefore, directly reflect on the significance of his historical research but rather on the general human need expressed in history, fiction, and myth for finding a meaning, structure, message or story, "in the formless flow of things and the monotonous flux of historical facts."[41] Man must always create meaning in order to live. The paradox here is that Eliade's ideal fiction about himself, having been creatively imagined and recorded, has fallen into history and becomes a meaningful fact about Eliade.

It should also be noted that Eliade is acutely aware of the need to keep his historical and fictional work separate in his own life. Indeed, he tells us that it is the oscillation between the two poles of the real and the unreal that is essential to his "spiritual equilibrium" and general creativity in both realms.[42] Granting a proper distinction between historical and literary activity, both, in their rhythmic interplay, show themselves as complementary "instruments of knowledge."[43] Dialectically in fiction one escapes time in the purely ideal in order to return to time to find the timeless in the real. The unreal rhythmically refreshes the real.

For Eliade, stories of the real and the unreal are "interdependent and express a profound unity, because they have to do with the same 'subject,' *man*—more precisely, with the mode of existence in the world specific to man and his decision to assume this mode of existence."[44] What Eliade means is that the "mode of existence in the world specific to man" is to live *as if* the world had some meaning. Man, in other words, decides to live as if the world was symbolic and discloses something meaningful amidst the accidental. "In the final analysis," Eliade says, "the world reveals itself as language."[45] The world discovered as language or symbol gives rise to meaning by a special act of language—the telling of stories. In this sense, the "only meaning of existence is the finding of meaning,"[46] and the finding or creation of meaning, the interpretation of experience, most fundamentally and organically involves the "mythical dignity of narration."[47] To be human is to interpret, and to interpret "is to narrate, to unfold stories from other stories."[48] History and fiction, therefore, intersect with myth as imaginative and narrative modes of finding meaning in the face of the "formless flow of things." All three represent modes of interpretation, narrative ways of both finding and creating a narrativity in experience.

In keeping with Eliade's idea of the interpretive or cognitive function of story telling, Paul Ricoeur emphasizes that the historicity of human experience "can be brought to language only as narrativity and that this narrativity itself requires no less than the intersecting interplay of the two modes (of history and fiction)."[49] "Historicity," Ricoeur goes on to say, "is *said* to the extent that we *tell* both stories and histories."[50] Extending this along Eliadian lines, could it not also be said that as a sacred history, as a story which by definition grounds historicity in the essential, myth represents the functional convergence of history and fiction? Like history, myth finds meaning in what was created and is real and, like fiction, myth imaginatively creates an original, essential, or hidden universe parallel to the everyday world. Myth says that human life had a dramatic and meaningful plot from the very beginning of the world. More fully than either history or fiction because it is both at the same time, myth tells the story of the meaning of the world as story.

The story that Eliade tells us by means of his scholarly remembrance of past myths and his literary creation of new fables is that religion is the most profound and meaningful way of interpreting the story of human existence. Most generally, culture is the human interpretation of the world, a fabulation of a cognitive or symbolic world of meaning parallel to the world of nature. Religion, as a cultural system, is a particular interpretation of the meaning of culture as creative interpretation. Religion specifies a symbolic content which asserts an essential continuity between human cultural creation and an original divine creation of the natural world.

The problem and paradox of religion is that it is a cultural institution which interprets cultural interpretations of experience as having more than just cultural, historical, or accidental significance. Religion in myth and rite says that culture is meaningful because, like the creation of the natural world, the human world is also a creation having a sacred, ultimate, or essential foundation. In a "primitive" or traditional sense, culture gives meaning to human life by finding a religious message hidden in the fact of existence itself. Myth says that the creation of culture has meaning because it is a reenactment of the first divine act of creation—the power to make something exist out of what was only imagined. Culture is a fiction which mythically becomes fact.

Another issue here is that while religion traditionally interprets human experience as being ultimately and essentially meaningful, the history of religions tends to tell of the progressively more difficult ability of man to be religious, to see any essential meaning in existence or cultural life. Eliade's history of religions most of all discloses the theme of the increasingly complete disguise of the religious significance of the world, the inability to find a sacred mystery in the merely anecdotal. In the history of religions the passage toward a more complete "unrecognizability of the sacred" is indicated by the replacement of myth as the sacred history of man by a situation where history explains reality as wholly accidental and fiction explains nothing at all. Thus in history, myth and religion progressively become just fictions and the real meaning of experience is interpreted as completely historical or only accidental.

This theme pervades all of Eliade's work and runs as a leitmotif throughout many of the interpretations of Eliade found in this book. It also represents another reason why, in the absence of a living mythic tradition, Eliade feels he must tell both scholarly and literary stories which, on the one hand, find an essential meaning in history by comparing past myths and, on the other hand, imaginatively prolong the cognitive function of the ideal or fantastic in fiction. Eliade's *yin* and *yang* of history and fiction, therefore, is finally his attempt to recapture for himself and others exiled in modern history the more meaningful rhythm of a religious interpretation of human experience.

Eliade's story or mock drama, "Good-bye!," published here for the first time in English, is especially revealing both for his interpretive understanding of the whole history of religions and his own vocational self-understanding as an historian of religions—a "would-have-been believer" or "a religious mind without religion."[51] This story suggests, to borrow again from Cioran, that it is Eliade's fate, as well as the fate of modern man in general, to stand, "on the periphery of every religion, by profession as well as conviction."[52] It is our destiny, then, to be almost completely deaf (aside from, perhaps, some children and women) to God's single word of farewell whispered at the beginning of human history. In distinction to primitive man, and the rare saints and religious founders of civilizational tradition who could periodically overcome the opacity of history by becoming actors in the mythic drama of God's first and last word to man, modern man is fated to be the bored and impatient spectator of a drama completely obscured by the curtain of cultural history. The problem is that in "waiting for Godot," modern man must, because of the crushing weight of his very historicity and secularity, find some meaning in boredom or just be bored to death.

That most modern men can only be saved by discovering the sacrality of the mundane is to say that for Eliade the experience of meaning-lessness and alienation in modern life really heightens the paradoxical tension whereby the essential is hidden in what is completely profane. For modern man it is the most accidental, the most utterly banal and ordinary experiences of secular life, that potentially disclose a mean-ingful message of the hidden spiritual continuity of culture, nature, and history. But this is the case only if men are historically and imag-inatively prepared to see and hear meaning in what appears to be completely absurd. In this way it can be said that it is especially difficult to rediscover an essential meaning in modern life because it is so en-tirely obvious, so seamlessly a part of what is wholly mundane and accidental. As Tom Robbins shows us, it is the improbable and ridic-ulous situation of modern man to have to wrest sacred meaning from the symbolic text of a Camel pack—"a vessel of symbolic truth un-precedented in the last quarter of the twentieth century, a virtual lunar Bible, compact, accessible and concise, befitting a transistorized age."[53]

III

. . . nous sommes très heureux, parce qu'il y a toujours des écureuils qui viennent mendier des amandes.

Mircea Eliade

All our language, all our thought and opinion, all our deeply felt symbolism, Burke reminds us, comes from the world of things, the world of bumping atoms, thoughtless squirrels and trucks, so that before we can get to the great idea True, an emotionally charged symbolic construct for which innumerable women and men have died, we must first stare thoughtfully and long at a tree, Old English treow, which gives us the word true (treow), the "deeply rooted" idea.

John Gardner

Lives, like religions and cultures, "contain their own interpretations," and "one has only to learn how to gain access to them."[54] One way to gain access to Eliade, therefore, is to listen imaginatively to some of his stories of self-interpretation and, in keeping with the principle of the "hiddenness of the obvious and the obviousness of the hidden"[55] outlined above, I would like to retell an utterly banal story told by Eliade about himself.

In a conversation with an anthropologist at the University of Chicago, shortly after his arrival from Paris, Eliade tells us that he was asked about what had most impressed him so far concerning the United States.[56] Eliade whimsically remembers that he quickly answered, "the squirrels," referring to those that inhabit the university campus. Reflecting later on the extreme bemusement of his anthropological colleague, and his apparent attempt to interpret this remark as some kind of symbolic or ironic illusion to the "American situation," Eliade notes in his journals that his experience of squirrels in Chicago was not symbolic in terms of any hidden sociological reference but rather referred to his experience of a miniature and fleeting epiphany of religious significance. It was an occasion for the imaginative rediscovery of some of the lost religious meaning of the relation between man and animal.

In retelling this story later in Europe, Eliade offers us an interpretation of the meaning he found in that experience "when the first squirrel had approached my outstretched hand to take an almond":

> Every time distrust, enmity, the struggle for life, everything that characterizes the relations between man and beast seems to me to be abolished—even if it's only for an instant—a powerful and obscure emotion takes over inside me. As if the actual condition of man and of the world were canceled and the paradisiac epoch glorified by the primitive myths were reestablished. Then, *in illo tempore*, before the "Fall," before "sin," men lived in peace with the wild beasts; they understood their language and spoke to them as friends. Friendship with the wild animals and the understanding of their language are both paradisiac and eschatological syndromes. The day the suckling child plays with the viper and the young kid gambols beside the leopard, history will be nearing its end and the Messianic age will be at hand. Hermits and the saints recover—but only for themselves— that friendship with the beasts.[57]

Eliade concludes by saying that "what is encouraging is that a man of today," a man lost in the meaningless grey concrete landscape of Chicago, can still "be so deeply moved by the friendship of an untamed animal."[58]

For his critics it is discouraging to find that a distinguished scholar at the University of Chicago would admit to such imaginative nonsense which reads like a particularly overwrought scene from "Bambi" as it might be written by Ingmar Bergman. Indeed Eliade acerbates this critical impression by repeating and elaborating upon his story about squirrels and almonds. Thus in a recent interview Eliade again remarks on his fondness for squirrels as a signal of transcendance and adds that he was equally impressed by the appearance of cardinals in Chicago, a bird which is rarely seen in Europe. Eliade continues by observing that the cardinal is a species of bird which poses the theological problem of Providence. How, without Providence, he asks, could this flamboyantly red bird have survived, especially since "it is unable to camouflage itself, even to the extent that in a tree it is particularly visible . . ."[59]

Darwin would not be amused, but what is remarkable is that, with respect to the significance of Eliade's squirrels and cardinals, many theologians would be as embarrassed as any sociologist. This is only to say that Eliade is not entirely acceptable within the main cultural currents of scholarly and literary opinion. Eliade has the old-fashioned audacity to trust the meaning of meaning to his "powerful and obscure emotion" for squirrels. Eliade is consequently often ignored or dismissed because he is so naively uncynical, so given to a "hermeneutics of trust" rather than a "hermeneutics of suspicion."[60]

In taking religion and the creative imagination seriously, Eliade has been intellectually unfashionable within some influential academic circles for so long that his scholarly and literary works, as well as their unity of interpretive intent, may yet be found to be more than quaintly romantic. It is therefore noteworthy that there has been a growing cultural response and critical celebration of the return of a readable fiction where storytelling is given precedence over the idea of literature as a semiotic exercise. The return of a fiction which raises questions of the essential meaning and value of human experience is seen, for example, in the increasing popularity of the mythically episodic narrative genres of science fiction, fantasy, and horror novels and, more seriously, in Doris Lessing and Nabokov's work (especially *Ada*), the importance of the "magical realism" of recent Latin American fiction, and the reappearance of an American literature that displays more of what Elizabeth Sewell calls the "Orphic voice" and John Gardner calls "moral fiction."[61] With regard to scholarship, this turn of affairs may also be suggested by the increasing influence of the more phenomenologically interpretive and humanistic anthropology-sociology of such figures, among others, as Clifford Geertz, Victor Turner, Mary Douglas, and Robert Bellah.[62] The same is true, in different degrees, for other academic disciplines and, despite the continued popularity of Wilson's "sociobiology," Harris's protein-depleted cannibals, Jayne's "breakdown of the bicameral mind," and Lévi-Strauss' neo-rationalist "structuralism," there is at least a rumor that Gödel, Escher, and Bach can be meaningfully compared and that, perhaps after all, "chimps don't chat."[63]

These are only a few random examples of what can be called an inchoate "post-modernist" shift toward a sensibility that in some important ways comes close to Eliade's hermeneutical vision.[64] Whatever such developments portend by way of a more profound critical appreciation of either Eliade's scholarly or literary works remains to be seen. It will, of course, depend on how these accidental cultural signs, and Eliade, are interpreted—what story is told about their comparative significance. Some of those stories are told here.

Returning to Eliade's fondness for squirrels it should simply be remarked that, despite one's critical persuasion and preparedness to suspend disbelief, Eliade is, after all, only telling us a story about what that incident meant to him. It represents only a small and absurdly mundane event that imaginatively allowed him to remember other forgotten stories and myths of a meaningful relation between man and animal. Eliade's interpretation of his own experience is made-up, but not just personal, since the history of religions shows us that the chance encounter between men and wild animals did once have a religious significance and was told of in traditional tales. While "hermits and the saints" recover the full experience of sacredness, they live outside of modern history and achieve it "only for themselves." Having an "educated imagination," knowing the history of religions, however, allows the meaning of the sacredness of life to be shared culturally and rediscovered historically by all men.[65] Knowing the history of religions, therefore, allows a modern man to see the universal human and cultural significance of experiences that seem only personal, irrelevant, and accidental.

Eliade in his history of religions, novels, short stories, journals, and other writings makes us appreciate that we have not seen what is most simple, obvious, and true—because it is so "deeply rooted" in ordinary human experience. This was something which was seen and expressed mythically in the past but is now hidden because of its sheer familiarity and triviality, because such an encounter and sentiment is interpreted as meaningless. Knowing myths and stories, then, helps us to remember and recover part of our essential humanity. It helps us to know that we can rediscover the hidden religious meaning of our own lives, even if it is only an imaginary creation. Although we may not be able to share Eliade's "powerful and obscure emotion," especially when we face a situation where all the squirrels are stuffed, we are still left with his stories.

Notes

1. For the head quotations to each section see: John Hargrave, *The Life and Soul of Paracelsus* (London: Victor Gollancz, 1951), p. 72; Paul Ricoeur, "The Narrative Function," *Semeia* 13 (1978), p. 198; Mircea Eliade (Conversations with Claude-Henri Rocquet), *L' Epreuve du labyrinthe* (Paris: Pierre Belfond, 1978), p. 126; and John Gardner, *On Moral Fiction* (New York: Basic Books, 1978), p. 67.

2. E. M. Cioran, "Beginnings of a Friendships," p. 407 in Joseph M. Kitagawa and Charles H. Long, ed., *Myths and Symbols, Studies in Honor of Mircea Eliade* (Chicago: University of Chicago Press, 1969).

3. Ibid.

4. Mircea Eliade, *No Souvenirs* (New York: Harper & Row, 1977), p. 72.

5. T. O. Beidelman, review of Eliade's *Zalmoxis* in the *Journal for the Scientific Study of Religion* 12 (1973), p. 365.

6. Northrop Frye, "World Enough Without Time," *Hudson Review* 12 (1959), pp. 430–431; and "The Odyssey of the Reluctant Professor," review of Eliade's *Fragments d'un Journal* in *Times Literary Supplement*, January 18 (1954), p. 50.

7. Mircea Eliade, *Soliloquies*, unpublished trans. by M. L. Ricketts, xerox copy, p. 41. Originally published as *Soliloquii* (Bucharest: Editura Cartea cu Semne, 1932). See part IV in this book for the passage in question.

8. Ibid.

9. Eliade, *Souvenirs*, p. 192.

10. Quoted by Gardner, *Moral Fiction*, p. 9.

11. It should be noted that *māyā* is here taken in its original non-Vedantist sense which suggests the magical creative power of change or transformation; see, for example, Mircea Eliade, *A History of Religious Ideas* (Chicago: University of Chicago Press, 1978), pp. 201–202.

12. See, for example, Mircea Eliade, "Crisis and Renewal," in *The Quest* (Chicago: University of Chicago Press, 1969), pp. 54–71; and also Adrian Marino's discussion in this volume.

13. Maurice Mandelbaum, *History, Man, and Reason: A Study in Nineteenth Century Thought* (Baltimore: Johns Hopkins, 1971), p. 6.

14. See Robert A. Oden, Jr., "Hermeneutics and Historiography: Germany and America," *Society of Biblical Literature 1980 Seminar Papers*, ed. Paul J. Achtemeier (Chico, California: Scholars Press, 1980), pp. 135–157.

15. Eliade, *Souvenirs*, p. 72.

16. See Philip Wheelright, *The Burning Fountain, A Study in the Language of Symbolism* (Bloomington: Indiana University Press, 1954), pp. 88–89.

17. Ibid.

18. Eliade, *Labyrinthe*, p. 162.

19. J. W. von Goethe, "Vorwort zur Morphologie," quoted by Jonathan Z. Smith, "*Adde Parvum Parvo Magnus Acervus Erit*," *History of Religions* 11 (1971), p. 84.

20. Eliade, *Labyrinthe*, p. 162.

21. Ibid.

22. Ibid.

23. Edgar V. McKnight, *Meaning in Texts* (Philadelphia: Fortress Press, 1978), p. 25.

24. Ibid.

25. See P. Ricoeur's review of *Histoire des croyances et des idées religieuses* in *Religious Studies Review* 2 (1976), p. 3.

26. Ibid., pp. 3–4. See also Seymour Cain's "Mircea Eliade: Attitudes Toward History," *Religious Studies Review* 6 (1980): 13–16.

27. Claude Lévi-Strauss, *Tristes Tropiques*, quoted by Clifford Geertz, "The Cerebral Savage: On the Work of Claude Lévi-Strauss," in his *The Interpretation of Cultures* (New York: Basic Books, 1973), p. 356.

28. Ibid.

29. Jonathan Culler, "Phenomenology and Structuralism," *The Human Context* 5 (1973), pp. 37–38; see also Eliade's comments on Lévi-Strauss in *Occultism, Witchcraft, and Cultural Fashions* (Chicago: University of Chicago Press, 1976), pp. 13–17.

30. *Times Literary Supplement*, p. 50. See also Seymour Cain's discussion in this volume.

31. Ibid. See also Edmund Leach's acerbic comments in his "Sermons by a Man on a Ladder," *New York Review of Books* (Oct. 20, 1966), pp. 28–31.

32. See, for example, Eliade's "Autobiographical Fragment" published here and also Eliade's "Preface" to *The Forbidden Forest*, translated by Mac Linscott Ricketts and Mary Park Stevenson (Notre Dame: University of Notre Dame Press, 1978), pp. v–x.

33. See Guilford Dudley III, *Religion on Trial: Mircea Eliade and his Critics* (Philadelphia: Temple University Press, 1977) for a positive evaluation of Eliade as a Foucaultian "anti-historian." See also the review of this work by Ninian Smart for a more negative point of view in *Numen* 25 (1979), pp. 171–183.

34. Eliade, *Souvenirs*, p. 85.

35. From Bulwer Lytton's alchemical melodrama, *A Strange Story* (Berkeley: Shambala, 1973), p. vi.

36. See in this volume, Matei Calinescu, " 'The Function of the Unreal,': Reflections on Mircea Eliade's Short Fiction," and Geertz, "Deep Play: Notes on the Balinese Cockfight," in *Interpretation of Cultures*, pp. 448–453.

37. See in this volume, Mircea Eliade, "The Fact."

38. See Eliade's remarks in the "Foreword" to Douglas Allen, *Structure and Creativity in Religion* (The Hague: Mouton Publishers, 1978), pp. vii–ix.

39. See in this volume, Mircea Eliade, "Autobiographical Fragment."

40. The works of Dudley, Allen, and especially Marino, are the first substantial efforts in this direction.

41. Eliade, *Souvenirs*, p. 85.

42. Eliade, "Preface," *Forbidden Forest*, p. vi.

43. Ibid.

44. Ibid.

45. Mircea Eliade, *Myth and Reality* (New York: Harper Torch Book, 1963), p. 141.

46. Eliade, *Soliloquies*, p. 1.

47. See in this book, Eugen Simion, "The Mythical Dignity of Narration."

48. Calinescu, "Function of the Unreal." See also Stephen Crites, "The Narrative Quality of Experience," *Journal of the American Academy of Religion* 39 (1971), pp. 291–311.

49. Ricoeur, "Narrative Function," p. 195.

50. Ibid.

51. Cioran, "Beginning of a Friendship," p. 413.

52. Ibid.

53. Tom Robbins, "Meditations on a Camel Pack," *Esquire* 94 (July 1980), p. 37.

54. Geertz, "Deep Play," p. 453.

55. See Calinescu, "Function of the Unreal."

56. Eliade, *Souvenirs,* pp. 6–7.

57. Ibid.

58. Ibid., p. 7.

59. Eliade, *Labyrinthe,* p. 126.

60. See Calinescu, "Function of the Unreal."

61. See, among other works, Elizabeth Sewell, *The Orphic Voice* (New York: Harper and Row, 1971); John Gardner, *Moral Fiction;* and Joseph Epstein, "Rx for the Novel," *Commentary* (July, 1978), pp. 57–58.

62. See especially Geertz in his *Interpretation of Cultures.*

63. Borrowing here from Martin Gardiner's review essay entitled "Do Chimps Chat?," *New York Review of Books* 27 (1980), No. 4, pp. 3–6.

64. For a discussion of the ambiguities of a "post-modernist" movement in literature see John Barth, "The Literature of Replenishment," *The Atlantic* 245 (January, 1980), pp. 65–71; and, more generally, Crites, "Narrative Quality" pp. 308–311.

65. From a literary standpoint see Northrop Frye, *The Educated Imagination* (Bloomington: Indiana University Press, 1964).

Part I

Meaning and the Scholarly World

We shall not cease from exploration
And the end of all our exploring
Will be to arrive where we started
And know the place for the first time.

T. S. Eliot
Four Quartets

Adrian Marino

Mircea Eliade's Hermeneutics

In my work I have tried to elaborate this hermeneutics; but I have illustrated it in a practical fashion, on the basis of documents. It now remains for me, or for another, to systematize this hermeneutics.

Journal, 24 June 1968

The aim of this study—the first taken from the Romanian "bibliography" of Mircea Eliade—is to make a systematic reading and critique of his hermeneutical method, to reconstruct it and evaluate it using all the fragments explicitly or implicitly of a theoretical-methodological nature which have hermeneutical content found in this Romanian author's works on the history and phenomenology of religion and the philosophy of culture.

It must be specified at the outset that such an investigation can be productive and conclusive only from the perspective of the general, "traditional" hermeneutical theory as defined and practiced from Schleiermacher onward. It is noteworthy that Eliade never refers to the lectures on *Hermeneutik* by this author, just as he makes no reference to Dilthey or Spitzer. Among "moderns" he cites Bultmann (but as a theologian, not for *Das Problem der Hermeneutik*), Hans-Georg Gadamer, and several others, but without any particular emphasis. Enthusiasm for methodology, although evident, is not accentuated. But, we hasten to add, what is significant is not this attitude, but rather the fact that Eliade discovered "by himself" a series of traditional, essential hermeneutical procedures by simple intuition, and he discovered hermeneutical—I should say "empirical"—reflection by direct, concrete, and authentic contact with "texts."

Mircea Eliade reconstructs, in a genuine way, the whole fundamental problematics of hermeneutics. He rediscovers *all* the classic positions and solutions of hermeneutics, he poses and resolves all its basic problems simply by confrontation with an essential hermeneutical situation: the necessity of explaining and interpreting "texts." The only difference is that in his case it is not a matter of Biblical texts, the classical point of departure of hermeneutics (these are discussed only in the broad context of the history of religions), but of the whole aggregate of mythico-symbolic texts, of the entirety of "documents" of religious ethnography and the history of religions. In this fashion Eliade reinscribes a circular situation no less typically hermeneutical: from the interpretation of Biblical texts (the Schleiermacher phase) to the exegesis of universal mythology (the contemporary phase) through the same essential relation: hermeneut/text—a relation qualitatively equal in all historic phases and moments.

Therefore I do not hesitate to see in Mircea Eliade's hermeneutics a very important, *modern* moment in the history of this method, enriched and developed—a major contribution in my opinion—by an attitude and approach typically hermeneutical: intuitive, inductive, via direct experience with texts of the history of religions, without much theoretical discussion; from text to method, in an experimental way. It is not a matter of a programatic application of a method, but of an *elaboration*, of a "live" discovery of a method, which is crystallized and theoretically formulated—progressively and fragmentarily—in the very act of being constituted: text-hermeneut-text/hermeneut-text-hermeneut. A relationship which is reciprocal, alternating, progressive, circular, and of the purest essence of the "hermeneutic circle": *Zirkelschluss* (Schleiermacher), *Zirkel in Verstehen* (Dilthey), to-and-fro movement (Leo Spitzer). Whence also the "creative" aspect—if we may so express it—under our very eyes, in the framework of an open, uninterrupted process.

I

The essential object is defined with distinct clarity: ". . . To illustrate the possibilities open to a hermeneutics of the archaic and folk-religious universes, in other words, of religious creations that have no written expression and, in general, no valid chronological criteria." These "religious universes" produce and are constituted by "hierophanies," "manifestations of the sacred expressed in symbols, myths, and supernatural beings," perceived by the modern hermeneut under the form of "structures," as elements of a "prereflective language which necessitates a particular hermeneutics." These investigations as a whole represent the systematic hermeneutics of the sacred and its historical manifestations.[1] It follows therefore that what Eliade will call "my hermeneutical method"[2] is to be extracted, clarified, and defined from the totality of its practical applications which cover—as proved especially by *Patterns in Comparative Religions* and *Histoire des croyances et des idées religieuses*—the whole domain of the religious morphology and phenomenology of humanity. This is a considerable, captivating enterprise, with few equals in the present era.

This being the point of departure of a long process running from crystallization to systemization, we will not be surprised to find at the same time something of a terminological, hence semantic, instability. For both Eliade and many other contemporaries, the idea of "hermeneutics," "exegesis," "decipherment," "interpretation," "understanding," etc. are somewhat synonymous, or at any rate overlapping and circular. It is possible, nevertheless, to distinguish two major—I should say preferred—meanings of hermeneutics: 1) The creation, deposit, and transmission of the totality of meanings of sacred texts, with hermeneutics being the unveiling of the ultimate reality implied in the sum total of texts from a particular category;[3] 2) The method of study of these meanings, the organized effort to "understand" them, to "comprehend the religious values of prehistoric societies less imperfectly."[4] Hermeneutics therefore is the method or "science" for "deciphering" religious meanings and those of any other nature. Very often there occur in Eliade's writings—it is unnecessary to give references—expressions such as "to decipher," "decipherment," "to describe," "description," as well as "the preoccupation with" or "the necessity for deciphering" or "decoding" one meaning after another of a religious text or "document." But the method of "deciphering" demands "decipherment" itself, both in its causality and in its objective functional mechanism.

If hermeneutics has become and continues to prove to be an essential "scientific" necessity, it is a consequence—a phenomenon grasped and defined already in Antiquity—of the fact that myths cannot truly be understood in their literal sense, that they have "hidden meanings," "subconscious" (*hypónosai*) senses. In fact, every religious phenomenon constitutes a "cipher;" it is the bearer of a "message" which calls for decipherment. Moreover, the whole cosmos, all cosmic planes and rhythms—viewed from this perspective—prove to be "ciphered." "It is necessary therefore to decipher what the cosmos 'says' through its multiple modalities in order to understand the mystery of life." Culture and civilization have likewise their "secrets," whose cultural value, according to Eliade, is still insufficiently studied: "All the great discoveries and inventions—agriculture, metallurgy, various techniques, arts, etc.—entail, in the beginning, secrecy; only 'initiation' into the secrets of the profession could guarantee the success of the operation." Hence the result that these secrets presuppose a decipherment, and thus a hermeneutics. If secrecy, according to Plutarch (in a text recalled by Eliade)[5] "augments the value" of revelations, their decipherment and interpretation will be all the more rich and their hermeneutics will be all the more necessary and stimulating the deeper, more numerous, more enigmatic the "secrets" are. Moreover, everything begins by being secret, mysterious, enigmatic, initiatory. Hermeneutics is nothing but the extension and consequence of this kind of existential and ontological situation.

Viewed from this perspective, the whole spiritual life of humanity is transformed into a vast deposit of *meanings* or—perhaps better said— into a considerable "hermeneutical deposit." We find ourselves in the presence of an enormous "system" of obscure meanings expressed through a specific, "pre-reflective language" which can be deciphered only through a "specific hermeneutical method." This secret language consists of myths, rituals, hierophanies, theophanies, symbols, etc. which "manifest themselves," "speak," transmit "messages," reveal hidden "meanings."[6] Mythology becomes equivalent to a true religious seminology ("some *sign* suffices to indicate the sacredness of a place") which is combined ultimately with the image of a live, articulate cosmos, meaningful and polyvalent. This is because, in the last analysis, in Eliade's hermeneutical vision, *the world reveals itself as language.*[7] Once again we have a circular situation of a "textual" essence: the whole cosmos becomes the text of a "secret language" (allegorical, symbolic, legendary, emblematic), while hermeneutics is called upon to decipher this entire universe of meanings, expressed by an infinite series of "messages" which await decipherment and understanding.[8] Whence the profound analogies of substance between ancient *exegetai* who interpreted the oracles at Delphi (and even poets who, in the conception of the ancients, preserved via the phenomenon of *anamnesis* the memory of lost primordial meanings) and modern hermeneuts who rediscover, disclose, decode, and interpret the obscure religious significations of the mythic languages.[9] Of course, this pansymbolism leads to the institution of a global, universal hermeneutics, applicable to the whole historical, cultural, and utilitarian sphere: historical events, cultural currents, intellectual fashions, practical attitudes.[10] A discipline (as we shall see) which appeared and was situated at first under the sign of totality, hermeneutics subsumes and integrates ever broader planes of meaning. Its ultimate end is the decipherment of the whole cosmos of meanings; and Mircea Eliade has rediscovered with keen insight the same traditional objective.

II

The key idea of *meaning*—which plays an essential role in any hermeneutics, hence also in that of Eliade—calls for some clarification and a short commentary. We observe again a certain terminological—as well as generalized—oscillation, this time between the concepts of "sense" (*sens*) and "signification" (*semnificație*), both of which may be translated "meaning." Sense, defined in accordance with a series of texts and contexts, is in most instances understood as general orientation, the fundamental, essential understanding of a "text." "Signification" often expresses one of the attested or possible connotations of the essential "sense," the different "semantic" interpretations of the "text' (myth, symbol, etc.). But in many other contexts, the two ideas are synonymous, the contexts specifying the definition of hermeneutics as a method of deciphering either "senses" or "significances." Sometimes Eliade puts the question, "What may be the meaning (*sens*) [of the data]?" At other times, pursuing exactly the same objective and program, he states that "specialists have neglected sometimes to study the significance of these data."[11] The interdependence, if not the identity, of the two terms is evident.

What does it mean to have "significance," to be a bearer of "significances," etc.? According to Eliade, the realm of significance is established by the "spiritual sense" of a document, by the "traditional sense of a science."[12] A "spiritual," "traditional" sense means essentially a magical, metaphysical, prophetic sense, all that expresses a sacred, transcedent significance.[13] We refer intentionally to these old definitions in order to demonstrate the continuity and coherence of Eliade's system of thought. Mystico-magical sacrality is by definition "deep." Hence, in newer formulations, we find a constant preoccupation with deciphering "deep significances" (declarations of this sort are quite numerous[14]), i.e., absolute, ultimate ones. To have a "significance" means to make reference to a sacred, "absolute reality." Therefore, in the final analysis, significance reveals a reality that is ultimate and sacred.[15] Its domain is the sphere of hidden "truths"—secret and essential ones. The fundamental hermeneutical question will be, therefore: "What does the 'true significance' of the domain X mean?"[16] Sacred, deep, hidden, absolute, and true significance is at the same time "virtual," hence multiple and polyvalent. In numerous places Eliade insists upon this point, which is also one of the common positions of the "new critics." If for Roland Barthes all coherent interpretations are "valid," for Eliade all meanings are true, in the context of an open virtuality, unfolded on multiple planes of reference: religious, but also psychological, psychoanalytic, etc.[17]

It is not out of place to dwell upon these assertions—and we shall return to enlarge upon them when we evoke the theory of symbol in the conception of our author—because Eliade spoke about the "inexhaustible polyvalence"[18] of meanings long *before* the current vogue of the "New Criticism." Parallel to this direction, but in a way independent of it (which moreover precedes it and confirms his priority in this domain by specialized analyses which are stricter, more technical, and hence more convincing), Eliade brings out the "simultaneity" of meanings of a (religious) symbol. From this derive two completely justified assertions: 1) "No hermeneutic is excessive," being legitimated by every possible discovery of meaning; and 2) hermeneutics is in fact inexhaustible, since meanings are by definition polyvalent, open, "superimposed," "multistoried," situated on several planes, on several scales.[19] This is because religious meanings are never "pure." A religious phenomenon is at the same time also an historical, sociological, cultural, or psychological fact—to mention only its profane and more important aspects. Since purely religious concepts do not exist, neither will purely religious meanings exist.[20] This leads to the establishment of a plural hermeneutics, realizable for each meaning individually, the result of polysemeia, the coexistence of meanings of a religious, historical, sociological, cultural, psychological, etc. type in one and the same symbolic document. All these meanings are born and deposited in aluvial forms in successive strata. The new meaning (Christian) does not cancel out the old (polytheistic). The ancient, ancestral meanings do not disappear, are not destroyed, but are only agglutinated or absorbed into the composition of a new synthesis. New meanings are evidence of new *"prises de conscience."*[21] Finally, a last note characteristic of "significances": any profound significance has its "beauty," its "nobility," and therefore value.[22] The discovery of a meaning equals the discovery and consecration of a value.

The decipherment of meanings constitutes an essential but very difficult hermeneutical operation, scrutinized by Eliade with full lucidity. He has established a true list of obstacles, a quasi-complete inventory of hermeneutical barriers, beginning with what he called in a work of youth, "the law of the *degrading of meaning (sensul)*, understanding by this any adulteration, any *loss* or *forgetting of an original significance."* The primordial meanings are supressed by a process of decomposition, corruption, adulteration. The most current form of this degeneration is the transformation of profound meanings into simple superstitions, legends, decorative motifs, phenomena duplicated or perpetuated by rationalization, "infantilization," a fall into the "profane."[23] In short, degradation through secularization. These erosions often amount to a real "emptying" of any original significance, and end in "disappearance." Hence the intervention of hermeneutics with its aim of rediscovering one or more of the lost meanings.[24] Sometimes Eliade speaks of meanings "forgotten," the natural process of amnesia of the symbolic memory of humanity which ends in "abolishing," "obscuring," or "demythicizing"[25] its entire religious content—and, by extension, its whole original potential for signifying. Hermeneutics becomes necessary also owing to the "camouflage"[26] of myths and symbols— a phenomenon no less frequent in the current era of mass secularization, of the appearance of "atheistic theologians," of the "death of God," etc. In these circumstances, it is precisely by means of an adequate hermeneutics that we succeed in identifying myths that today are degraded, hidden, "camouflaged" under various ideological and artistic forms. To draw out into the light these apparently abolished contents, contents which at any rate have been degraded to the point of their complete disfiguration, and to decipher their deep significance is what might be called "hermeneutical archeology." The operation is not without analogy to *L'Archéologie du savoir* or *Des sciences humaines* by Michael Foucault.

Of course, other obstacles of an objective order intrude, capable of provoking the most doughty specialist: the lack of written texts, or the absence of written or oral documentation of any nature. And when these *do* exist, they offer a certain resistance because of their fundamental obscurity.[27] The sort of thing which imposes limits on any capacity for deciphering: the case of the mysteries of Eleusis or of Dionysos. The sort of thing which determines also the typical hermeneutical question in *Histoire des croyances:* "Can the Mysteries be known?" Nor does Eliade escape ultimately from the fact that many of these difficulties derive from the "opacity" of the European or Western spirit for which many of the primitive or Asian symbols are and remain quasi-hermetic, quite lacking in transparency, difficult or impossible to decipher in a correct and complete way. To everything else is added further the restricted condition of the modern historian of religions: his positivist-scientistic prejudices, philosophical timidity, flight from the dangers of synthesis and general theories, etc.[28] It is not difficult to observe that the same obstacles stand in the way of critical and historical-literary hermeneutics.

The penetration of meaning—its explanation, clarification, definition—is the product of a hermeneutical problem of *interpretation*. Hermeneutics represents—using a very general formulation—the theory and general methodology for interpreting texts; and it is rather surprising that Eliade seems to dissociate the two ideas which are in fact synonymous or at any rate convergent. He speaks in one place about "scholastic interpretations and hermeneutics"[29] without making clear whether it is a matter of an ideational or methodological dissociation or only of a terminological redundancy. The decipherment of meanings presupposes their interpretation, and the whole hermeneutical strategy consists in the establishment of valid principles of interpretation in accordance with precise criteria. On this crucial point hermeneutics separates itself from any other possible "method" of interpretation. It establishes the most general objective conditions of interpretation, its functional "model"; and the difficulty lies, in the case of Eliade's hermeneutics (applied to the totality of manifestations of the "sacred") in the discovery of the objective, stable, general, and universally valid criteria of interpretation which he uses. We are aware, of course, of the perfect symmetry between the polyvalence of meanings and the inevitable plurality of interpretations: myth, for instance, is an extremely complex cultural reality which can be "approached and interpreted from multiple and complementary perspectives." There is a "multiplicity of possible interpretations."[30] Nevertheless, among these multiple possible perspectives and interpretations a hierarchy exists. Some meanings and therefore some interpretations are more important, more to be preferred than others. So, once again, what are the basic criteria?

For Eliade, interpretation begins and ends in the recovery and decipherment of the *true meaning*, the *first* or *original* one,[31] of a mode of behavior, a creation, or a religious document, and, by extension, of any category of documents or texts. "True," "primordial," and "original" become thus synonymous concepts and hermeneutically interdependent. The difficulty—an enormous one—does not lie in the acceptance of this principle, but—on the one hand—in grasping the original meanings and—on the other—in explaining their genesis through an investigation on the order of "depth psychology," undertaken in both directions. The validity of the solution is in function with the acceptance of the basic premises: the recognition of the existence of a metaphysical theory, an ontology implied in the documents of religious and cultural ethnography. And this presupposes that the human spirit is capable of "fundamental intuitions," that it is our nature to define man's existential situation and position in the cosmos and at the same time to construct a true cosmic vision made up of planes, spaces, and times that are "absolute," and hence "real," "true." These theses appear already in works of Eliade's youth,[32] and the great syntheses of his later life do nothing in essence but verify and develop them.

Eliade postulates—and I do not see how he could proceed otherwise—the existence of a primordial, elementary, spontaneous spiritual

experience which is combined with the *first* sacro-metaphysical revelations of humanity. The situation of man in the cosmos and the consciousness of this situation are products of primordial reflective acts
of contemplation: the discovery of a different, sacred "space" identified
with the heavenly vault or with regions sacralized by signs, cosmic
rhythms which become hierophanies, etc.[33] The result is that meanings
are born "spontaneously" in the primitive mentality, that their origin
is not—if we may express it so—"physical," but rather the result of a
"creation" of the human spirit. Many of these are nothing but the
products of "language," but not in the sense of theories about the
origin of myths as a "disease of language"; rather of language's capacity
to create an imaginary universe, full of fabulous creatures, paramyth-
ological and parapoetic.[34] At any rate, the older thesis according to
which there was a primacy of theory in societies of an archaic type[35]
is taken up anew, amplified, and consolidated by reference to the
ontological principle of meaning: the human spirit cannot function
without discovering and recognizing meanings. Consciousness confers
meanings in an organic and "original" way. Any profane action *has* to
receive also a meaning (sacred or other). Any act of repetition implies
a complex of meanings, while meanings in turn compel repetitions,
returns *ab origine*,[36] to archetypes.

From this perspective, hermeneutics becomes no less an "original"
and spontaneous creation of the spirit. It postulates, *ab origine*, the
existence of a meaning of the spirit, it founds an intelligible spiritual
universe, it actualizes a latent potential for interpretation as well as an
uninterrupted effort at interpretation. It has in essence the same primordial origin: the appearance of the first meaning is accompanied
inevitably by its initial interpretation. In other words, any significance
has *ab origine* an accepted, validated, communicated meaning. The
proof is that all myths and hierophanies are accompanied by traditional
interpretations, very old, historically attested, that all ancient "secrets"
conceal a meaning, stimulating at the same time the interpretation of
that meaning: the classic case is the mysteries of Eleusis. One can
therefore assert—and Eliade all but does so—that the impulse to describe, to discover signs and significances, is ontological and essential,
and that one can effectively speak of the existence of *homo significans*
even at this level of deep archaic obscurity. As a matter of fact, the
bringing to light of the "genesis" of a meaning has no other role than
a hermeneutical one: "The genesis of a god is interesting only to the
extent it helps us to understand better the religious spirit of his be-
lievers."[37] Meanings are discovered and conveyed by just a few individuals, while their content only becomes accessible thanks to the

information furnished by members of the respective societies.[38] This information forms the object of hermeneutics, first as traditional interpretation, then as scientific discipline.

Even if the idea is not strongly emphasised by Eliade, it is self-evident that modern hermeneutics does no more than to continue and perfect, with documentary methods and finer instruments, the original impulse. A development which one cannot avoid, in the light of modern scientific consciousness, is the problem of the validity of this hermeneutics, a method not devoid of difficulties old and new. As a matter of fact, some difficulties appeared even in Antiquity along with the appearance of the "authentic" exegesis of the Gospels. Origen proclaimed—among the first—the obstacles to the establishment of "historical truth"[39] (and not only in cases of this kind). The same question—draped in long philosophical robes—rises maliciously today also.[40] The problem of the "objectivity" of the history of religions and hermeneutical ethnology reappears continually, but Eliade does not elucidate it. On the contrary, he openly poses the question of the "validity"[41] of the hermeneutics which he practices, fully conscious of its limits: the existence of an irreducible core of any explanation in a whole series of meanings; the inevitable "opacity" of the modern consciousness which necessitates our according priority to traditional interpretations, closer to their original source; the accessibility of the pure, initial meanings, today degraded, etc.[42] And he is constantly obsessed with the same key question: to what extent can the modern, profane mentality realize—in all its complexity—the primordial experience of sacrality? What can we understand *today* of *primitive* spirituality? To what extent can the past be made accessible to contemporary understanding? And this puts squarely in the center of any hermeneutics the problem of understanding, the clarification of its conditions, possibilities, and limitations.

The idea of *understanding*—as fundamental in classical hermeneutics as it is in that of the modern day—betrays the ultimate objective of interpretation: to decipher and interpret meanings in order to "understand" them. Understanding is the final goal and supreme act in the hermeneutical process. In the whole *oeuvre* of Mircea Eliade one can distinguish as a constant theme the same preoccupation: "to understand the meanings," "a series of 'messages' waiting to be deciphered and understood," "to try to understand what they reveal, to try to decipher their message," etc.[43] The object of this effort to understand is global: it aims at both the entirety of religious meanings and the totality of cultural creations.[44]

The question, no less essential, arises: what does it mean "to understand," and in what sense does Eliade use this idea whose role in hermeneutics is so important? What is meant by "understanding"? In a very general sense—equivalent to the objective of any traditional "explanation of a text"—it is a matter primarily of "understanding correctly . . . the religious manifestations," of "demonstrating in the text that which a certain symbol 'means to say.' "[45] The meaning of religious symbols proceeds to become "intelligible" and "clear" for both the hermeneut and for those who follow him: "to understand and clarify for others," "to make intelligible a theoretical universe." Hence the necessity for "translating into our everyday language."[46] Decipherment constitutes therefore a basic condition for understanding. The operation unfolds on two convergent planes: that of the consciousness of the interpreter, and that of his readers who accept his interpretations: "to understand and to make understood"[47] even the most obscure meanings. But all this represents merely the minimal preliminaries and so to say "formal" conditions of understanding.

The operation presupposes—at its core—a system of references and integrations on a series of specific planes of meaning. First, the recognition of religious behaviors (however strange, barbarous, excessive) as "human acts, cultural acts, creations of the spirit—and not pathological eruptions of instinct, acts of beastiality, or infantilism." This is equivalent to the effort to grasp the "ideological" meaning "implicit," latent, hidden, "subadjacent" in all myths and symbols interpreted. Only this approach distinguishes subjective impressions and opens an objective perspective capable of understanding the "normality" of a given religious behavior. In order to understand a group of meanings it is therefore absolutely necessary that we "reconstruct the ideology which assumed them and valorized them."[48] We do not understand unless we decipher the "ideological" meanings: i.e. aspects of a concept of the world, of a cosmogony or a metaphysics.

Already in a work of his early years Eliade made it specific—essential—that we are in danger of understanding nothing of the "natural sciences" of old Mesopotamian cultures "if we do not keep constantly in mind their conception of the world, their cosmology."[49] The key to any interpretation is the reference to a specific *Weltanschauung* which elaborates, articulates, and valorizes original "situations" (note existentialist influence), analogous to empirical "situations" (psychological, historical).[50] Each of these calls for adequate understanding, but the only significant elements, which lie at the base of the religious life of humanity, are "original experiences," fundamental, existential ones, which express the perception or intuition of a situation of man in the cosmos. Summing it up: "The ambition of the historian of religions is to arrive at the existential situation assumed by religious man, . . . and to make this primordial experience intelligible to our contemporaries."[51]

To "understand," in this sense, does not mean therefore—to use a conventional expression—to "demystify," but on the contrary to transpose oneself and think in cosmogonic, symbolic, metaphysical terms. It means to intuit concrete "revelations" of these processes of knowledge and to raise oneself to them through intellectual clairvoyance. It means, in a word, to experience again in an inverse, rational, analytic, and scientific sense the primordial revelations, and having reached this stage to understand them and describe them from within. "Those who understand" are individuals capable of thinking symbolically, cosmogonically, metaphysically, and of transposing themselves, of identifying themselves spiritually with that kind of position and situation.[52] To understand means, in the last analysis, to realize an ontological situation, to have access to other realities, and in this way to assume *another* ontological status. This allows us to penetrate into the "essence," "destiny," and "mystery" of myths and symbols, to situate ourselves "inside" them, to distinguish between their deep sense (the only revelatory one) and the infantile, degraded, or ridiculous forms which they may sometimes embrace.[53]

The final result of understanding is the realization of the unity and intelligibility of man and the cosmos—of the situation of man in the cosmos. Understanding assures order and unity of the cosmos and of life, existence itself being an act of understanding. Man exists in the cosmos to the extent that he understands, that he can give an answer, through "engagement," to the problems of existence. Understanding the ultimate meanings of existence, we penetrate into the generality of human life and therefore into the essence of each individual separately. By understanding man in his mysteries, symbolisms, and mythology, we end in understanding ourselves in depth.[54] Understanding, therefore, according to Eliade, is cosmic and total.

II

If this is the object of hermeneutics (in the "traditional" conception, but adapted to a new field of investigation), the method of realizing it presents new identities, similitudes, concordances, and symmetries with the "classic" or "traditional" hermeneutics. The same series of obligatory circuits, and inevitable circularities, the same type of reciprocal relations realized on various well-known planes, theorized and practiced by historical hermeneutics.[55] The only difference is that Mircea Eliade reinvented and rediscovered by himself a series of procedures (actually topics) which for a long time have been part of a true pattern of hermeneutics. A brilliant demonstration—we keep returning to this idea—of hermeneutical vitality and "spontaneity," of concrete experimental confirmation in the very contents of the analytic mechanism of the necessity and viability of certain procedures which prove their existence, their obligatory character, and hence their effectiveness in the course of the effort to decipher, interpret, and understand meanings. Eliade speaks about "my own method of work and the perspective which defines it specifically."[56] It remains to be seen in detail in what this method consists and what his specific perspective is.

We shall refer in passing to a few elementary precautions which belong to any deontology of research: the use of documents which are authentic, numerous, convergent, intelligible, etc. In short, the mastery of a good philological discipline, a term which in this case denotes the knowledge of the language, history, culture, and society whose religion is being studied. Any exegesis is founded on a philology.[57] Decipherment and interpretation are not possible without documents which are "reliable and sufficiently well known."[58] Decipherment and interpretation are themselves "the product of documents which call for decoding, describing." With this (essential) observation: that for this type of hermeneutics, the documents alone are not enough. The exegete intuits, has the feeling that "these documents tell him something more than the simple fact that they reflect historical situations." This "something more" is precisely their significance, their deep meaning, the expression of a symbolism which is obscure but well articulated. For this reason: "When it is a matter of spiritual values, the contribution of psychology, however indispensible, does not exhaust the richness of the object." Eliade even displays irritation (in his journal) when his colleagues recognize the primacy and factual content of historical documents and do not continue their hermeneutics on the plane of the meaning of the documents.[59]

More important are two other methodological attitudes which by themselves are capable of circumscribing with precision the domain of the interpreter. In the first place, the phenomenon (religious, etc.) submitted to exegesis must be considered "in itself," that is, the specificity of its essential elements, in reference to its own structures.[60] Any "document" therefore must be understood in itself, for what it signifies, in its being. In the second place, it is necessary to eliminate any confusion of planes and points of view. Hermeneutics can only be operative and conclusive when it studies phenomena (in this case religious) "on their own plane of reference," when it analyses a myth in the "frame of reference which is its own," in accordance with its specific value. He insists time and again upon the fact that any interpretation of myths and symbols must be undertaken only "from the perspective which is proper to them." Understanding is possible only on "the plane of specificity," and only in reference to the proper modality of the object of interpretation. A religious phenomenon is not in its essence either sociological or ethnographical. No phenomenon can be understood, consequently, except in its irreducible, original meanings and structures. This is a hermeneutical rule of universal validity, applicable also to art, literature, aesthetics, and literary criticism. Eliade's hermeneutics has therefore as its point of departure—to use his own language—a true phenomenological "reductionism." Any ignoring or surpressing of the essences and structures specific to a phenomenon can only be fatal to the effectiveness and validity of interpretation.[61]

It must be stressed at the outset that the hermeneutical method of Eliade is enclosed—by its very structure, even by its functional mechanism—within a circular situation well known under the name of the *hermeneutic circle*.[62] In other words, the hermeneutical process has a circular development. It traverses various circuits which involve a continuous succession of alternative relations, returnings, cumulative repetitions, and spiral demonstrations. Anyone who has read the works of Mircea Eliade knows very well that the author repeats himself, that he takes passages and illustrations from one book and develops them in another, that his analyses often are reassembled and superimposed. Much of the contents of *Techniques du Yoga* is extracted and developed in *Le Yoga, immortalité et liberté*. The theme of "Mysteries and Spiritual Regeneration" (in *Myths, Dreams, and Mysteries*) is taken up again in *Birth and Rebirth, Rites and Symbols of Initiation*, etc. The significant thing is that the author shows a distinct sensitivity—and by no means coincidentally—for all repetitive cosmic and archetypal phenomena. He is vitally preoccupied with "cosmic renewal," the "Myth of the Eternal Return," etc. Eliade has intuited keenly the existential-circular dimension of the human being implicit in his spiritual life. But in the case of Eliade's exegesis, it is a matter of something more, a phenomenon as precise as possible.

Although in no circumstance does he state the theory of the "hermeneutic circle" and all it entails (the necessity of determining precisely the beginning point of the circular demonstration, of avoiding tautology and the vicious circle, etc.), the typical circular situation appears in the simple determination of the process of interpretation. In other words, the interpretation and understanding are given, in a certain sense, at the very beginning. You find, decipher, interpret—in fact—exactly what you want, what you are seeking. The aim of the interpretation is, in reality, only the rediscovery of and return to the point of departure—a situation ascertained and theorized (more than once!) in connection with the interpretation of literary texts also.[63] In order to be able to decipher a hierophany, a myth, symbol, etc., you must first know—to put it simply—what a hierophany, myth, symbol, etc. *is*. You work, in other words, with a set of preconceptions which include in their definition an outline of the essential solution to the problem. Without this preliminary "given," the hermeneutical process could not begin. And it is quite remarkable that Eliade is fully aware of the fact that his entire exegetical activity is, in actuality, prescribed and preconditioned. He knows very well that "the analysis of a foreign culture principally reveals what was sought in it or what the seeker was already prepared to discover."[64] Philosophers such as Heidegger and Merleau-Ponty, linguists such as Leo Spitzer, critics such as Jean Starobinski, etc. do not say in essence anything different. The convergence of these positions goes still further, even if it is no more than a truism with which we have to do. "One understands principally what one is predestined to understand by one's own vocation, by one's own cultural orientation and that of the historical moment to which one belongs."[65]

Numerous passages from Eliade's works demonstrate that there is no other way to solve problems. Nay, in not a few instances it clearly results that the solution is given, known, assumed, and even validated from the start, before any analysis has been made. For instance: "Without in any way anticipating the conclusions that will come from analyzing that evidence, we may note at once that the tree represents . . . the *living cosmos,* endlessly renewing itself."[66] The homology of the tree-cosmos is therefore prescribed, as is also that of the tree-*axis mundi,* tree-microcosm, etc. The structure of the symbol can be presented only as an extension of the hierophany, as an autonomous form of revelation.[67] But the definition of "hierophany" must be known beforehand, etc. Just as "the scale creates the phenomenon," so here the point of view creates the object of its observation. Eliade knows (and repeats) that "the perspective adopted in the observation of a phenomenon plays a considerable role in the very constituting of the phenomenon."[68] The situation is analogous to Heisenberg's principle of indetermination in physics. But no less inevitable is the fact that it brings up again the whole problem of the validity of the hermeneutics. In a large number of instances it is more than doubtful that we can utilize the enormous mass of hermeneutical writings which have been transmitted on the subject of the "mysteries" for the purpose of deciphering the original meanings of the Eleusinian, Orphic, or Hellenistic mystery cults. But, on the other hand, all commentators "read into the ancient rites their own spiritual situation, determined by the profound crises of their times,"[69] nor could they do otherwise. Eliade's hermeneutics finds itself in exactly the same situation.

His point of departure is found in a "revelation," an original intuition of a global solution to a problem. It is the *declic* of which Leo Spitzer speaks in one place. The hermeneut studies a file, a mass of documents, and at a given moment he has, in a flash of lightning, a "vision": the answer to his essential questions. It is the beginning of the hermeneutical process which sets in motion the whole "hermeneutic circle." It is interesting to observe that Eliade, finding himself in such a situation, intuited even in his youth that the exegetical mechanism can begin in no other way. Erudition not only has the advantage of preventing the investigator from making any hasty generalization, but "it enriches him with a certain power of divination"[70] which allows him to distinguish between what is archaic and permanent and what is secondary and local in all folkloric creations. The method is specified even better in the sense that the most appropriate attitude for penetrating "the meaning of an exemplary human situation is not the 'objectivity' of a naturalist, but the intelligent sympathy of the exegete, the interpreter."[71] This operates through a transposition and, in a sense, through an identification, a hermeneutical *Einfühlung*. "Intuitionism" nevertheless has nothing in common with the irrationalism of a message received in a state of trance, but it is—in an essential way—the effect of the qualitative leap of the act of knowing, in addition to numerous quantitative accumulations made beforehand of a documentaty, scholarly nature. It is the result of a long "cohabitation" with the "facts" being investigated, of the investigation of them "in the mental universe which gave birth to them," of the understanding of them "within the whole from which they have been extracted." Hence, a certain sympathetic solidarity between the original revelation submitted to exegesis and the modern ulterior decipherment of these original revelations. The contemporary historian of religions validates in this way meaning given anciently and well defined. For instance: "The cry of the Kwakiutl neophyte, 'I am at the Center of the World!' reveals to us again one of the most profound meanings of sacred space."[72] Likewise, the same hermeneut declares himself wholly in accord with mythical representations of the Great Goddess, according to which "sacrality, life, and immortality are found at a 'center.' "[73] Primordial intuition meets, and in a certain sense provokes, the modern hermeneutical intuition with which it is identified. The modern hermeneutical intuition discovers, recovers, and valorizes the primordial intuition which confirms it: a reciprocal, alternating situation, eminently circular. In both cases it is a matter of an "interpretation" and an "understanding" qualitatively equal.

That it is not some kind of intuitive irrationalism is proved by two other categories of facts which are worth examining in some detail. (At a suitable place I shall call attention to other proofs.)

Intuition operates on the mass of facts subjected to interpretation by making a "selection," an "initial choice." "We must choose," declares Eliade in more than one place.[74] It is unnecessary to multiply examples and citations endlessly. The abundance of facts calls for a sorting, a "hierarchizing." The question immediately arises, According to what criteria? How does this inevitable selection work? The answer seems, at first glance, tautological: religious phenomena are selected from "among the most significant." Hence, the significance was, in fact, anticipated, prescribed even in the moment of selection. We shall see immediately that that significance is actually the product of a confrontation, of an intuitive-reflective, inductive-deductive circuit, the effect of an alternating "coming and going." In other instances it is specified that the selection was made from among documents which were the "most permeable," i.e., more easily decipherable—which implies the same preliminary decipherment. Or, finally, a selection from among the "most favorable"[75] manifestations of sacrality, etc. In all these instances there is operative the same *incipit*, preanalytic moment, revelatory and profoundly anticipatory, of the hermeneutic circle.

Intuition is objectified in documents. This is yet another of the profoundly objective aspects of Mircea Eliade's hermeneutics whose infrastructure is oriented to an intuition-text-intuition/text-intuition-text relationship. Between these two planes there is a continuous collaboration and verification, a reciprocal change accomplished by suggestion, stimulation, and retouching. A single example: in one place the formula of aquatic symbolism is given; "water" is defined as always implying regeneration; then follow texts which confirm this definition.[76] The whole of *Patterns* (to cite only one work) is written according to this objective method. Moreover, Eliade is interested above all in objective aspects of the religious experience. And these objective aspects can be studied only through "historical documents" with religious content—documents comparable to any other aspect of culture: artistic creations, social phenomena, economics, etc. It is this perspective, further, which separates Eliade's hermeneutics from the speculative, philosophical type of Paul Ricoeur, for example. "Ricoeur, being a philosopher, appeals to a hermeneutics which I, for my part, did not use in *Patterns*. I first had to convince 'savants'—Orientalists, sociologists, philosophers—that I had the right to base my argument on documents and not on 'speculations.' "[77] The primacy of documents implies the postulate of latent-objective meaning included in the original "texts." Hence the conclusion—essential for the demonstration of this objective attitude—that any symbolism *exists* and persists regardless of its being understood or not, degraded or not, camouflaged or not. The proof is the existence of numerous prehistoric symbols lost for millennia and later "rediscovered."[78] Nor can we overlook Eliade's repeated declarations that his essential aim is the establishment of an objective perspective in the history of religions—an "objectivity" defined, of course, in accordance with orientations of our time.[79] We shall see that in Eliade's conception the role of the historical perspective is considerable—and furthermore it is consubstantial with his entire hermeneutics.

The decipherment of meanings *in* documents and *through* documents implies inevitably a long and painstaking exegesis.[80] In other words, a long and painstaking analysis, the essential and indispensible hermeneutical operation: "We shall be content, for a clear understanding of the structure of human sacrifice, to mention just a few examples, but with sufficient detail."[81] These details can be well circumscribed and defined only through analysis: "It is always instructive to know in detail at least one rite from the category we wish to study."[82] All the details, in turn, demand to be subsumed under a pattern, integrated into a synthesis. The passage from *analysis to synthesis* belongs, moreover, to the beginnings of hermeneutical theory, to the prehistory of the philological circle, and it has no other function than to recognize an inevitable dialectic correlation, a necessary alternating and reciprocal passage from analysis to synthesis and from synthesis to analysis.[83] Undoubtedly, any analysis is undertaken with a view to a synthesis, just as a synthesis can be realized only through a number of analyses. Analysis cannot have an intrinsic hermeneutical finality, and Eliade calls attention insistently to the limitations of his methodology. He knows that "the risk of any analysis is that it become fragmented and pulverized into separate elements which, for the consciousness which it represents, compose a single unit, a Cosmos." "We are obliged to return repeatedly to the *synthetic* character which every archaic religious act preserves . . . in order to avoid the danger of understanding it *analytically* and *cumulatively*." Investigation separates into fragments that which was perceived intuitively as a whole. Ontological situation is transformed into methodological principle. That is why Eliade so insistently calls for liberation from the tyranny of the superstition according to which only analysis represents "truly" scientific work, as well as the elimination of the prejudice that one must not propose a "synthesis" or a "generalization" until very late, at the end of one's life.[84]

Mircea Eliade's reaction to excessive and inconclusive analyses which lead only to fragmentation and paralysis of thought is energetic and very welcome. We hasten to add that this position is diametrically opposed to present-day tendencies which are oriented toward the infinitesimal, toward microscopic examination, toward the cult of the detail—not only in the history of religions, but also in the whole field of philological sciences. For it is no longer a matter of literary history, properly speaking, when the same prejudice is propagated, namely that in our times works of synthesis cannot be elaborated except by broad collectivities and only in collaboration. As if this work of collaboration did not need a coordinating spirit, a synthetic head which would insure unity, cohesion, and a common conclusion to the collaboration. Moreover, the history of religions (and any type of history) cannot be fragmented to infinity and entrusted to philologists and specialists,[85] experts in a single religion or a single period of a religion (or in one literary era, a single author, etc.). This is a fatal, paralyzing timidity which accomplishes nothing, but propagates the prejudice against taking a risk, the prejudice of the impossibility of syntheses and general theories.[86] In reality, as Eliade himself shows, "the road to synthesis passes through hermeneutics"—synthesis which constitutes at the same time a hermeneutical stage, alternative, and conclusion. The study of symbolic structures involves necessarily not an operation of *reduction,* but one of *integration*—hence, once again, of a synthesis of all its polyvalent meanings.[87] It is self-evident that this operation of synthesis can only integrate the results of ethnology, psychology, sociology, history—synthesize, for example, all the specialized investigations of shamanism,[88] or any other religious phenomenon in a global, total investigation.

For Mircea Eliade, exegesis begins with a fundamental dissociation of *sacred* and *profane* meanings. The problem is put in the most categorical terms in *The Sacred and the Profane,* but it recurs throughout his *oeuvre.* The dissociation and opposition sacred-profane constitutes the deepest and broadest hermeneutical relationship possible. It represents a true "universal key." "Explanation" is impossible without the preliminary delimitation of the domain of the sacred from that of the profane—two exemplary, paradigmatic situations for the whole hermeneutical process. What he institutes in this vision is, in fact, a profound—perhaps the most profound—existential situation: the "choice" between the sacred and the profane planes, an option followed by a radical, absolute separation which splits and organizes the whole cosmos.[89]

Meanings, therefore, begin to arise out of an "embryonic dualism," equivalent to a true, original dialectic. Because, the domains are alternative, reciprocal, and complementary: the sacred appears and is defined by its opposition to the profane; the profane appears and is defined by its opposition to the sacred. That is to say that meanings are conditioned by a double process: one of continuous sacralization and secularization. This is a phenomenon with major consequences in the history of culture, literature, and the arts, one which delimits a specific, autonomous domain only by a more or less accentuated tendency toward separation and emergence from sacrality.

To enumerate the attributes of "the sacred" means, from this perspective, to define the deepest character of the meanings. The sacred is original, essential, a structural element of the spirit, inherent in the human condition.[90] The sacred expresses essential human nostalgias, constitutes the basic reference, institutes "true" meaning. While the sacred is *par excellence* "true," the profane is by definition "false," i.e., "non-meaningful," neuter; as is said today, of zero-degree significance.[91] For Eliade, only the experience of the sacred confers meaning. It alone opens and reveals significances (those continually retained: deep, essential, complete, original ones—which demonstrates once again that meanings of this type cannot be described, interpreted, and understood except on their own plane of reference, which is sacred reality.[92]

The alternating, "circular" situation of the sacred and the profane proves to be of the greatest hermeneutical importance: the interpretation, explanation, etc. are conducted according to the relationship of the sacred to the profane, or of the profane to the sacred. Between these two planes there is a permanent continuity and interference.[93] This means that in the sphere of the profane we can identify sacred signs and meanings. The most elementary and fundamental form of polyvalence of the religious phenomenon is precisely this: to participate, in quite variable proportions, in one side or the other and at the same time, in sacred and profane realities. Hence the permanent possibility of the appearance of ambivalent meanings and obvious ambiguity.

If modern man has desacralized the cosmos and life, a phenomenon discussed at length in numerous texts and contexts, one might say that Eliade on the contrary has "sacralized" it. While the emptying of religious significance becomes ever more pronounced, Eliade tenaciously makes a goal and method out of reactualizing it, recovering it, revalorizing it. One might say that what preoccupies him essentially is the operation of reverse demystification: the discovery of all the sacred meanings in the modern secularized world, the valorization of all "camouflaged" symbols and myths. A typical text is "Survivals and Camouflages of Myths," chapter 9 in *Myth and Reality*, and also appendix I of the same volume, "Myths and Fairy Tales." But in numerous other places Eliade analyzes at length the way myths are manifested, limited, and secularized in the modern world.[94] His whole hermeneutical perspicacity consists in deciphering them and making them intelligible—thus accessible—to the modern spirit, in spite of all the new forms in which they are clothed. Of course, the same hermeneutics acts also in the inverse sense, in the aim of deciphering sacred behaviors hidden in profane manifestations, or of demonstrating the thesis that some contemporary profane forms constitute in essence new forms of sacrality.[95] The reversibility is obvious and, on the plane of its own circular method, convincing.

The sacred experiences of humanity are reducible to a number of prototypes or *archetypes* and, without discussing in this connection the theory of archetypes elaborated by C. G. Jung,[96] it is quite obvious that in Eliade's hermeneutics the archetype plays a fundamentally heuristic role. Decipherment and interpretation, analysis and synthesis, begin with identifying and defining archetypes, with the establishment of significant relationships drawn from a series of archetypal situations. These express the totality of primordial experiences, and reference to their content constitutes the decipherment of essential meanings of religious phenomena. Interpretation and understanding for Mircea Eliade consist precisely in the transposition and the assumption of the original, primordial, essential phenomenon of the archetype. This is the initial and fundamental hermeneutical moment in the deciphering of all archaic ontological structures.[97] Hence the special preoccupation with ascertaining the "original," "genetic" moments, a method which permits the apprehension of the oldest meanings, the most authentic and most pure.[98] For this reason, any archetype, beginning, embryonic moment, etc. is meaningful in itself and for itself. Its ferreting out can be considered accomplished whenever hermeneutical analysis reaches the point of discovering an original, irreducible situation which cannot be translated in *any other way:* by another image, symbol, myth, concept, etc.[99]

To decipher archetypes means to decipher original existential situations, bearers of fundamental meanings. Primordial revelation, primordial meaning, and meaning obtained by exegesis of this primordial revelation are convergent operations, and they converge at an essential point. Primal intuitions of primal existential situations[100] constitute consequently so many "explicative" moments. "Primal meaning" is essential and truly "meaningful," inasmuch as it continues the totality of latent-physical valencies characteristic of an essential order of value. In short, the archetype confers basic meaning, and to follow the archetype (mythical and symbolic prototypes, archaic theories, etc.) means to find the "key," the "explanation," the essential "interpretation." Man requires archetypes precisely because he feels the need of an essential referent. That is to say that the totality of meanings to which the individual has access—his whole meaningful universe—is, in fact, archetypal.[101] It corresponds to a residium, to prototypes of the collective unconscious—the deposit, according to Eliade (wholly Jungian in this respect), of the global religious experiences of humanity. In this regard, at least, his hermeneutics is a true hermeneutics of the collective unconscious and of its mythico-symbolic expressions.

But the exegetical virtues and aspects of the archetype do not stop here. Being a prototype, it establishes an exemplary model, a schema of essential exemplary situations capable of generating new categories of meaning. To the extent to which any archetype requires acts of repetition and imitation, the reproduction of manifestations which took place *in illo tempore*—the simple participation, assumption, and imitation of this kind of model are capable of revealing meanings, but these meanings can only be infinite in number, inasmuch as infinity, inexhaustibility, is the very cause which generated them.[102] The archetype is by definition polysemic and polyvalent. Any reference to a mythic model, any act of imitation of a mythical prototype, reveals meanings and multiplies to infinity a series of meanings. Inversely, all that cannot be related to an exemplary model seems lacking in meaning, betrays a situation devoid of significance.

The effectiveness of the archetypal method is verified not only in the case of traditional cultures ("This tendency to interpret life and history in terms of exemplary models and categories is characteristic of traditional cultures")[103], but also of modern ones: references to certain "patterns" which survive under various camouflages help us to decipher certain modern behaviors.[104] Further: thanks to this hermeneutics, one can arrive at the establishment of a general archetypology, not only of the imaginary universe in the sense of Gilbert Durand[105] (indebted to Eliade), but also of real life. Just as all archetypes reduce ultimately to a single one, the primordial archetype, the cosmogonic myth, so also the sum total of all existential situations, the prime intuitions and revelations of men, group themselves in a single complex: the archetypal situation of man in the world.[106] Finally, a series of central myths and symbols can be characteristic of the spirituality of a people. They have in this case also a national significance. Thus, the *Miorița* can be considered as the spiritual "archetype" of the Romanian people.[107]

The "symbolic" situation of this technique of deciphering and interpreting is the *symbol*, the true *locus hermeneuticus*. Its exegesis determines (and even requires) the discovery or rediscovery, total or partial, of all traditional hermeneutical principles and procedures. The symbolic can become accessible only through interpretation. For this reason it is the preferred *locus* of hermeneutics. If this sort of method exists, it is explained by the fact that symbol exists, has its structures and valencies, its peculiar exigencies, its intrinsic-exegetical necessities. It constitutes a mystery, an enigma which demands penetration. The symbol is itself the "archetype" of the symbolic situation, on the ontological and gnoselogical planes alike.

Decipherment becomes necessary because symbol, before anything else, *says* something, *reveals* something, *shows* something, *expresses* something, using its own "language," predominantly figurative, pre-literate, and often even prearticulate (the gesture, etc.).[108] Hence the first typical hermeneutical question: what does the symbol *say?* Eliade's reply derives from the totality of his principles of thought and his method: the symbol reveals—we know this very well—a limit-situation, an ultimate reality: total, sacred, ontological. Through it we recognize original intuitions, the deepest creations of the psyche: "The majority of religious symbols show *the World in its totality* or *one of its structures* (Night, Water, Sky, Stars, seasons, vegetation, temporal rhythms, animal life, etc.), or they refer to *situations fundamental to the human condition,* to the fact that man is sexual, mortal, and in search of what today is called 'ultimate reality.' "[109] Therefore, the symbol has a certain significance which can be deciphered only through reference to symbolic structures and mechanisms. Symbol constitutes a "sign" and at the same time a "cipher" of absolute realities, of the deepest cosmic regions. This causes Eliade to be constantly defining and explaining symbols: "the snake symbolizes . . ." etc., "the house symbolizes . . ." etc.[110] Through the clarification of meanings we will understand not only what symbol "explains,"[111] but also why symbol (myth, etc.) constitutes an instrument of knowledge; except that the symbol can attain planes which totally escape profane understanding. This is tantamount to saying that the experience of the sacred is accessible only via the symbolic road. "Everything not consecrated directly becomes sacred by participation in a symbol." The production of a meaning, finally, confers a value on the symbol. All these ideas appear already in Eliade's early writings. "Every sign is a symbol." "The origin of a symbol is worth as much as the discovery of a dynasty of pharaohs," etc.[112]

The anatomy and morphology of symbol bring out other characteristic traits. Its significance depends on the fulfillment of certain conditions. Symbol achieves plenitude only in its mature state, not in its germinal phase. The entire meaning-potential of the symbol is revealed only in the phase of its complete realization. The essential meaning is given at decisive cosmic moments, moments of changes in the life of the cosmos.[113] Because, symbol has its own life, it passes along an evolutionary curve: it is born, develops, then becomes adulterated, darkened. The circumstances in which the symbol was meaningful pass away.[114] This meaning is universal. The same symbols and the same meanings are met with everywhere. Symbol therefore opens and expresses general and universal meanings. Consequently: *"The one who understands a symbol not only 'opens' himself to an objective world, but at the same time succeeds in emerging out of his particular situation and arriving at an understanding of the universe."* Moreover, symbol not only "opens" upon, but it has also a direct connection with the objective world. It represents in itself an objective reality, in the sense that symbols are given, imposed; they precede individual consciousness.[115] Symbols always have a transindividual, universal-objective existence. Their totality constitutes the symbolic order of the world, an archetypal stratum of the "noosphere."

The manipulation of symbol, both through representations of symbolic mentality and through interpretations of the same mentality, is effected in accordance with a symbolic "logic." In other words, symbol has an autonomous, *sui generis* structure, and a functional mechanism which is peculiar to it. There exists a logic of symbolic "behavior" which causes certain groups of symbols to demonstrate coherence and their replacement to be logical, which causes them to be formulated in a systematic way and expressed in rational terms.[116] There exists, therefore, a "chain-effect" in symbolization, following the line of force of an ontological schema. Because, this logic is, in fact, the expression of an ontological order, of an essential restructuring of reality. Symbol ontologizes the reality which incorporates it, deriving its validity precisely from this incorporation. It discloses an ontological region inaccessible to rational, superficial experience.[117]

Incorporating reality in all of its aspects through the association and unification of various sectors of the real (aquatic symbolism reveals the structural solidarity between water, the moon, becoming, vegetation, femininity, seeds, birth, death, rebirth, etc.—an example Eliade himself gives), adding at the same time new values and meanings to its old values and meanings, symbol, for all these reasons, cannot but be "polyvalent."[118] The expression has become very common in the contemporary era, especially through the success of the "New Criticism" which explores and valorizes the polyvalent meanings of the text; it is truly a basic postulate of these critics. But it is equally true that Eliade spoke about the "coexistence of meanings" already in the Romanian writings of his early years, prior to 1940.[119] All his subsequent studies speak in like manner of the "multivalence" of symbol, of its capacity *"to express simultaneously several meanings whose solidarity is not evident on the plane of immediate experience,"* of the coexistence and convergence of the natural and symbolic planes which are full, due to the very fact of their semantic density; about the "openness" of symbol, capable of revealing "transcendent" meanings which are not given, not evident, to immediate experience, transcendent inasmuch they comprehend homologies which escape the simple "imagination of matter."[120]

All these elements can prefigure, undoubtedly, a symbolic anthropology, which Eliade has indeed sketched. His hermeneutics becomes the instrument of investigation of this symbolic anthropology. Man is by definition a symbolizing animal, a *homo symbolicus*. Traditional society speaks, similarly, through the sum total of its members, the same symbolic language, "a language more simple, more beautiful, more fantastic because it was created in fantastic communion with cosmic hierarchies." Moreover, this language voices in a unified way a community's whole capacity for symbolic expression. "Symbol acquires valorization and expresses reality only when it participates in the life of a culture, when it is the language current among men, is accessible and alive to everyone, and is produced by the fantastic, mythical activity of the entire society." In this world, man is not isolated, "thrown into the world," cloistered in his own mode of being. On the contrary, he is "open" to life and can have communication with the world because he uses the same language: symbol. All his activities—we are speaking of traditional man of course—entail a certain symbolism. They are, in other words, freighted with meanings. These, in the last analysis, are symbolic, inasmuch as they refer to supernatural values and figures. Finally, it is necessary to underscore the existential value of religious symbolism. Symbol "visualizes always a reality and a situation which engage human existence." The religious symbol reveals not only a structure of the real or a dimension of existence, but it gives at the same time a meaning to human existence.[121] In contrast to this *homo symbolicus* for whom anything, any time and anywhere, can be a symbol, the omnipresent phenomenon *par excellence*, modern man is by definition antisymbolic, or, says Eliade, "desacralized." Paul Ricoeur makes, in effect, the same analysis when he shows that the progress of modern language has done nothing but empty it of its symbolic capacity.[122] Though presented in a much more expanded form, the theories of this philosopher do not say in essence any more about symbol—nor, we might add in passing, about hermeneutical *method*— than Eliade has said. It is sufficient to reread carefully, "Observations on Religious Symbolism" from *Mephistopheles and the Androgyne* to be convinced of this fact.

No one can miss the objective-hermeneutical value of this theory of symbol. The spiritual life and human existence are not fully understood except through the decipherment and interpretation of their symbolisms. Eliade pleads energetically and in a strongly convincing way for the recognition and "restoration of symbol as an instrument of knowledge." "The document falls on the second plane; there remains *sign*, symbol." "What is of primary interest is the *understanding* of the document," i.e., of its symbolic values and meanings.[123] That this knowledge is qualitatively equal to any other, if only it be situated on its own plane of reference, is a self-evident conclusion. What must be made emphatic, however, is the fact that both the existence of symbol as well as investigation by means of symbol have, in the same hermeneutics, an *objective* value. The validity of symbol (an idea urgently emphasised) does not depend on the degree of understanding of the individual who uses it or transmits it. Neither does symbol depend on statistical criteria or international factors. Existence can disregard the consciousness of symbol, since the status and functioning of symbol are autonomous— a conclusion with many methodological consequences: "The historian is now free to conduct his hermeneutics of a symbol without asking how many individuals of a particular society and of a certain historical moment understand all the meanings and implications of the symbol."[124] The understanding of the contemporary historian derives exclusively from consideration of the meanings of the symbol as objective manifestations extracted from the totality of "documents," through a method capable of interpreting them in all their implied systematic polyvalence and coherence.

The underscoring of the action of the *"systematic"* factor, first at the level of archetype and symbol, and then at that of the *method* by which archetypes and symbols are deciphered, is important in that it brings out an essential character of the archetypal-symbolic-mythic mentality. The hermeneut is directed to speak of the "logic of symbol" since symbols of any nature, regardless of their form of manifestation, are always "coherent and systematic," while "mythical thought is always coherent," "systematic." To have a "logic of its own" means to have an "intrinsic coherence."[125] Better said—an essential hermeneutical element—to have a series of traits perfectly conformable to a "coherent system of meaning,"[126] schema, or structure of interpretation. Therefore, in this respect at least, Eliade is in his own way a "reductionist." It is just that his reduction operates only in the sense of the consideration and assumption of a basic reality whose decipherment necessarily requires recognition of the existence of coherent systems of sacred modalities. The interpretation starts from the premise that every hierophany "presupposes" a complex system of coherent statements about ultimate reality (a system which can be considered a metaphysics), from the idea that all meanings and values are produced and articulated within a "system" (*axis mundi, coincidentia oppositorum,* etc.).[127] This system is organized around a "center" (meaning that every religion has a "center"), while the elements which comprise it demonstrate an obvious cohesion, in the framework of which "everything is contained."[128]

The typical complex of this systematic universe of meaning is symbol. Every symbolism integrates and articulates in a system common elements and heterogeneous or isolated realities. Becoming symbols— that is, signs of a transcendent reality—these objects "nullify their concrete limits, they cease being isolated fragments in order to be integrated into a system." Better said, these fragments, in spite of their precarious and fragmentary character, incarnate the whole system in question. All myths and rituals are coherent, in the sense that they form a "symbolic system which, in a sense, is anterior to each component element considered separately."[129] The symbolic system precedes, assimilates, and organizes the totality of symbolic signs.

The essential hermeneutical objective consists, consequently, in ferreting out, deciphering, and setting forth the mode in which the meanings of a symbolic complex are articulated in a coherent vision; it consists in "making transparent and coherent what is 'allusive,' cryptic, and fragmentary" in the theoretical content of an archetype or symbol. This is equivalent to demonstrating the mode in which meanings are linked together and organized in a system which constitutes—in the final analysis—a "universe of meaning."[130] In consequence, explanation will have to proceed through the identification of the meaning of the system, in accordance with its cause and "center." "These elements have no chance of being understood if the investigator does not realize that every religion has a 'center,' a central conception which inspires and animates the whole corpus of myths, rites, and beliefs."[131] All are generated by an *etymon* (a term used by Leo Spitzer in connection with the *Weltanschauung* of literary works), and to explain a system means to ascend to its source—which is equivalent to a progressive understanding of systems of meaning on increasingly higher planes of reference, in accordance with a "symbolic code." There is also, of course, the risk of integrating, in an artificial way (in a system which is coherent and unitary, but too rigid), elements of an infinite variety.[132]

We know, moreover, that in the hermeneutical process, intuition expresses itself necessarily through a heuristical operational schema. In the beginning it is imprecise and confused, then it becomes clearer and clearer, to the extent that—through operations of induction-deduction/deduction-induction, intuitive-reflective/reflective-intuitive,[133] direct contact with texts, permanent confrontation and rectification *in* and *through* documents—it clarifies it and consolidates it. Intuition meets the reality of the texts and the "model" becomes conscious of its own reality and modality of function through this textual verification. At the same time, the verification and confirmation through texts transforms the model from an abstract and imprecise schema—of the species "system of meaning of a symbol"—into a valid construction, well articulated and integrated into historical reality. And in the case of Eliade's hermeneutics, the two convergent planes end by superimposing themselves integrally: the "system" of the symbol meets and is identified with its own system of interpretation, elaborated precisely in view of the discovery and understanding of the "meaning-system" of the symbol—a situation once again eminently circular: we decipher and construct just the "system" we were seeking and which we knew in advance we had.

The reduction to unity (archetype, system, universe of meaning, etc.) is not possible without the intervention of a *schema* and a *typology*, Eliade insists quite emphatically. His method of interpretation is founded on the constant referral to a series of schematic, theoretical, and heuristic constructions, to operations of simplification, unification, and summarization of myths and symbols, and to the organization of "scenarios." The same schema (cosmogonic, initiatory, etc.), recurring in all "mysteries," is enough to establish the contours and lines of force, the basic coordinates, which integrate the morphological variety of the mythico-symbolic universe and make possible its reduction to a unity.[134] The historian of religions forms a schema of a verified validity and relates all his data to it.

Schematicization therefore necessarily entails typology, the grouping of characteristics distinctive of certain religious, cultural, and historical categories of phenomena and their classification and systematization in accordance with a number of common and characteristic general elements. The works of Mircea Eliade are full of such morphologico-typological schemas having to do with symbols and rites of rebirth, initiation, the experience of mystic light, etc.[135] In this way we arrive immediately at the idea of "structure," of the unitary, interdependent, and functional organization of convergent elements presided over by a unique principle of interior coherence. What most interests Eliade is not morphological analysis *per se*, but the discovery of "structures," "structurally coherent wholes," structural differences (sacred-profane, the typical example), or common structures (archaic ontologies, religious symbolisms, shamanistic phenomena, etc.).[136] We even find a definition which confirms these observations: "There is always a structure, that is, an intimate coherence between the different modalities [of a myth]." Its great stability leads to the recognition of the fact that *"every new valorization has always been conditioned by the structure of the Images,* so that one may say about an Image that it is simply awaiting the realization of its meaning."[137] On this plane of analysis, the meaning seems prescribed by its own archetype, by its own structural "model," which acts as an implacable mechanism. Moreover, the idea of *model* or *pattern* is frequently used by Eliade to define the origin and form of organization of meanings.[138] More than once he gives lists of patterns, and his *Patterns in Comparative Religion* is nothing but this kind of systematic inventory of *topoi* situations, as is shown very clearly by the English title (the French original was *Traité d'histoire des religions*).

From the hermeneutical point of view, the schematico-typological perspective is full of ramifications. For the time being we shall not inquire as to what extent (in this case also) the idea of pattern neces-sarily implies formalization, modelization.[139] In any event, it is not possible to constitute the model without the recognition of the existence of certain recurrent common elements. The idea appears under the form of the recognition of "characteristic and common features," or "coincidence in the history of the spirit," or "invariables."[140] In a broader sense, schematicization and typology have as their infrastruc-ture a series of "lines of force" (*les lignes maitresses*), thanks to which the interpreter can sketch a "map of magico-religious complexes of the same type."[141] This presupposes a general and generalizing perspec-tive, synthetic and as little as possible "positivistic."

Methodology appertains in fact to "comparativism," which inter-venes in order to associate and dissociate, to bring together and sep-arate elements, to confront results, for the purpose of integrating, systematizing, and identifying common notes. Understanding is pos-sible in this hermeneutics only through comparison,[142] in the frame-work of the same spiritual universe, in view of discovering both general structures and specific meanings. When strict parallelisms cannot be established or objective equivalents indicated, then resort is made to the establishing of similitudes, analogies, homologies, and symme-tries—a domain in which Eliade exhibits an extraordinary associative ability. The premise is always the same: "Everything is grouped by a tight system of correspondences and assimilations."[143] The investigator will proceed frequently therefore by identifying and establishing cor-respondences, by comparing systems and structural analogues, by rec-ognizing spiritual synchronisms, by homologizing on the basis of the recognition of certain common existential, metaphysical, or religious experiences. And yet homoligization is not confused with reductionism or mechanical parallelism. It constitutes, in fact, a method of assimi-lation and of "understanding" archaic and exotic spiritual universes, realizable on the one hand through the homologization implied in any reference to "depth psychology," to the ancestral background of hu-manity, and on the other through the recognition of structural variants, present both in Occidental and Oriental cultures, and in both modern and archaic ones.[144] We will find in Eliade therefore also homologies of type: Yoga—surrealism, the occident which discovers "Platonism" (archetypes, exemplary models) in Oriental spirituality, modern science which confirms Hindu philosophy, etc. *Fragments d'un journal* is a very instructive work in this regard, filled with examples of just this type. But let us note that the same Mircea Eliade urges us—naturally enough—to be very careful whenever we attempt to establish analogies between modern philosophy and philosophies of India.[145]

In the last analysis, the typologico-schematic perspective of Eliade reduces to what is called in modern criticism and hermeneutics "simultaneous reading."[146] It is accomplished by bracketing the chronology of texts and by using them on the same plane of meaning and structural invariance. When, in an early work, written documents were placed and cited on the same plane as symbolic architectonic "documents," Eliade made precisely this kind of simultaneous reading. The recent portrait of Prometheus (to give a single example) compiled from texts belonging to different eras but perfectly convergent as to meaning, appertain to the same method: "What matters is not the identity of philosophical terminology: it suffices that the problems be homologizable." The juxtaposition of religious facts gathered from peoples of different eras is therefore justified, fully valid, to the extent one seeks only the *description* of a "phenomenon per se," in its structure. In general, a structure can be described and interpreted through a few representative examples,[147] albeit intuited with keen insight. This type of hermeneutics is not, nor does it propose to be, exhaustive on the documentary plane; it only aims to provide sufficient conclusive examples to saturate its typological schemas.

Any schematization or typology presupposes an operation of synthesis which necessarily entails *totalization*. Schemas integrate, unify, totalize the partial component elements, and it is noteworthy that Eliade's hermeneutics operates only with and through aggregates. It has in an essential way the virtue of totality. He considers "the sacred in its totality." "The entire religious history of humanity"[148] verifies the thesis according to which, for mystical thought, "the particular mode of being is preceded of necessity by a *total* mode of being." This is because totality is ontological, essential, primordial, and therefore eminently meaningful. In the consciousness of archaic man, everything is linked together. Religious manifestations (hierophanies, myths, symbols) constitute a whole, through analogies, correspondences, participations which make up a cosmic "network" within which all elements are united and nothing remains isolated.[149] Any decipherment and objective hermeneutical interpretation therefore is obliged to begin from this basic reality.

The typical situation is offered by the structure of the symbol, whose polyvalence constitutes by definition a semantic totality. It does not "analyze," but only "synthesizes," integrates, unifies, structures, thereby embracing a totality of meanings without identifying them or confusing them. "Every symbol reveals the fundamental unity of several zones of reality." In its capacity of symbol it transforms "objects" into something else, into meanings different from those of profane experience. But, on the other hand, in becoming a symbol, any object tends to coincide with a *whole*, to incorporate sacrality in its totality, to exhaust by itself all manifestations of sacrality. In the context of symbolic experience, "the world is revealed as a totality," as a "network" whose "center" generates or structures into a system the aggregate of all its equivalents and correspondences.[150] The privileged hermeneutical situation is evident.

But the most conclusive proof is this: only the decipherment of the symbol permits an X-ray of a global meaning, since in the last analysis only the symbolic totality has meaning. "The different meanings of a symbol are interlocked, united, as in a system." Contradictions which can be discovered between different individual versions are, in most instances, only apparent: "they are resolved once we consider a symbolism in its totality, once we consider it as a structure." This demonstrates that an aggregate is not meaningful except insofar as it constitutes a coherent totality, and that it does not become a totality in some "symbolic" way. Only its solidarity and continuity are profoundly significant.[151] Hence, nothing can be described if it is not integrated into a system of meaning; nothing can be valorized if it is not related to a "symbolic aggregate."[152]

In accordance with these principles we rediscover also the fundamental hermeneutical relation, *part-whole*,[153] whose theorization receives an ontological grounding in the work of Mircea Eliade. Symbolic totalization achieves a true *coincidentia oppositorum:* the tree or stone "becomes *All* while remaining at the same time *part;* it is a sacred thing while remaining at the same time an ordinary object in the cosmos."[154] Hence a conclusion no less essential: the totality exists in and through the parts which compose it, just as in each of the parts totality exists. The relationship is reciprocal and eminently circular. Both components of this equation are grasped and defined with clarity by Eliade. He knows well that "in any fragment the whole is present," that "the original unity is implied in even the smallest fragment," that "any meaningful fragment *repeats* the totality"—just as the obverse is likewise true. This observation can be found even in an early Romanian work: "Every folkloric product . . . carries in itself the mental universe which gave rise to it." In accordance with this same principle, Christian symbolism does not become integrally significant until it is situated in the context of a "general" symbolism, one universally attested by the religions of the world. A simple reference to the Old Testament is not sufficient.[155]

Hermeneutics presupposes therefore the use of a continuous circular relationship: *whole-part-whole/part-whole-part*, and a decipherment from part to whole and from whole to part, a reciprocal verification and rectification in conformity with both bench marks, through alternating references and integrations. One can speak therefore in a metaphorical sense of a metonimic (*pars pro toto*) sense, but equally of a sinecdotic (*toto pro pars*) sense of the same method.

This appears clearly formulated in a Romanian study of 1937, "Folklorul ca instrument de cunoaştere" (Folklore as an instrument of knowledge, i.e., as a means of gaining "scientific" facts, etc.) where Eliade arrives at the following conclusion: "Having verified experimentally some of . . . the beliefs and superstitions (e.g., *cryptesthesia pragmatica*, levitation, the incombustibility of the human body), we have the right to suspect that at the basis of *other* folk beliefs lie *concrete facts*." Through the validation of some elements one can arrive at the validation of whole categories of elements—just as sometimes the existence of a single fossil makes possible the reconstitution of the organic whole of which this vestige was a part. But the opposite line is proved likewise operative and conclusive: only through "the decipherment of the fundamental ideological system which lies at the base of social and religious institutions is it possible to understand rightly a particular divine figure, myth, or ritual." The symbolism of the center—to give a single example—explains cosmological images and religious beliefs relative to a particular series of myths and rites about holy cities and sanctuaries which are located "at the Center of the World," temples which are replicas of the "Cosmic Mountain," and so forth.[156]

Another important methodological conclusion is the need to overcome the limits of fragmentation, the position implied in the dialectic *analysis/synthesis*, clearly resolved in favor of synthesis. It is not the fragment which is significant, but only the structure to which it belongs, i.e., the system, the totality. Only integration into a unit gives content and significance to the fragment: "How depressing," Eliade exclaims at a certain moment, "is the excessive fractioning and fragmenting of our historical vision!" The history of religions—as well as any other history, of ideas, literature, etc.—cannot but be lost through excessive specialization and exploration of minute fragments, just as an elephant cannot be studied with a microscope. A *single* aspect of religious life is not and cannot be significant and essential while all the other aspects are ignored.[157] The unifying spirit of this hermeneutic cannot but react with vigor against pulverization, microscopic analysis, the passion for the irrelevant detail, any rigorously compartmentalized "philology."[158] Need we repeat that this reaction is highly commendable *today?*

This methodological effort aims at the establishment of new and more objective bases for the whole process of interpretation. If only the whole has value, if a religion (or any other spiritual creation) can be understood only in the context of a whole and not in its isolated aspects, the result is that understanding can only be the product of a totalization. True meaning belongs only to the whole, ". . . because every symbolism 'makes a system' which we cannot know truly except insofar as we consider it in the totality of its particular applications." This too is a "position of youth," defined with acumen in an early work: "The only means of understanding an archaic belief is to try to reintegrate it into that whole to which it once belonged, endeavoring to represent that whole in its intimate coherence."[159] This is a program which becomes in later works that of "distinguishing the deep meaning and structural solidarity of all those symbols, rites, and beliefs." Or, even more precisely: "Only a scrupulous hermeneutical analysis of the totality of archaic religious manifestations will permit us to perceive and interpret the dimensions proper to this type of creativity." Hence the result that any *"partial, incomplete"* interpretation is inevitably "false," being taken out of the symbolism of which it is a part.[160]

The same situation and the same essential handicap exist in the case of any other critical analysis (literary, artistic) as well.

This kind of interpretation of the totality is realizable only through the elaboration of a *"total hermeneutics,"* a basic objective of Mircea Eliade. Its realization is not possible without a radical change of perspective. The hermeneut consequently adopts another spiritual attitude toward reality. He must prove receptive to the *totality* of sacred manifestations, he must arrive at a "global understanding of the real" without forgetting "to reveal at the same time the coherent and intelligible structures of the *sacred.*" At the same time—to synthesize our analysis up to this point—he consequently rejects any reductionism, any fragmentary limitation of the decipherment of meanings, any ignoring of the specific plane of reference: with regard to this type of phenomena "we do not have the right to reduce them to anything other than what they are: spiritual creations."[161] Everything is undertaken from an intuitive and generalizing plane of lofty height, going on to arrive at "an increasingly precise intuition of the whole" (the process being progressive). And when documents are lacking, we must make our case from that which we have called, without any scientific inhibitions, the "hermeneutical imagination." This is the case, for example, with the religion of Zalmoxis, "where we are reduced to imagining what might be the mysterious remainder"—what is left apart from the documents which tell us something about this religion. The objectivity of the interpretation is assured by the systematic validity, coherence, and integrity of all the sources we have at our disposal. Consequently, on the basis of a sure premise, "we have the right to 'generalize' in the history of religions—provided that we present the *essential* on the scale on which we are working, and that we be coherent."[162] In other words, provided that we present the entire interpretation in the framework of a rigorously consistent system, well articulated and documented.

So far as the idea of a "total hermeneutics" proper is concerned, one can distinguish in the case of Eliade several senses: 1) the study of all religions historic and prehistoric, literate and preliterate, and of "original" and "modern" religious phenomena; 2) the study of all religious morphologies through a series of large monographs grouped under chapter headings: Sky, Sun, Moon, Water, etc., according to the table of contents of his *Patterns in Comparative Religion;* 3) a "total hermeneutics" also in the sense of "describing and explaining all encounters of man with the sacred, from prehistory to the present," hence of the totality of meanings and experiences (religious, etc.) objectively attested; 4) a total discipline by virtue of the fact that "it must utilize, integrate, and articulate the results obtained by various methods of studying religious phenomena," by going beyond the alternatives *religious phenomenology* or *history of religions* to an "integral conception of the science of religions";[163] 5) an effort defined as "excellent for comprehending *everything*, for taking account of everything, for valorizing everything" (the model in this instance being Hegel); 6) results obtained also through the *total* transposition, participation, and engagement on the part of the hermeneut: "The whole of a man's being is engaged when he listens to myths and legends."[164] The hermeneutical object and subject are therefore implicated from the beginning to the end in the same total and profoundly existential "adventure" of interpreting and understanding.

The analysis of interpretation brings out the fact that interpretations new and old coincide ultimately in an essential point. This fact is explained by the existence of the no less essential hermeneutical relation: past-present-past/present-past-present,[165] as well as an alternating process of understanding that presides over and organizes all hermeneutical circuits: intuition-reflex, schema-model, preconcept-concept, analysis-synthesis, whole-part, etc. The past can be deciphered and interpreted only by means of instruments of knowledge and, on the horizon of the present, from a contemporary perspective, while the present can be deciphered and interpreted only by means of data, findings, and conditionings of the past. This is the determinative situation for a modern historian of religions like Mircea Eliade, whose field of investigation is the totality of the domain of the archaic or traditional religious mentality.

One may say for a certainty that the circular relationship *past-present* runs throughout the entire methodology and exegesis of our author like a red thread. Interpretations start, depending on circumstances, from traditional documents or contemporary observations, but the two planes overlap and complete each other permanently. The past becomes accessible only through modern analysis, while the modern become intelligible only through historical references which anticipate it. Whence, once again, the reappearance of the alternating "going-coming" relationship, the uninterrupted exchange of ancient-modern/modern-ancient meanings. It is not a matter of our deduction only, but of the methodological position of Eliade himself, quite clearly expressed. Of course, it is a matter—as is also the case of other hermeneutical circuits—of two ideal theoretical moments, dissociable only by analysis. In the concrete synthesis of investigation, the two planes coexist, interact, and collaborate with full efficacy.

Consequently, any "hermeneutics" begins with an investigation of an "archeological," "historical" type, and Eliade's is no exception. His preoccupation with "primitive" and "traditional" documents and situations is more than obvious. Every one of his exegeses begins by evoking the "historical" data and meanings of the problem. We are reminded that science itself begins by being "traditional" in the sense that any scientific knowledge preserves a "totalitarian" structure, which implies cosmogonic, ethical, and existential principles. In a sense one could say that hermeneutics uses only given, traditional rules of interpretation, that the totality of documentary material is, in substance, pre-modeled by our whole vision of the "primordial situation," "archaic thought," etc., referred to so often by Eliade. There is no doubt that all his interpretations proceed from the past to the present and begin with a reference to a primordial (archetypical, mythical, symbolic, etc.) situation. They aim to discover above all "living fossils" (spiritual or cultural), "beginnings," "origins" (whose survival is traced in modern science, in Freud, etc.). Let us recall two programmatic citations: "The hermeneutics necessary for the revealing of meanings and messages hidden in myths, rites, and symbols will help us . . . to understand depth psychology as well as the historic era into which we have entered." The text defines in a concise way both terms of the equation. At the same time, "to understand the structure and function of myths in traditional societies . . . does not mean to elucidate a stage in the history of human thought, but to understand better a category among our contemporaries."[166]

But the investigation must pursue the same direction in the opposite sense also, since any hermeneutics is undertaken from its concurrent historical plane. The past is assimilated and deciphered only through an actualization in the present. In this operation of recovering the past, one makes either 1) "an immediate and direct reintegration into a primordial situation," or 2) "a progressive return to 'the origin,' taking

us back in Time, from the present moment to the 'absolute beginning.' " In this way the resurrection of the "total past of humanity"
becomes possible, the uniting with all vanished and peripheral peoples.
"In studying rural European societies we have an opportunity to understand the religious world of neolithic hunters." Analogies, "ethnographic parallelisms," comparisons with contemporary situations,
are in this way fully justified. Without this kind of method, the symbolism of the stone age or of megalithic cultures would remain forever
obscured. Regressive deduction is therefore justified: "If, at a given
moment of history, a religious symbol could express with clarity a
transcendent meaning, we are justified in assuming that at an earlier
time period this meaning could have been vaguely anticipated."[167]
Equally well founded is the interpretation of present-day spiritual tendencies through their projection onto a background of a very far-off
and broad history. Some contemporary Western phenomena of regres-
sion—the rediscovery of the paradisal myth, the "myth of the noble
savage," regeneration via return to nature, a whole series of messi-
anisms, etc.—likewise find their true dimensions and significance
through the same retrospective reference. A great associative capacity
presides over this whole system of relationships: a mysterious illness
of a savant like Fechner cannot be explained without resort to the
shamanistic initiatory scenario. The history of religions can decipher
current philosophical movements, etc.[168]

Homologies of this sort are not possible without the recognition of
continuities between these two worlds, contemporary and past, united
through the same systems of meaning (archetypal, mythical, symbolic,
etc.). Myths of the modern world rediscover and repeat myths of the
ancient world. There are an obvious structural analogy and stability of
hierophanies realized in a given "historical moment," which are able
to repeat the same hierophanies thousands of years older or newer.
"Any new valorization of an archetypal image crowns and absorbs the
old."[169] The universal meaning therefore is unitary and permanent. In
order to decipher it and understand it, the interpreter must displace
it from a temporal axis. He will most certainly find the same spiritual
contrasts and therefore the same meanings.

In fact, the whole operation consists in a contiuous and inevitable
actualization by means of a reading which can be made only on the
contemporary plane. Even the archetype is defined only on this plane,
since every interpretation takes place exclusively in the *hic et nunc*, in
accordance with certain objective temporal coordinates. Just as the
archetype, model, or symbol is imitated and can only be imitated
through conditioned historical metamorphoses which are given (we
shall return in the following paragraph to this important aspect), so

this way, out of the totality of religious meanings, only those intelligible to the spirit of modern man will be selected,[170] valorized by the spirit of a modern hermeneut. It is evident that the "understanding" of Mircea Eliade (as an exponent of this situation) is of a different quality and is produced on a different level from that of the primitive, however great may be his capacity for intuition, transposition, hermeneutical imagination, etc. Willy-nilly, he lives and studies in *another* era—a rationalized, demythologized one—even if he maintains that the imaginary world of prehistoric cultures "is still accessible to us through experiences of our own imagination."

Granted that "in the final analysis, the history of religions is obliged by its hermeneutical effort to 'relive' a host of existential situations and to dismantle a large number of presystematic ontologies."[171] One can admit, likewise, for the sake of symmetry, that primitive philosophical anthropology is "qualitatively" equal to modern, in spite of its poorer means of expression and the typification which the former always enjoys. However, it remains an indisputable fact that *any* interpretation, any signification, even if qualitatively equal, must be formulated, defined, and interpreted by a contemporary consciousness with all that this sort of determinism presupposes. Any meaning varying in accordance with the historical horizon of the receiving consciousness and referring to Gadamer or others is not obligatory for this *topos* of hermeneutical theory. Both interpretations (past and present) are "objective," but neither is superior to the other. Time and again Eliade is confronted with just this key situation, of deciding between the validity of an aboriginal meaning or a modern one originating with a present-day observer or critic.[172] His tendency is to homologize, to equate, so that in any fused meaning, in the last analysis, there is an original "sense" and a modern one. How "historical" and how "personal" this distribution is, no one can declare with certainty. Hermeneutical knowledge is always the product of a synthesis through the collaboration and intersection of two planes of historical consciousness: of historical formation (of the historian) and of the "history" recovered and assimilated by this historical formation. In the case of Eliade, it seems obvious, to define it with an inevitably simplified formula, that he is preeminently "an arbitrating spirit."

The past/present relationship is not possible without the recognition and perpetual intervention of *history* in all phases of the hermeneutical process. The latter unfolds, draws its sources from history, from its documents and texts, and in general from its whole substance. For anyone who has read Eliade attentively there can be no doubt: his point of departure (which does not coincide wholly with his final point of view) is fundamentally historical. The author reflects upon historical conditions, upon the meanings and ambiguities of this idea ("that which has passed," but also "historiography," etc.),[173] he recognizes the necessity of "historical documents" as well as the primacy of the historically "concrete" and "authentic" in any interpretation.[174]

This kind of orientation makes its presence felt in works of Eliade's youth, where he draws attention to the "grave errors of an historical perspective" (in a case where definitions of nature in non-European cultures do not coincide with a series of scientific truths of our own), as well as to the necessity of "historical perspective" which means to "take account of all that connects you with the past, to know all the stages of scientific progress." Moreover, even if the majority of the religious actions and principles of primitive societies and archaic civilizations were long ago superseded by history, they have not disappeared without a trace: "they have contributed to the realization of what we are today; they participate in our own history."[175] Man, as a concrete, historical, authentic being, is found always in an "historical" situation; sacrality is manifested only "in a certain historical situation."[176] All these theses would be only so many "truisms" if there were not at their base a whole technique of concrete and objective interpretation.

To summarize: Eliade's point of departure consists in a triple historical determination: 1) any spiritual phenomenon has an historical genesis and conditioning: "Ethnology does not know a single people which has not changed in the course of time, which has not had a 'history' "; "Everything is manifested in the historically concrete and everything is conditioned in some way by history"; "Every historical being carries within him a large part of historic humanity from before him"; "Since the religious life of humanity incarnates itself in history, its expressions are inevitably conditioned by multiple historical moments and cultural styles."[177] 2) Historical conditioning gives birth to new historical contexts: for instance the new cultural context in Europe of the nineteenth and twentieth centuries of the myth of the "Golden Age."[178] 3) Historical conditioning gives birth to new values and meanings, each of which has its own "history." Any symbol has a history, in the sense that it appears at a certain historical moment and that its meanings become diversified and enriched in the course of history.[179] Concerning the solidarity and circularity of these historical determinations, which are so self-evident, there is nothing to add. . . .

III

In the course of this study I have noted in passing a number of implications and convergences that exist between Eliade's hermeneutics on the one hand, and aesthetics and literary criticism on the other. By extending this hermeneutics creatively, one can extract from it easily a number of ideas and suggestions essential to a theory of art and literature, as well as to a critical, systematic theory. Besides, the whole hermeneutics is, in itself, nothing but a theory of interpretation, a method of "deciphering" texts, of exegesis, and thus a form of objective criticism carried out with dexterity and finesse, but also with rigor, at the far extreme from "impressionistic" improvization. The hermeneutics is neither pedantic nor dilettantish, but rather coherent and consistent with its own premises. In what follows, we propose to pursue only a few of the more important paths which the whole hermeneutical reflex of the author opens up, without in the least trying to exhaust them. We confine ourselves only to those contributions which seem to us truly essential. We shall proceed as heretofore in this methodological introduction to Eliade's thought by the extraction, selection, and organization of fundamental, revelatory citations. Our aim, we repeat, has been to achieve an analytic reading, focused directly upon the *texts* of some of Eliade's more important hermeneutical works.

First of all, there are a goodly number of indications of adhesions to a theory of art which is ritualistic, archetypal, metaphysical, and symbolic. Following J. Evola and, especially, Ananda K. Coomaraswamy (whose writings he reviewed, discussed, and published[180]), Mircea Eliade considers the creation of art as a sacred act, a ritualistic, canonical operation, an integral participation in the world of archetypes and symbols[181]—a thesis verified especially in Indian art, wholly typical for this kind of traditional aesthetics. In the same way, myths: "Myth expresses graphically and dramatically that which metaphysics and theology define dialectically."[182] The content of art is fundamentally ontological, while aesthetic contemplation becomes an act of knowledge. The idea of "novelty" and "originality" is devoid of any meaning, as is true also of *mimesis* and "realism." Art only recreates primordial archetypes through a gesture of mythico-magical recurrence of an initiatory stamp. The infrastructure of myths and symbols sustains the totality of styles and cultures.[183] Eliade's theory of artistic symbols cannot be dissociated from ample consideration of the structure, logic, and meaning of symbol surveyed above. These principles—to give but a single example of contemporary comparison—are not without analogy to the symbolic aesthetics of Susanne K. Langer in *Philosophy in a New Key* (1942).

Eliade's conception of literature has the same metaphysical-mythico-symbolist orientation. The perspective is radically antiformalist, anti-aesthetic, anti-belletristic. In the course of literary history the same archetypal tendencies, the same patterns, reappear. In a modern tragedy one can discern traces of traditional metaphysics, in modern novels we rediscover archaic myths (such as that of the androgyne in Balzac). Moreover, there is a real structural solidarity between the central myth and the central literary motif of a work. Myths find their way into literary works without the "intention" of the creator. They belong to the anthropological structures of the creative imagination.[184] So also do the entirety of eschatalogical, initiatory, messianic, and paradisal themes. Even more significantly, a series of myths reappear or can easily be discovered in the midst of modern avant-garde literature; for example, the apocalyptic myth of radical destruction: to make a *tabula rasa* and begin the artistic cycle over again, starting from a recovered absolute purity.[185]

Like myth, symbol intervenes also in literary works without the author's awareness. Its reality is stronger than any graphic, iconic representation; hence the fundamentally nonrealistic, abstract character of symbolic art. In the majority of instances, creation only actualizes the latent existence of the symbol, just as modern language takes up and perpetuates a number of exemplary images.[186] The phenomenon of the degrading of archetypal symbolic meanings (which we have noted before) reappears also in literature. A great many epic scenarios are in reality nothing but degraded or camouflaged myths. In *Myth and Reality* this situation is discussed at length; it was evoked previously in *Comentarii la legenda Meşterului Manole*. Paradisal islands become "exotic" islands. The opposite phenomenon is also illustrated in literature: the biography of an historical hero can become mythical through the repetition and remaking of an archetype, that of the stylized life of an exemplary hero. Nor are observations lacking about the relationship of myth and poetic inspiration,[187] revelation, initiation, "enthusiasm," "mania", etc. The sum total of these observations about the great efficacy of myth and symbol in literature rehabilitates all forms of traditional spiritual creativity. All are "equal." "We have no right to treat them differently from the way tragic Greek poetry is considered."[188] Carried to its logical conclusion, this orientation profoundly undermines a certain conventional literary hierarchy: the primacy of purely artistic creation loses all real justification. "Literature" (secularized, desacralized, formal, aesthetised) can no longer aspire to supreme, unique, essential valorization. Mythico-symbolic creation is—and proves itself continually to be—of an equally sensitive "quality." A certain "anti-literary" process, very accentuated in our century, is nourished consequently from considerations of this sort referring to the authenticity, exemplarity, permanence, universality (and implicitly, the superiority) of traditional spiritual creations. Mircea Eliade is working to actualize and legitimatize them on all planes.

Ideas about synthesis and totality associated with the message of the new universal humanism and the emergence out of "provincialism" lead to the rediscovery of the concept (no less traditional) of *Weltliteratur*, presented this time in an original way from the new hermeneutical perspective of the history of religions and the "primitive" spiritual universe. The totality of the spiritual creations of humanity form one world, and literature does not make an exception to this reality. From the universal perspective, Occidental or European literature constitute only a part, a fragment, a "province" of the great "republic of literatures," to use an expression from the eighteenth century. Nothing could be more natural than to find in Mircea Eliade, at the end of a study about Balzac and Goethe who sensed it, precisely this concept: "European literature arises from beyond Greece and the Mediterranean, from beyond the ancient Near East and Asia; myths that reappear in *Faust* and *Séraphita* come to us from a great distance in time and space: they come to us from prehistory." Between all these creations there is a continuity and a unity; literature cannot be—in its essence, morphology, syntax, and semantics—fragmented. Aesthetic and eternal creations are completed, explained, and "understood" reciprocally, while the critic, the aesthetician, and the literary theoretician can only situate him- or herself for this reason in a universal perspective: "I share the conviction likewise of those who believe that the study of Dante or Shakespeare, yes or even of Dostoievski or Proust, is illuminated by a knowledge of Kālidāsa, the *Nō* theater, or of *Singe pèlerin*."[189] This is a viewpoint expressed enthusiastically among contemporary comparitivists by Etiemble, to whose latest work in this field we refer only: *Essais de littérature (vraiment) général*. The identity of positions is striking.

To this object (which we have so very schematically evoked) corresponds a critique of a special type, a technical, ideological, non-impressionistic, non-belletristic one, a critique not at all preoccupied with "creating," with "explaining emotion," or with "provoking perception." These preoccupations have been extirpated from the New Criticism of the present day, with which Eliade has a number of obvious affinities which do not, however, turn him into a "critic"—although, in his Romanian phase, he wrote literary essays and did literary criticism on certain favorite authors and themes. His convergences with the New Criticism cover the entire area of thematic and archetypological criticism (in the genus of Maud Bodkin: *Archetypal Patterns in Poetry*), of psychocriticism, and—in a very broad sense—even of structuralism. But what obviously predominates are his affinities with "depth" criticism, which his whole hermeneutics of archetypes, myths, and symbols anticipates and, in a way, even practices. Mircea Eliade even tends—if it may be put in this way in his case—toward a "total" criticism, knowing that there exists "a continuity and a solidarity between the work of the literary historian, the sociologist of literature, the critic, and the aesthetitician." It is the consequence of his whole orientation toward universality, toward the integration (in his work of exegesis and interpretation) of several complementary sciences. "The circulation, assimilation, and evaluation of a literary work presents problems which no one discipline can resolve *by itself*."[190] His critico-hermeneutical vision is interdisciplinary.

This is why Eliade tends also in the literary field to dissociate and associate the phenomenological and historical perspectives, the analysis of structures, and the historical content. He knows that the study of the psychology of an author and the historical dimensions of his work do not suffice "to disclose and explain the values of the poetic universes." For this it is necessary that the work be "studied in itself." Consequently, "a whole exegesis remains to be made after the historian of literature has concluded his mission, and then the literary critic intervenes. It is he who approaches the work as an autonomous universe, having its own laws and structures."[191] Eliade knows that "hermeneutics of literary works" has as its basic postulate the consideration of works *"on their own plane of reference,* in their particular universe,*"* that the discovery and understanding of their meanings is possible only to the extent to which the work of art "is considered as an autonomous creation, that is, to the extent we accept its model to be *that of artistic creation*—and do not reduce it to one of its constituent elements (in the case of the poem: to sonnet, vocabulary, structure, linguistics)," or to one of its ulterior functions (message, sociological or ethnographic document, etc.[192] It is the principle which defines also the essential object of literary hermeneutics: the decipherment of "structures of imaginary universes revealed by various poetic creations."[193] It stands under the sign of "revelation" and "mystery" and has, in the last analysis, an "initiatory" character.

This language is only apparently esoteric. What Eliade is seeking is the same discovery, interpretation, and understanding of systems of meaning which legitimate his whole hermeneutics of myths and symbols. The method remains the same; only the object becomes different: literary and artistic works. His explanation seeks, beyond any formal, historical, sociological, or ideological analysis, the discovery of "the secret message in the *oeuvre* of great writers," "the revelation of secret meanings." This is not possible if "we do not reintegrate them into the mystery from which they were taken,[194] if we do not reestablish them, in other words, in their germinal moment and system, in their latent structures. This program recurs frequently in the theses of the New Critics, with the observation that for Eliade genetic, archetypal, etc., criticism becomes in his case a hermeneutics of the mythological-symbolical infrastructures of literature: the total destruction foreseen by the avant-garde revived in the apocalyptic myth of "the end of the world," the renewal of time in Proust, the "rediscovery" of the myth of the eternal return, etc.[195] The fact that the writers are in no wise conscious of this mythic *anamnesia* proves on the one hand the extraordinary persistence of archetypal structures in the process of creation, and on the other the legitimation of this kind of expertise, which has nothing in common with the objectives of literary lampoonery.

In his entire orientation, Eliade thus aligns himself quite spontaneously with the essence of the program of the "new critics" who propose to discover structures, to apprehend meanings (*sensuri*), to explore significations, to reconstruct imaginary universes. And it is indeed a "significant" finding that the author appeals to the idea of "signification" with a special insistence. Systematic reference to depth psychology, to archaic and primitive spiritual universes, can lead only to the conclusion that "the philosopher, theologian, and literary critic can make use of the discoveries of worlds of meaning forgotten, distorted, or neglected." A good example of exegesis is offered by what Eliade calls the "folklore of Dacia and Eastern Europe," with his excellent commentaries on Zalmoxis, the Legend of Master Manole, the *Miorița*, etc. His method is expanded in fact to cover the whole of oral literature, the hermeneutics of which aims at the understanding and presentation of the spiritual universe of folk stories, etc., by precise reference to their mythical antecedents.[196] But it proves to be effective also in the case of modern artistic and cultural phenomena which *"must all have a significance,"* a meaning, a deep spiritual and existential sense.[197] The universe of meaning is explored from top to bottom, on all planes, and in all its manifestations.

Eliade's law of "meaning" (signification) calls for several supplementary specifications relative to its character, which is objective, permanent, universal, and nevertheless polyvalent. It is not simply that the "imaginary universes reflected in literary creations disclose a deeper, and secret, significance, quite independent of the artistic value of the respective works."[198] This is equivalent to saying that significance has an intrinsic, autonomous value in accordance with its own structure, its own system of reference, and relationships. Significance is not "faithful" or "unfaithful," neither "true" nor "false" (which would lead to the recognition and installation of an inverse objectivism), but only pertinent, valid, coherent in the framework of its own system of interpretation (or, to use a current expression, system of "reading"). This type of hermeneutical interpretation neither distorts nor betrays nor recreates a text, but only "deciphers" it according to the grammar of an intelligible and universal language. It uses a morphology, a syntax, and an objective semantics in the double sense of permanent textual attestations and of strict obedience to the object in the specificity of its autonomy.

It is self-evident that all the technical principles and details of this kind of method can be found and deduced from the overall analysis of Eliade's hermeneutics undertaken here. In literary criticism also, all the circuits[199] described above function, with inevitable but nonessential peculiarities. In several instances references to literary works are direct and quite conclusive. The relationship *whole/part*, for example, is proved wholly effective when able to explain the meaning of certain uninspired fragments only by reference to the whole corpus of a literary genius. An apparently paradoxical aspect, how God could be "sympathetic" toward Mephistopheles, can be understood only by "integrating it into the whole *oeuvre* of Goethe." The discovery of the meaning of one work by an author can disclose and save the meaning of his whole previous production, etc.[200] The relationship *past/present* resolves in its turn the whole problem of making archaic texts contemporary, of recovering a "simultaneous reading." The hermeneutical role of this recovering is clear: mediation between past and present, tradition and modernity.[201] The validity of simultaneous reading, of which we have spoken, in literary criticism and history is justified, similarly, by the necessity to "decipher the poetic phenomenon as such," to "demonstrate the essential difference between poetic and utilitarian language."[202] It is a procedure which asks and fully verifies in this area also the necessity and effectiveness of parallelism, comparativism, and typology based on invariants, on literary and theoretico-literary constants. Associations between surrealism and certain powerful longings of the Indian spirit can find no other justification. The transfer and homologization of meanings is produced in both senses: "The work of a writer increases in value and reveals unrecognized aspects primarily through his later literary creations and experiments."[203]

All these observations are reducible once again to the discussion of the essential problem of understanding, which presupposes an analytic-rational process, but also an eminently creative one, of the continuity of imaginary activities, and hence of the homoligization of archaic "imaginations" through our modern ones. A book must be more important than others, in order to be understood. Even when the reader is not competent, he *can* and *must* think about "solutions" to the book he reads, he must articulate it into a "system" of reflexes and references, to understand its logic and orientation. "No artistic Asiatic monument has been 'savored' until it was 'understood.' Indian temples, for instance, were for a long time looked upon as perfect examples of 'barbarian art.' It was necessary first to understand Indian aesthetic canons—which incidentally are quite coherent and intelligible—before Indian architecture and sculpture became 'pleasing.' "[204]

About the hermeneutical act of understanding there is talk in European criticism from at least the time of Schleiermacher, and Mircea Eliade continues effectively in the same tradition.[205] The analysis can continue also in the sense of demonstrating the "creative" character of this literary hermeneutics, first of all in the proper sense of the word, by the elaboration of some critical works, some works of interpretation, in which the critical reading supplements and amplifies the mythico-existential function of the reading brought to light by Eliade,[206] and secondly by the inner "transformation" of the critic, who develops spiritually by assimilating any new understanding of literature.[207] A typical creative moment—perhaps the most profound of all[208]—is that of "intuition" itself, which sets in motion the whole hermeneutical circle. Another consists in the prolongation and re-elaboration of this hermeneutics in view of the interpretation of theoretico-literary texts, of the type of our *Critica ideilor literare* (Criticism of literary ideas, 1974). We do not hide the fact that we have undertaken this lengthy analysis with a view to connecting our hermeneutics with this kind of preoccupation which establishes—through the contribution of Mircea Eliade—the first Romanian hermeneutical moment of international dimensions and significance. Our effort needs to be integrated into this tradition, which must be studied and defined with clarity. In any event, the idea of "critical creation" has, in this kind of perspective, a wholly different meaning from the aesthetic-impressionistic concept of critical "re-creation," of "creation on the margin of another creation." The latter is a belletristic concept and an eminently tautological one: what interest can there be in remaking, repeating, or paraphrasing the *same* creation? True hermeneutical creation is wholly alien to this "artistic" velleity, so minor and so obsolete.[209]

Notes

[Translated from the Romanian by Mac Linscott Ricketts; first published as "Hermeneutica lui Mircea Eliade," in *Revista de istorie și teorie literară*, Academia de Științe și Politice a Republicii Socialiste România, vol. 26, no. 2 (1977), pp. 223–50; and vol. 26, no. 3 (1977), pp. 371–99. Part of the original article has been deleted in this English translation (i.e. that preceding section III). The epigraph from the Journal is from *No Souvenirs*, p. 313.] It will be observed that Marino customarily groups several references from the same paragraph in one footnote.

1. Mircea Eliade, *De Zalmoxis à Gengis-Khan* (Paris, 1970), p. 11; *idem, La Nostalgie des origines* (Paris, 1971), pp. 9, 14.

2. ———, *Fragments d'un journal* (Paris, 1973), p. 67.

3. ———, *Histoire des croyances et des idées religieuses, I* (Paris, 1976), p. 220.

4. ———, *De Zalmoxis à Gengis-Khan*, p. 11.

5. ———, *Aspects du mythe* (Paris, 1963), p. 189; *Le Sacré et le profane* (Paris, 1965), p. 126; *La Nostalgie des origines*, pp. 30–31; *Histoire, I*, p. 314.

6. ———, *Fragments*, pp. 555–556; *Le sacré et le profane*, p. 15; *Fragments*, p. 301.

7. ———, *Le sacré et le profane*, p. 26; *Aspects du mythe*, p. 174.

8. ———, *Traité d'histoire des religions* (Paris, 1964), pp. 197–98; *La Nostalgie*, p. 10.

9. ———, *Histoire I*, p. 284; *Aspects du mythe*, p. 149.

10. ———, *Le Mythe de l'éternel retour* (Paris, 1969), p. 176; *Méphistophélès et l'androgyne* (Paris, 1962), p. 14; *Occultism, Witchcraft, and Cultural Fashions* (Chicago, 1976), pp. 11, 26.

11. ———, *Mythes, rêves et mystères* (Paris, 1957), p. 276; *La Nostalgie*, p. 18.

12. ———, *Comentarii la legenda Meşterului Manole* (Bucharest, 1943), p. 7; *Cosmologie şi alchimie babiloniană* (Bucharest, 1937), p. 17.

13. ———, *Fragmentarium* (Bucharest, 1939), p. 156; *Insula lui Euthanasius* (Bucharest, 1943), p. 128.

14. Just one reference: *Le Sacré et le profane*, p. 66.

15. *Traité*, p. 143.

16. *De Zalmoxis*, p. 183; *Méphistophélès*, p. 195; *Occultism*, pp. 2–3.

17. *Traité*, p. 131; *Images et symboles* (Paris, 1952), p. 18; *Le Sacré*, p. 180.

18. *Comentarii*, p. 48.

19. *Insula*, p. 18; *Traité*, p. 368, 378; *Aspects*, p. 242.

20. *Nostalgie*, p. 50; *De Zalmoxis*, p. 146.

21. *Images et symboles*, p. 241; *Le Sacré*, p. 117; *Mythes, rêves*, p. 142.

22. *Le Sacré*, pp. 8–9.

23. *Cosmologie*, pp. 18, 128; *Mitul reintegrării* (Bucharest, 1942), pp. 56–57; *Traité*, pp. 361, 369, 378.

24. *Aspects*, p. 186; *Mythes, rêves*, pp. 294–95; *Occultism*, pp. 37, 92.

25. *Comentarii*, p. 18; *Aspects*, pp. 138–40; *Le Sacré*, p. 93; *Nostalgie*, p. 134; *Histoire I*, p. 385.

26. *Aspects*, p. 88; *De Zalmoxis*, p. 10; *Histoire, I*, p. 296.

27. *Aspects*, p. 193; *Techniques du Yoga* (Paris, 1975), p. 12; *Traité*, p. 16; *Histoire I*, p. 17.

28. *Traite*, p. 116; *Yoga, immortalité et liberté* (Paris, 1968), p. 13; *Méphistophélès*, p. 246.

29. *Traité*, p. 132.

30. *Aspects*, p. 14; *Histoire I*, p. 26.

31. *Nostalgie*, p. 247; *Mythes, rêves*, p. 295.

32. *Comentarii*, pp. 26, 36; *Insula*, p. 103; *Cosmologie*, p. 11.

33. *Le Sacré*, pp. 21, 100; *Le Mythe de l'éternel retour*, p. 14; *De Zalmoxis*, p. 63; *Histoire I*, p. 38.

34. *Le Mythe*, p. 14; *Occultism*, p. 118; *Histoire I*, p. 38.

35. *Fragmentarium*, p. 49.

36. *La Nostalgie*, p. 8; *Histoire I*, p. 7; *Le Mythe*, pp. 16, 41.

37. *Méphistophélès*, p. 118; *Histoire I*, pp. 251, 63, 95, 314.

38. *Aspects*, p. 180; *Histoire I*, p. 25.

39. *Aspects*, pp. 202.

40. Note signed R. B. ("Nos correspondents"), in *Nouvelle Revue Française*, no. 213, 1 Sept. 1970, pp. 124–26.

41. *Images et symboles*, p. 29.

42. *Le chamanisme* (Paris, 1968), p. 12; *Méphistophélès*, p. 266.

43. *Religions australiennes* (Paris, 1972), p. 197; *La Nostalgie*, p. 10; *Mythes, rêves et mystères*, p. 208.

44. *Le Sacré*, p. 78; *La Nostalgie*, p. 333.

45. *Religions australiennes*, p. 14; *Images et symboles*, p. 29.

46. *Méphistophélès*, p. 241; *Le Sacré*, p. 137; *De Zalmoxis*, p. 163; *Le Mythe*, p. 13.

47. *Traité*, p. 19; *Le Chamanisme*, p. 12.

48. *Aspects*, pp. 12, 94, 98; *Mythes, rêves*, pp. 98, 119.

49. *Cosmologie*, p. 20.

50. *La Nostalgie*, p. 19; *Méphistophélès*, p. 19.

51. *Traité*, pp. 19, 133; *Le Sacré*, p. 140; *Naissances mystiques* (Paris, 1959), p. 22.

52. *Le Sacré*, p. 9; *Mythes, rêves*, pp. 264, 302; *Traité*, p. 139; *Comentarii*, p. 123.

53. *Le Mythe*, p. 111; *Traité*, p. 48; *Le Sacré*, p. 139; *Fragments*, p. 232.

54. *Traité*, p. 60; *Le Sacré*, p. 171.

55. A systematic survey in Chapter VIII, "Hermeneutica ideilor literare," in our book, *Critica ideilor literare* (The Criticism of Literary Ideas; Cluj, 1974); German translation, *Kritik der literarschen Begriffe* (Cluj-Napoca, 1976).

56. *Le Chamanisme*, p. 11.

57. *La Nostalgie*, p. 127, 158.

58. *Fragments*, p. 67.

59. *La Nostalgie*, p. 116, *Le Yoga*, p. 5; *Fragments*, p. 484.

60. *Comentarii*, p. 126; *La Nostalgie*, p. 332; *Traité*, p. 46.

61. *Fragmentarium*, p. 87; *Mythes, rêves*, pp. 7, 97; *De Zalmoxis*, p. 10; *Le Mythe*, p. 91; *La Nostalgie*, pp. 26–27; *Religions australiennes*, p. 14; *Traité*, p. 11.

62. A simple reference for orientation: Wallace Martin, "The Hermeneutic Circle and the Art of Interpretation," in *Comparative Literature* XXIV (1972), pp. 97–117.

63. Adrian Marino, *Critica* (see note 55), pp. 258, 402.

64. *Le Yoga*, p. 5.

65. Ibid., pp. 5–6.

66. *Traité*, p. 231.

67. Ibid., p. 376.

68. *Mythes, rêves, et mystères*, p. 176.

69. *Naissances mystiques*, p. 240.

70. *Comentarii*, p. 6.

71. *Méphistophélès*, p. 11.

72. *Le sacré*, p. 34; *Comentarii*, p. 6.

73. *Traité*, p. 246; other examples, pp. 141, 267, 370.

74. *Images et symboles*, p. 46; *Traité*, p. 15; *Mythes, rêves*, p. 252.

75. *Traité*, pp. 8, 230; *Le Yoga*, p. 6.

76. *Traité*, p. 165.
77. *Méphistophélès*, p. 242; *Fragments*, p. 299.
78. *Traité*, p. 377.
79. *Mythes, rêves*, p. 98; *Images et symboles*, p. 35.
80. *Naissances mystiques*, p. 219.
81. *Traité*, p. 290.
82. *Mythes, rêves*, p. 261.
83. Adrian Marino, "Two Hermeneutical Circuits: Part/Whole and Analysis/ Synthesis" in *Dialectics and Humanism* 2 (1976), pp. 132–34.
84. *Traité*, pp. 141, 155; *La nostalgie*, p. 126.
85. *La nostalgie*, p. 128; *Méphistophélès*, p. 253.
86. *Méphistophélès*, p. 246.
87. *La nostalgie*, p. 128; *Méphistophélès*, p. 253.
88. *Le chamanisme*, pp. 10–11.
89. *Histoire I*, p. 373; *Le chamanisme*, p. 10; *La nostalgie*, p. 260.
90. *La nostalgie*, p. 143; *Aspects*, p. 115; *Histoire I*, p. 7; *Naissances*, p. 214.
91. *Aspects*, pp. 18–19; *Traité*, p. 386; *Le mythe*, p. 41.
92. *Aspects*, p. 171; *La nostalgie*, passim; *Naissances*, p. 124; *Méphistophélès*, p. 206.
93. *Le sacré*, pp. 10–11; *Traité*, pp. 357.
94. *Fragmentarium*, pp. 97–98; *Images et symboles*, pp. 20–21; *Naissances*, pp. 24, 261; *La nostalgie*, pp. 13, 247: *Mythes, rêves*, p. 168.
95. *Le sacré*, pp. 10–11, 173.
96. A precise reference: *La nostalgie*, p. 56.
97. *Comentarii*, pp. 23, 26; *Mythes, rêves*, p. 270.
98. *Histoire I*, p. 283; *Traité*, p. 231.
99. *Méphistophélès*, p. 237.
100. *Mythes, rêves*, pp. 34, 208; *La nostalgie*, pp. 55, 92–93, 99, 101, etc.
101. *Images et symboles*, pp. 158–59; *Aspects*, p. 48; *Le sacré*, p. 180; *Le mythe*, p. 21; *Traité*, pp. 292, 324; *Histoire I*, p. 314.
102. *Aspects*, pp. 16, 129, 177; *Le sacré*, pp. 83–84; *Le mythe*, p. 21; *La nostalgie*, p. 180; *Traité*, pp. 352, 360.
103. *Le mythe*, p. 48.
104. *Histoire I*, pp. 104–05; *Le sacré*, p. 159.
105. Gilbert Durand, *Les structures anthropologiques de l'imaginaire* (Paris, 1969).
106. *Le sacré*, p. 41; *Traité*, p. 346; *Images*, p. 55.
107. *De Zalmoxis*, p. 232.
108. *Le mythe*, p. 14; *Méphistophélès*, pp. 248, 254.
109. *Images*, pp. 13, 43, 232–33; *Méphistophélès*, p. 238.
110. *Images*, p. 233; *Méphistophélès*, p. 238; *Le sacré*, pp. 48, 50, 52.
111. *Occultism*, p. 33; the example of Christianity: *Naissances*, p. 248.
112. *Traité*, p. 374; *Aspects*, p. 10; *Fragmentarium*, pp. 38, 91.
113. *Mythes, rêves*, pp. 162–64; *Méphistophélès*, p. 267; *Histoire I*, p. 113.
114. *Méphistophélès*, p. 249.
115. *Insula lui Euthanasius*, p. 29; *Le sacré*, p. 179; *Méphistophélès*, p. 262; *Fragmentarium*, p. 135.

116. *Traité*, p. 41; *Images*, p. 46; *La nostalgie*, p. 316.

117. *Traité*, p. 232, 350.

118. *Fragments*, pp. 9–10; *Images*, p. 234.

119. *Cosmologie*, p. 29; *Insula*, pp. 62, 67, 130.

120. *Méphistophélès*, p. 156; *Traité*, p. 231; *Fragments*, pp. 9–10.

121. *Fragmentarium*, pp. 61, 65; *Aspects*, p. 175; *Méphistophélès*, pp. 257, 261.

122. Paul Ricoeur, *Le conflit des interprétations* (Paris, 1969), p. 284; notes on symbolism, p. 313.

123. *Fragmentarium*, p. 37.

124. *Images*, pp. 29, 30; *De Zalmoxis*, p. 175; *La nostalgie*, pp. 44–45.

125. *Mitul reintegrării*, p. 25; *Traité*, pp. 368, 380.

126. *Méphistophélès*, p. 198; *Le mythe*, p. 164; *Traité*, p. 14; *Histoire I*, p. 204.

127. *Traité*, p. 21; *Le mythe*, p. 13; *La nostalgie*, p. 144.

128. *La nostalgie*, pp. 34, 159; *Cosmologie*, p. 114.

129. *Méphistophélès*, pp. 50, 257; *Traité*, p. 377, 379; *Histoire I*, p. 204.

130. *Naissances*, p. 26; *Images*, pp. 44, 215; *Traité*, 274; *Histoire I*, p. 63.

131. *Le mythe*, p. 117; *La nostalgie*, p. 34.

132. *Méphistophélès*, p. 266; *Histoire I*, p. 34; *Le mythe*, p. 65.

133. Adrian Marino, *Critica*, pp. 264–66.

134. *Traité*, p. 80; *Comentarii*, pp. 98ff.; *Le sacré*, p. 166; *Méphistophélès*, pp. 209, 212; *Naissances*, pp. 195, 259.

135. *Traité*, p. 230–31, 284; *Images*, pp. 135, 145; *Méphistophélès*, p. 91; *Naissances*, pp. 22, 26, 59.

136. *Comentarii*, p. 7; *Mythes, rêves*, pp. 103, 152; *Le sacré*, pp. 56, 76; *Méphistophélès*, p. 252; *Traité*, p. 230.

137. *Images et symboles*, pp. 127, 210.

138. *Mythes, rêves*, p. 159; *Naissances*, pp. 192, 266.

139. Adrian Marino, "The Mechanism of the Theoretical Literary Model," *New Literary History* VII, 3 (Spring, 1976), pp. 449–465.

140. *Mythes, rêves*, p. 263; *Traité*, p. 14; *Fragments*, p. 557; *Occultism*, p. 3.

141. *Traité*, p. 209; *Le mythe*, p. 10; *Images*, p. 124.

142. *Méphistophélès*, p. 249.

143. Ibid., pp. 244, 249; *Le chamanisme*, p. 12; *De Zalmoxis*, p. 10; *Occultism*, p. 93.

144. *Images*, p. 234; *Histoire I*, p. 129; *La nostalgie*, pp. 74, 77; *Fragments*, p. 287.

145. *Insula*, p. 13; *Mythes, rêves*, p. 8; *Méphistophélès*, pp. 10, 71; *Fragments*, pp. 63, 219, 224, 329, 375, 410–11, 440, 444; *Techniques du Yoga*, p. 14.

146. Adrian Marino, *Critica*, pp. 296–310.

147. *Cosmologie*, p. 21; *Histoire I*, pp. 266–72; *Le Yoga*, p. 10; *La sacré*, pp. 18–19; *Traité*, p. 210.

148. *Le sacré*, p. 14; *Naissances*, p. 22.

149. *Naissances*, p. 65; *Mythes, rêves*, p. 239; *Traité*, p. 142.

150. *Insula*, p. 85; *Images*, p. 214; *Traité*, pp. 151, 379.

151. *Images*, p. 215; *Naissances*, p. 65; *La nostalgie*, p. 35; *Mythes, rêves*, p. 279.

152. *Histoire I*, p. 17; *Le sacré*, p. 112.

153. Adrian Marino, "Two Hermeneutical Circuits."

154. *Mitul reintegrării*, p. 63.
155. *Traité*, pp. 140, 154, 232; *Comentarii*, p. 17; *Images*, p. 206.
156. *Insula*, p. 45; *Traité*, p. 23; *La nostalgie*, p. 79; *Le sacré*, p. 36.
157. *Fragments*, p. 65; *La nostalgie*, pp. 30, 51; *Méphistophélès*, p. 100.
158. *La nostalgie*, p. 148.
159. *Images*, p. 201; *Mythes, rêves*, pp. 159, 177; *Commentarii*, p. 104.
160. *Fragments*, p. 22; *Religions australiennes*, p. 11; *Images*, p. 18.
161. *Traité*, pp. 116–17; *La nostalgie*, p. 259; *Mythes, rêves*, pp. 157, 161 (against Freudian reductionism).
162. *Traité*, p. 140; *De Zalmoxis*, p. 60; *Fragments*, p. 439.
163. *La nostalgie*, pp. 124–25, 30–31.
164. *Fragments*, p. 64; *Méphistophélès*, p. 101.
165. Adrian Marino, *Critica*, pp. 282–93.
166. *Histoire* I, p. 95; *Aspects*, pp. 10, 95–99; *Fragments*, pp. 310, 403.
167. *Aspects*, pp. 111, 168; *Le sacré*, p. 138; *Histoire* I, pp. 19, 22, 26, 28, 35, 43, 135; *Méphistophélès*, p. 267.
168. *Mythes, rêves*, p. 51; *La nostalgie*, p. 180; *Fragments*, pp. 383, 385; *Occultism*, pp. 4, 47.
169. *Mythes, rêves*, pp. 17–36; *De Zalmoxis*, p. 130; *Le chamanisme*, p. 13; *Images*, pp. 215–16.
170. *Histoire* I, p. 99; *La nostalgie*, p. 19.
171. *Histoire* I, p. 46; *La nostalgie*, pp. 33–34.
172. *Traité*, p. 323; *Naissances*, p. 108.
173. *Le chamanisme*, pp. 12–13.
174. *Méphistophélès*, p. 247; *La nostalgie*, p. 14; *Images*, p. 226.
175. *Cosmologie*, pp. 16–17; *Fragmentarium*, p. 108; *Le sacré*, p. 171.
176. *Comentarii*, p. 21; *La nostalgie*, p. 82; *Images*, p. 39; *Traité*, p. 16.
177. *Aspects*, p. 173; *Le chamanisme*, p. 13; *Images*, p. 14; *Le sacré*, p. 57, etc.
178. *Méphistophélès*, pp. 194–95.
179. Ibid., p. 263; *Images*, pp. 263–65.
180. Ananda K. Coomoraswamy, "The Philosophy of Medieval and Oriental Art," in *Zalmoxis* I (1938), pp. 20–49, 234–35; Eliade, *Insula*, pp. 265, 275, etc.
181. *Insula*, pp. 134, 140; *Comentarii*, p. 139.
182. *Mitul reintegrării*, pp. 39, 53; *Traité*, pp. 350–51.
183. *Images*, pp. 228–29.
184. *Mitul reintegrării*, pp. 14, 74; *Insula*, p. 210; *La nostalgie*, p. 243.
185. *Aspects*, p. 232; for more details, see our study: "L'avant-garde et l'histoire retrouvé," in *Synthesis* IV (1977).
186. *Insula*, pp. 17, 27, 54–55, 129–32; *Comentarii*, p. 48; *Le sacré*, p. 45.
187. *Comentarii*, p. 142; *Le mythe*, pp. 53–54; 58.
188. *La nostalgie*, p. 259.
189. *Méphistophélès*, p. 154; *Histoire* I, p. 10.
190. *La nostalgie*, pp. 24–25.
191. *Insula*, p. 152; *La nostalgie*, p. 25.
192. *La nostalgie*, pp. 26–27.
193. *De Zalmoxis*, p. 174.
194. *La nostalgie*, p. 25; *Fragments*, p. 232.

195. *Aspects*, p. 94; *Fragments*, p. 390.

196. *La nostalgie*, p. 13; *De Zalmoxis*, pp. 240–44; *Aspects*, p. 240.

197. *Aspects*, p. 228; *Occultism*, p. 5.

198. *Occultism*, p. 54.

199. A study of them, in our work: *Critica ideilor literare* (Cluj, 1974), pp. 233–310.

200. *Fragmentarium*, p. 13; *Méphistophélès*, p. 96; *Fragments*, p. 167.

201. Hans-Georg Gadamer, *Le problème de la conscience historique* (Louvain and Paris, 1963), p. 69.

202. *Le sacré*, p. 19.

203. *Fragments*, p. 63; *Fragmentarium*, p. 110.

204. *Histoire* I, p. 46; *Cosmologie*, p. 7; *Insula*, p. 139.

205. Frederick D. E. Schleiermacher, *Hermeneutik*. . . . Nachweise von Heinz Kimmerle (Heidelberg, 1968), pp. 20–23, 32.

206. *Le sacré*, p. 174; *Naissances*, p. 272; A. Marino, "Lectură critică—creaţie critica," in *Critica ideilor literare*, pp. 341–44.

207. *La nostalgie*, pp. 131–32.

208. A. Marino, *Critica*, pp. 255–60.

209. See now Adrian Marino, *Hermeneutica lui Mircea Eliade* (Cluj-Napoca, 1980; French translation: L'Herméneutique de *Mircea Eliade* (Paris: Gallimard, 1981).

Douglas Allen

Phenomenological Method and the Dialectic of the Sacred

The reaction of many professors of philosophy, after reading a few pages or a book by Mircea Eliade, has been disbelief at how methodologically uncritical this historian of religions tends to be. Many anthropologists, such as Leach, Kirk, and Wallace, and historians and others associated with history of religions, such as Baird, have similarly dismissed Eliade on methodological grounds. His approach is not empirical and historical; but rather subjective, mystical, and theological; and so on.

Even those who have admired Eliade's scholarship have tended to concede that his strength is not methodological. For example, Altizer writes that Eliade's approach is mystical and romantic and is not rational or scientific; he then extols Eliade as a prophet, seer, and shaman.[1]

Mircea Eliade himself lends considerable credence to the view that he has never really dealt with crucial methodological issues and consequently lacks a critical systematic methodology. Not only has Eliade written very little on his methodology, but when asked how he arrived at his frequently unexpected and bewildering interpretations, he is apt to reply that he simply looked at his religious documents, and this was what they revealed. It is little wonder that such a seemingly uncritical approach is often viewed as incredibly naïve, that of a charlatan, or at best the brilliant intuitions of a true mystic. In any case, this approach would have little value for the methodological concerns of the rigorous phenomenologist.

Our position is that if Mircea Eliade represents a methodological improvement over previous phenomenological approaches, this is because of an impressive hermeneutical framework which serves as the foundation for his phenomenological approach to religious phenomena. Our approach has often taken a Kantian-like move in which we have analyzed Eliade's interpretations and then asked what it was necessary to presuppose methodologically to arrive at such conclusions. We have found that Eliade has a remarkable phenomenological approach grounded in his view of religious symbolism. Eliade usually attempts to interpret meaning through structure and grasps the meaning of a particular religious phenomenon by reintegrating it within its structural system of symbolic associations. If permitted, we could illustrate all of the following analysis from philosophical phenomenology in terms of Eliade's framework of "autonomous," universal, coherent structural systems of symbolic associations.

Beginning with a very general formulation of the phenomenological method, and then presenting what may be the most common criticism of Eliade's methodology, we shall introduce a notion of phenomenological induction as countering that criticism and suggesting an alternative explanation of what Eliade may in fact be doing. Finally, we shall summarize Eliade's key methodological notion of the dialectic of the sacred and shall suggest a remarkable similarity between the approach of the phenomenologist and the approach of *homo religiosus.*

Phenomenological Method: Insight and Variation

Let us begin by paraphrasing two methodological passages from "Symbolisms of Ascension and 'Waking Dreams,' " in which Mircea Eliade seems to emphasize two different tendencies in relating the historical particular and the universal structure.

The first passage calls attention to the paramount methodological status of universal structures and the hermeneutical movement from universal structures to the particular historical expressions.[2] It is only after phenomenologists have clarified the whole structure of the symbolism of "flight" and grasped its essential meaning (as expressing "the abolition of the human condition, transcendence and freedom") that they can then begin to understand the meaning of each particular historical manifestation.

The second passage formulates the hermeneutical movement from particular historical expressions to universal structures.[3] It is only after deciphering or "decoding" each particular meaning in its own specific "frame of reference" that phenomenologists can begin to see "different but interconnected planes" (of the oneiric, of myth and ritual, of metaphysical speculation, of ecstatic experience) and to discern that particular symbolic revalorizations of ascension express a structural solidarity. From the diverse, particular contexts, phenomenologists begin to grasp "structurally indissoluble meanings which fall into a *pattern*." They attempt to integrate all of the particular meanings into a whole, to interpret each symbolism as a "system" which "can only be really understood as far as we study it in the totality of its particular applications."

It may be possible to relate several of the above methodological emphases in terms of a general phenomenological procedure for gaining insight into meaning. It is imperative that we acknowledge the impossibility of outlining a linear temporal procedure in which the phenomenologist moves from particular facts to universal essences or vice versa. The particular and the universal must be seen in constant interaction and must be brought into some dialectical relationship.

In the phenomenological *Wesenschau*, the phenomenologist of religion attempts to disengage the essential structure embodied in the particular religious fact. His or her starting point is a specific perceptual experience of *homo religiosus*, a particular datum of religious experience. This does not mean that one can collect and describe particular religious facts and then generalize to universal religious structures. The particular *qua* particular is unintelligible. Experience always involves the unity of fact and essence.

Our above analysis is not confined to some "mystical" or supersensible experience but expresses a precondition of any experience. Either consciously or unconsciously we make a distinction between the fact that we have an experience and what is experienced. It is in terms of this "whatness" of an experience that we can distinguish, compare, and relate it to other experiences; that we can classify it as an experience of a certain kind.

Now the central aim of the phenomenological method is to disclose the essential "whatness" or structure embodied in the particular facts, to gain insight into the essential meaning which constitutes the facts as facts of a certain kind. This is not to say that one begins with a clear understanding of the universal structure embodied in a particular datum. Rather the phenomenologist begins with a vague intuition of what is revealed in the particular fact. Without such a vague eidetic intuition, the phenomenologist could not even begin to distinguish, describe, and classify the particular datum.

When we examine a particular religious datum expressing snake symbolism, one phenomenologist of religion may see what is revealed in terms confined entirely to other snake phenomena; a second scholar may vaguely intuit an essential erotic structure; someone like Eliade may initially grasp the essential meaning of that same datum in terms of a lunar structure.[4] This diversity in the initial eidetic intuition, as well as in the completed or "fulfilled" *Wesenchau*, is attributable in large part to the diversity in the particular *Lebenswelts* of different phenomenologists.

The usual way to gain insight into meaning is by the method of "free variation." In certain cases, such as some mathematical phenomena, one may be able to grasp an essential structure by reflecting on one example only. However, in the case of religious phenomena, the phenomenologist of religion must compile and compare a great variety of examples before she or he can gain insight into the essential meaning of the data. There must be not simply a purely imaginative variation but also a *factual variation* of one's data.

By the "method of invariance," the phenomenologist of religion searches for the *invariant core* which constitutes the essential meaning of the religious phenomena. The snake example, which is already presumed to be a variation of a certain type (erotic, lunar, etc.), is subjected to a process of free variation. A variety of snake phenomena assume certain forms which can be considered "accidental," in the sense that the phenomenologist can go "beyond" the "limits" imposed by such structures and not destroy the basic character of his or her data. For example, a particular aquatic or earth structure disclosed by some examples of snake hierophanies does not reveal the invariable meaning of snake phenomena.

Through free variation, the phenomenologist gradually sees that snake phenomena assume forms which can be regarded as "essential," in the sense that such structures impose certain "limits" beyond which one changes the basic "whatness" of the data under investigation; one cannot "remove" such "elements" without destroying the basic nature of the data.

Such essential insight is not instantaneous. What Husserl calls an "empirical universal" is the vague appearance of certain permanence within the variations. Amidst the diverse revalorizations, one gradually deciphers a certain *structural identity*.

When the phenomenologist of religion has grasped the invariant core which constitutes the essential meaning of the data, he or she then has "achieved" the eidetic intuition. For Eliade, the invariant core which constitutes the essential meaning of the snake phenomena is generally understood in terms of a structural "web" of lunar symbolism. The essential structure embodied in the particular snake examples is grasped as inexhaustible life repeating itself rhythmically.

It is now possible to bring Eliade's two methodological passages into dynamic relationship. In actual religious experience, fact and essence are inseparable; although in analysis, the phenomenologist of religion can distinguish them and disengage or abstract the embodied universal structure.

In phenomenological analysis, especially by the method of free variation, there is a hermeneutical "movement" from the historical particular to the universal structure. This is not to deny that there is a continual universal particular interaction and that we could never even begin to distinguish and describe the particular unless we had already presumed some eidetic structure. However, once we have delineated a variety of such particular (snake) examples, we can then subject the particulars to free variation; begin to decipher certain structural similarities (erotic, initiation, etc.) and dissimilarities; and finally, ideally, grasp the invariant as a definite (lunar) structure.

Phenomenological analysis also involves a hermeneutical "movement" from the universal structure to the historical particular. The invariant (the lunar "web") serves as the hermeneutical framework in terms of which we can understand the meaning of a particular (snake) datum. Phenomenological understanding of the religious meaning of the particular phenomenon (expressing snake symbolism) involves reintegrating that phenomenon within its coherent universal (lunar) system of symbolic associations, within that totality which constitutes its universal (lunar) structure.

Uncritical Inductive Generalizations

By focusing on what is probably the most frequent criticism of Eliade's phenomenological approach, it may be possible to deepen our analysis of how the phenomenologist of religion gains insight into universal structures of meaning. This general criticism usually contends that Mircea Eliade, while claiming to investigate particular religious manifestations, arrives at his universal structures by means of highly subjective, uncritical, hasty generalizations; he "reads into" his specific religious data all kinds of "sophisticated" universal structures and meanings.

Underlying most of these methodological criticisms is the assumption that Eliade proceeds by some kind of empirical *inductive inference*. Critics submit that they cannot repeat Eliade's inductive process: they do not find it possible to generalize from the particular examples to Eliade's "profound" universal structures of religious experience.

Such criticisms have considerable merit. Eliade never formulates a comprehensive and critical methodological analysis in which he clarifies and justifies his phenomenological grasping of universal religious structures. The impression he often conveys is that his procedure is not unlike the "classical" formulations of inductive inference found in John Stuart Mill and other philosophers.

How did Mircea Eliade arrive at the universal structure of religious experience revealed in his analysis of the dialectic of the sacred? Did Eliade examine many particular religious examples and then detect certain common characteristics found in each particular phenomenon: a sacred-profane dichotomy, a sense of transcendence, etc.? It would then seem that Eliade might be able to claim varying degrees of *probability* for his generalized conclusions.

But Eliade has granted these universal structures of religious experience a sense of *necessity*, as if they had some synthetic a priori status. His generalized conclusions are supposedly dependent on the nature of the religious documents he has investigated, but they are not open to falsification: in the future, one could not investigate a religious datum which was without any of these structures. It does not seem possible for Eliade to grant these structures such a universal necessary status if they are arrived at by some inductive process of generalization.

Turning to Eliade's analysis of snake symbolism, it often seems that he has studied many snake examples, deciphered common characteristics in each datum, and then inductively generalized to his conclusion asserting their universal lunar structure. But then why don't other scholars discern in each of these particular facts that "inexhaustible life is repeating itself rhythmically"?

Without multiplying our examples, the above should suffice to establish our conclusion: if Eliade insists that he has inductively generalized from the particular religious facts to his universal religious structures, then many of the aforementioned criticisms of his methodology seem justified.

Phenomenological Induction

But perhaps the phenomenologist of religion does not arrive at his fundamental structures through some "classical" (Mill, etc.) inductive inference.[5] We would like to suggest that if one can formulate universal religious structures, such as those of the sacred and the profane, sacred time, initiation, ascension, etc., he or she may grasp such meanings through a kind of induction which bears some similarity to the phenomenological *Wesenschau*.[6] Our suggestion is submitted as one possible means to supplement, and not to negate, the recently elucidated general analysis of the phenomenological method and its use of eidetic variation.

The phenomenologist of religion proceeds by means of various "idealizing fictions" which are based on the particular facts. One recalls that there are no "pure" religious phenomena; the religious manifestation is viewed as spatial, temporal, conditioned, relative, "limited."[7] By reflecting on the particular, contingent, "imperfect" manifestations, the phenomenologist of religion attempts to disengage an *ideal religious structure*, to "read off" a conception of a "pure case." This ideal structure is actively constructed by the phenomenologist.

A key point in this analysis is the contention that such a conceived ideal structure or pure case is *founded on* the particular facts but is *not found in* the facts. In examining different expressions of flight and ascension symbols, the phenomenologist of religion conceives the ideal structure: transcendence and freedom, an ontological abolition of the human condition. Now a critic of Eliade's phenomenology analyzes the ascension phenomena and does not find such an ideal meaning expressed in each manifestation. Hence she or he assumes that Eliade is guilty of a highly subjective, uncritical inductive generalization; that Eliade has "read into" his data "pure," "sophisticated" religious meaning.

Our position concedes that "transcendence and freedom . . ." is not a generalized structure which is found in each particular, historical fact. Rather it, like other atemporal and ahistorical universal structures, is a "pure" or "perfect" structure which has been actively conceived or constructed by the phenomenologist. It is founded on the particular, historical, "imperfect" facts, but is not found fully in any of them.

The phenomenologist of religion may attempt to analyze "the difference" between the ideal structure of ascension and any specific ascension datum in terms of the particular, historical, cultural, and other relevant conditionings of the existential situation within which the ascension manifestation is experienced. Perhaps this is one clue to Eliade's frequent evaluations of a phenomenon as a "higher" or "more perfect" religious manifestation. The Indian yogi, for instance, may achieve a "higher" spiritual realization in the sense that the experience is "closer" (is less conditioned, etc.) to the ideal meaning or "pure case" of ascension symbolism.

The phenomenologist of religion attempts to verify the ideal structure by showing how it illuminates the meaning of the particular empirical facts. According to Merleau-Ponty,

> That which gives its probable value to the induction and which finally shows that it is truly founded on things is not the number of facts involved to justify it. No! It is rather the intrinsic clarity which these ideas shed on the phenomena we seek to understand. . . . [Induction is] a process of intellectual analysis whose verification consists in the total, or at least sufficient, clarity which the group of concepts worked out in this way bring to the given phenomena.[8]

The above view of induction can be compared with the phenomeno-logical *Wesenschau*. Both are based on facts; both involve a "reading" of the universal. But they can be "differentiated with respect to their elaboration": (Husserl's) *Wesenschau* "moves on the plane of the ima-ginary," involving an imaginary variation of certain facts; induction moves "on the level of actual facts," involving "effective variations in considering the different cases that are actually realized."[9]

The above formulation by Bednarski must be qualified. What Mer-leau-Ponty and other existential phenomenologists object to in Hus-serl's transcendental phenomenology is not that it involves the imagination. Phenomenological induction also involves the imagina-tion. But Husserl proposed that all data were constituted by conscious-ness and that in the phenomenological *Wesenschau* we could eliminate the particular actual given example and move on the plane of *pure possibility*. In the hermeneutical relation between the universal and the particular, Merleau-Ponty and other existential phenomenologists pro-pose that the actual examples have a kind of priority, that we cannot get rid of the particular given examples and operate on the level of pure possibility, that the actual example is not constituted by us but is the source of our constitution and judgment. In this regard, Mircea Eliade's phenomenology is similar to much of existential phenomenology.[10]

We may also recall Altizer's broad criticism of Eliade's method as being "mystical," brilliantly intuitive, but completely divorced from any "rational" and "scientific" approach. If the paradigm for a "ra-tional" and "scientific" approach entails some form of "classical" in-ductive generalization, then this criticism seems justified. But Husserl argued that intuiting essences is not something "mystical" or "super-sensible," but something we all do with varying degrees of insight. If our suggested inductive approach has any value, then certainly a tre-mendously creative phenomenologist such as Eliade, who can for-mulate ideal universal structures of religious meaning, would have to be "brilliantly intuitive."

The crucial methodological point is that such a brilliant intuitive conception of essential religious structures is not completely arbitrary and subjective. Such a phenomenological procedure is not arbitrarily superimposed on the religious data but is largely *derived* from the nature of the religious facts. Thus, Eliade analyzes the specific snake examples, subjects them to an "actual variation," begins to decipher structural similarities, etc.[11] What emerges is some sense of a hermeneutical foun-dation derived from the religious phenomena, a structural "web" of religious symbols. Now by reflecting on this foundation, Eliade is able actively and creatively to conceive an ideal lunar structure, which then helps to illuminate the meaning of the particular manifestations. This is not to minimize the brilliant creativity in gaining insight into such ideal meanings, but rather to indicate that such insights are founded on the facts and are not simply arbitrarily imposed.

Phenomenological Insight and the Dialectic of the Sacred

We may conclude our analysis by noting a similarity between the (philosophical) phenomenological method for gaining insight into meaning, especially the inductive procedure for "reading off" essences, and Mircea Eliade's account of the nature of religious experience.

Eliade's key methodological notion for distinguishing religious from non-religious phenomena and for analyzing how the sacred manifests itself in experience is the dialectic of the sacred.[12] The sacred and the profane are two modes of being in the world, and religion exists where the sacred-profane dichotomy has been made. Religion refers to the experience of the sacred, and the sacred always entails some sense of transcendence. Religion involves a radical break with the secular modalities, pointing us "beyond" the relative, historical, natural world of "ordinary" experience. Eliade describes the principal function of religion as rendering human existence "open" to a "superhuman" or sacred world of absolute, transhistorical, eternal, exemplary, transcendent values.

In the distinction of the sacred and the profane, there is always the separation of the hierophanic object. What interests the religious person are hierophanies. The manifestations of the sacred are never unmediated: the sacred is always revealed through something natural, historical, ordinarily profane. The process of sacralization involves the "radical ontological separation" of the thing which reveals the sacred from everything else.

The sacred-profane dichotomy is experienced in terms of a certain dialectical tension: the sacred and the profane coexist in a paradoxical relationship. What is paradoxical is that something profane, ordinary, limited, imperfect, finite, historical, while remaining a natural thing, can at the same time manifest that which is sacred, extraordinary, unlimited, perfect, infinite, transhistorical. What is paradoxical is that the sacred, which is transcendent, wholly other, ultimate, infinite, transhistorical, limits itself by incarnating itself in something profane, relative, finite, historical.

Implied in the dialectic of the sacred is an evaluation and choice. The religious person faces an existential crisis. Because of the dichotomy of sacred and profane, value and meaning are introduced into one's existence. The sacred dimension of being is now experienced as more significant and as containing a surplus of meaning, as powerful and ultimate, as paradigmatic and normative in judging one's existence. It is in terms of the sacred exemplary models that religious persons interpret their mode of being in the world and define the future possibilities of their existence.

Let us recall that in the phenomenological method, the phenomenologist attempts to disengage an ideal religious structure, to conceive the pure or perfect case. In the dialectic of the sacred, *homo religiosus* experiences that which is paradigmatic, perfect, the ideal structure, the pure case. The phenomenological essence, the ideal structure, is founded on the actual, concrete examples but is not found in those particular facts. In the dialectic of the sacred, the ideal sacred structure is not found in the particular, spatial, temporal, historical, limited facts *qua* particular, spatial, temporal, historical, limited facts. Eliade often analyzes those methodological approaches which have attempted to find the religious structure in the "natural" profane facts as naturalistic and historicistic reductions which negate the basic intentionality of the dialectic of the sacred.

What verifies the ideal structure for the phenomenologist is that he or she can use that structure to illuminate the meaning of the particular facts, to shed light on dimensions of experience otherwise unintelligible. What verifies the sacred model, the paradigmatic structure, for the religious person is that he or she can use it to illuminate the nature of one's specific existential situation; to give meaning to the chaotic, isolated, finite, "impure," "imperfect" facts of one's profane existence. In terms of such exemplary structures, the religious person can experience what were chaotic, isolated, profane phenomena as now part of a coherent, meaningful, spiritual *Lebenswelt*.

We should note that for Eliade the ideal religious structures, such as those of ascension or of the moon, do not constitute "original" constructions by the phenomenologist. Eliade's position seems to be that the ideal religious structure is actually experienced by *homo religiosus* in at least a few cases. The religious structure is not revealed in the profane facts *qua* profane facts. And it is not revealed fully in the vast majority of religious phenomena. But at certain highly creative moments in the history of humankind, *homo religiosus* did conceive fully the "pure case," the ideal religious meaning of ascension, of agriculture, of the moon, etc. Hence, in reading off these ideal structures, the phenomenologist of religion is attempting to empathize with, participate in, and reenact within his or her own experience the ideal meanings which *homo religiosus* has experienced.

Notes

1. For example, see Robert D. Baird, *Category Formation and the History of Religions* (The Hague: Mouton & Co., 1971), pp. 75–77, 86–87, 152–53; Thomas J. J. Altizer, *Mircea Eliade and the Dialectic of the Sacred* (Philadelphia: Westminster Press, 1963), pp. 17, 30, 36, 41, 84. It is true that many of Mircea Eliade's controversial assertions reflect unacknowledged ontological moves and highly normative judgments. Nevertheless, scholars such as Baird, Altizer, and most other interpreters of Eliade overstate the arbitrary, subjective, normative, romantic, theological, etc., nature of his history of religions. This is because they do not recognize that Eliade has developed a comprehensive sophisticated phenomenological approach, so that much of what they take to be subjective and unscientific, Eliade can in fact handle in terms of a rigorous descriptive phenomenological analysis.

More recently, Guilford Dudley has submitted that Mircea Eliade should admit that his approach has nothing to do with some empirical, historical, data-bound, inductive method, but should be seen as having a radical antihistorical approach involving paradigms and deductive analysis. See Guilford Dudley III, "Mircea Eliade as the 'Anti-Historian' of Religions," *Journal of the American Academy of Religion* 44 (June 1976): 345–59. This analysis has been expanded in Dudley's fine book *Religion on Trial: Mircea Eliade and His Critics* (Philadelphia: Temple University Press, 1977). Our disagreement with Dudley is that he seems to accept the classical epistemological dichotomy of empiricism and rationalism and then "saves" Eliade by identifying him with some French rationalist, antihistorical, deductive model. We would simply like to suggest two important points from contemporary epistemological analysis. First, much of both Anglo-American and Continental philosophy has been directed at undermining that classical view of empiricism. (In the final chapter of his book, Dudley does indicate that contemporary philosophers of science have rejected such a methodologically naïve and inadequate empiricism.) Second, modern philosophical phenomenology—not to mention Marxism and other philosophical approaches—has been directed at undermining the sharp empiricism versus rationalism dichotomy.

2. Mircea Eliade, *Myths, Dreams and Mysteries*, trans. Philip Mairet (New York: Harper and Brothers, 1960), p. 110.

3. Ibid., p. 118.

4. The primary source for our analysis of the snake and lunar symbolism is Mircea Eliade, *Patterns in Comparative Religion*, trans. Rosemary Sheed (New York: World Publishing Co., Meridian Books, 1963), pp. 154–87. See especially pp. 154–59 and 164–71. Our analysis is also based on sections of *Mephistopheles and the Androgyne, Rites and Symbols of Initiation, The Sacred and the Profane, Shamanism: Archaic Techniques of Ecstasy*, and *Yoga: Immortality and Freedom*.

5. The interpretation which follows is not what Mircea Eliade ever claims he is doing. As was just stated, Eliade tends to convey the impression of some "classical" method of generalization, and such an approach is not commensurate with the status he grants his conclusions. Our interpretation is intended to suggest an alternate approach which might render more acceptable the

phenomenological insight into universal religious structures.

6. The following suggestion is very similar to the analysis of induction found in Maurice Merleau-Ponty, "Phenomenology and the Sciences of Man," *The Primacy of Perception,* ed. James M. Edie (Evanston: Northwestern University Press, 1964), pp. 66–72.

7. This point is made throughout the writings of Mircea Eliade and will be emphasized in our analysis of the dialectic of the sacred.

8. *The Primacy of Perception,* pp. 69–70.

9. See Jules Bednarski, "The Eidetic Reduction," *Philosophy Today* 6 (1962): 22; Merleau-Ponty, *The Primacy of Perception,* p. 70.

10. The direction of existential phenomenology describes much of Eliade's phenomenology. At one point, Eliade specifically dissociates himself from the phenomenological approach, but this is on the same grounds that existential phenomenology rejects Husserl's "transcendental phenomenology." (Actually one could make a good case that Husserl himself rejected this transcendental project when it came to "inexact essences" and the *Lebenswelt.*) See Mircea Eliade, *Shamanism: Archaic Techniques of Ecstasy,* trans. Willard R. Trask (New York: Pantheon Books, 1964), p. xv. In criticizing earlier approaches in the history of religions, Eliade repeatedly insists that we begin with the concrete, historical, particular, religious expressions and that we must pay special attention to the specific nature of our data. It seems wrong to conclude that Eliade simply disregards this dimension of his data. Elsewhere we have attempted to show that Mircea Eliade places primary emphasis on the "givenness" of his data, especially the structures which are given to *homo religiosus* (and to the phenomenologist) through the dialectic of the sacred and the coherent universal symbolisms. Yet the religious experiences of *homo religiosus* and the interpretations of meaning by the phenomenologist do not simply consist of a passive reception of structures that are given. Here we find the model from Merleau-Ponty and other existential phenomenologists of a "constituted given" helpful. The actual example, with its religious structure, is given but must be made existentially relevant, must become a part of consciousness, must be constituted by us. Thus, in terms of the dialectic of the sacred, we have the sense of the religious person experiencing, evaluating, and choosing the sacred and constituting her or his life-world in terms of such a sacred exemplary model. See Douglas Allen, "Givenness and Creativity," *Journal of Thought* 8 (November 1973): 270–78.

11. This is not to deny our previous methodological point that there must be some eidetic intuiting even to begin this procedure.

12. Some of the following analysis of the dialectic of the sacred can be found in Eliade's *Patterns in Comparative Religion,* pp. 1, 26, 29–30; *Images and Symbols,* trans. Philip Mairet (New York: Sheed and Ward, 1961), pp. 84, 178; *The Sacred and the Profane,* trans. Willard R. Trask (New York: Harper & Row, Torchbooks, 1961), pp. 10, 14; "Structure and Changes in the History of Religion," trans. Kathryn Atwater, in *City Invincible,* ed. Carl Kraeling (Chicago: University of Chicago Press, 1960), pp. 353, 366. For a more complete account of the dialectic of the sacred, see Douglas Allen, "Mircea Eliade's Phenomenological Analysis of Religious Experience," *Journal of Religion* 52 (April 1972): 170–86.

Mircea Eliade

The Fact
(from *Fragmentarium*)

Everyone agrees that the really important thing for human knowledge is not *facts*—but *the fact*. You can look at a thousand plants without understanding the essential "fact" of vegetal life. You can read a thousand documents about the French Revolution without coming one step closer to that unparalleled "fact" in European history.

But how do we *choose*, out of millions of facts, those few essential ones? How do we obtain one "fact" out of a thousand documents, and how do we transform it into an act of knowing? And then this further question: do we *choose* and do we *transform* one significant "fact" out of millions, or is this "fact" in itself qualitatively different from the millions of facts which precede and follow it?

Take, for instance, friendship between a young man and a young woman, friendship which sometimes is transformed into love. A great many things happen between the two young people in the course of the friendship—things of no consequence (gestures, conversations, glances, etc.)—"facts" which pass away without issue, without "organic sequence." (We say so many words to each other which are lost; there are so many gestures, so many smiles, so many sentimental outbursts which last but a moment and vanish the next without any result, any meaning, any "knowledge" having been created in my consciousness or yours.) Then suddenly a trifle, a chance event transforms an ordinary friendship between two young people into love! A trifle (a glance—just *one* out of the thousands they have exchanged; a word, preceded by millions of words; a scene, a nuance,, etc.)—a trifle which detaches them from the normal, neuter milieu drowned in "facts," and enchants them, "hurls" them into a unique madness which we can without fear call Absolute.

The same thing is found throughout the biological world. In the history of an organism a million "facts" occur (innumerable tropisms, innumerable phenomena related to nutrition, innumerable vague processes). And yet in the life of that organism, the only ones that have importance—that is, significance for "organic sequence," for "destiny"—are a few: above all, the act of germination, the act of fecundation: *creation*.

In the history of peoples, in the history of the human spirit, only *creative acts* have importance. Only from them can another man learn anything. And what is the virtue of learning, if not to learn about an aspect of eternity?

One might say that "destiny" is just this struggle with yourself, this choosing of the *essential fact* out of the millions which are continually occurring around you and in you; the struggle with yourself, with the significance (fruitfulness, children, glory—the creative act or, at any rate, one with "organic sequence") which you can or cannot give to your personal life.

Notes

With regard to the title, the Romanian *faptul*, literally the "thing done," may be translated as fact, act, deed, etc. The various meanings should be borne in mind in this essay, which was first published in *Vremea* 10 (1937), 469, p. 13. (Tr.).

Part II

Coincidentia Oppositorum: Reflections on Parallel Worlds

I must confess, that, personally I have learned many things I never knew before . . . just by writing.

St. Augustine
De Trinitate

Seymour Cain

Poetry and Truth: The Double Vocation in Eliade's Journals and Other Autobiographical Writings

I

Mircea Eliade's *Fragments d'un journal*,[1] comprising entries from 1945 to 1969, provides a record and a testimony of the author's responses to the life he lived from the time he began his exile in Paris to the midpoint of his illustrious career at the University of Chicago. The English translation, *No Souvenirs*,[2] for some strange reason omits the crucial entries of the Paris years, in which Eliade struggled to cope with his exile status, composed his major works in the history of religions, and reestablished himself as a creative writer of fiction. Prior journals, begun in his early teens, are apparently lost forever, left behind in Bucharest when he chose not to return to Romania at the end of World War II. One should perhaps except *Şantier*, the "indirect novel," which, with some adaptations and excisions, is practically a transcription of the journal of his Indian sojourn.[3] Also his prize novel *Maitreyi*[4] admittedly "lifts" material verbatim from his Indian journal.[5]

This is not the time and place to enter into a full-scale consideration of Eliade's literary works, written in Romanian, the sole medium of his literary creativity. (Both Matei Calinescu and the anonymous *Times*

Literary Supplement reviewer of the *Fragments* see the journal as a well-wrought novel of exile, the "Odyssey" of Eliade's life.[6]) Many entries indicate his own critical, self-conscious assaying of the journal genre and its most appropriate style and contents. The central purpose of a journal, he states, is to preserve "certain fragments of concrete time,"[7] to pull them out of the temporal flux and fix them on the written or printed page so that they may be recalled and relived at a later time. This "fixation" of temporal fragments includes all kinds of things: banal visits and conversations, noisy neighbors, a screeching alley-cat, moments of boredom or angst as well as those of elation or serenity, travels to foreign climes, hopes and dreams, reflections on one's life and work, projects for new books, etc.

He perceives that writing a good journal requires a particular gift, like that of the novelist, a special literary talent and nisus. The most petty details become interesting in the hands of a writer so endowed, whose very urge to jot them down, to preserve these ephemeral moments in words, gives them light and life. The simple fact of being written down raises up the seemingly insignificant to the meaningful. The act of writing is inherently transformative or revelatory.[8]

As in the case of many other journals, we are presented here with a selected, edited version of the original manuscript, a winnowing that Eliade himself admits risks "a distorted or one-sided portrait."[9] Hence the title *Fragments d'un journal* is well chosen and no mere tautology, as Ernst Junger declares.[10] (It is an almost exact replication of the title of Maxim Gorki's published journals, *Fragments From My Diary*.) Thus in dealing with the journals as we have them, we must be aware that the earlier journals are lost and that of the later ones we have "something less than one-third of the original manuscript."[11] However, as regards our subject here—the relation between Eliade's fictional and scholarly work—we certainly have abundant materials in the *Fragments* and other autobiographical writings (e.g., Eliade's autobiography and the tape-recorded interviews with Claude-Henri Rocquet[12]). It is a good guess that what is omitted would not change the picture very much. Of course, one must always be alert to the possibility of self-regard and self-interest in autobiographical writings, and one is by no means always bound to accept the author's interpretation of his life and works.[13] But in the journals, at least, we are enabled to come as close as possible to Eliade's immediate experience of the double vocation.

II

In the Preface to *No Souvenirs* and more systematically and coherently in "Literary Imagination and Religious Structure,"[14] Eliade states his own view of his double vocation as scholar and writer. In the first place, he tells us, he comes out of a cultural tradition in which the combining of scientific and artistic productivity was not regarded as anomalous. In the second place, he found that he personally *had to* combine the two, so that no matter how fascinated he might become with history of religions studies, he could never give up writing fiction. It was an absolute psychological and spiritual necessity which impelled him from time to time to break off serious religio-historical inquiries and the composition of major scholarly works in order to write fiction. The latter was his safety valve which preserved his mental health and provided the inner freedom that only literary creativity could bestow. But *both* activities, scientific research and imaginative literature, were necessary to his "spiritual equilibrium" and, by extension, to man universally—an alternation, as he phrases it, between the "diurnal" and "nocturnal" phases of the spirit.

Not only did he discover mutually illuminating insights in his two activities but, most significantly, he discovered the cognitive function of literature. "Just as a new axiom reveals a previously unknown structure of the real (that is, it *founds* a new world), so also any creation of the literary imagination reveals a new universe of meanings and values."[15] And he notes that it is through narrative, the telling of stories, that the literary imagination reveals possible worlds and modes of human existence, responding to a universal human necessity which is also met in the parallel ways of myths and dreams. Then comes this startling sentence: "For me, a historian of religions and an Orientalist, the writing of fiction became a fascinating experience in method."[16]

Both the historian of religions and the fiction writer encounter new, strange modes of viewing the world, and deal with the creation of new universes. Both literary works and religious phenomena are characterized by the expression of exemplary value and meaning via ordinary, profane, historical objects, events, and persons—in a "camouflaged" form. "Investigating and understanding the universal and exemplary significations of literary creations," Eliade ventures, "is tantamount to recovering the meaning of religious phenomena."[17]

Whatever the merits or demerits of this position, generally speaking, it is obvious that there is something askew here. The proper analogy is between the literary creator and the religious myth-maker (individual or ethnic) on the one hand, and between the literary critic or historian and the historian of religions on the other. Eliade seeks to stress the imaginative component in scholarly or scientific knowledge, as well as the cognitive value of creative literature. Granted that the analogy between the literary critic-historian and the historian-phenomenologist of religions is a valuable, illuminating one, still, it would be salutary to preserve some distinction between the student and understander of myth (or of fiction) and its makers. That is, unless one is to endorse Thomas J. J. Altizer's view of Eliade as a master myth-maker—not interpreter of myths—and thereby provide ammunition to Eliade's most invidious critics.[18]

III

The preceding consideration of the double vocation by Eliade is just that: a considered, deliberate view, done at leisure and at some distance, in a preface or paper written many years later. What we get in the journals, on the contrary, are jottings written down in the very middle of things, in the confusion and tension of actual existence, and thereby we are presented with a vividly authentic portrait of what it actually was like for Mircea Eliade to pursue the dual vocation of scholar and writer. The beautiful balance implied in the later discursive statements is not always so beautiful or so balanced in the lived experience revealed here, nor is the preestablished harmony hinted at always so established or harmonious. We should note, by the way, that even as regards the allegedly propitious atmosphere of Romanian culture for such a double-sided activity, it was not always so propitious for the young Eliade. In his autobiography he notes that there was a certain bias in Romanian academic circles against scholars who dabbled in fiction-writing, thereby impelling the beginning scholar to couch his scientific writings in a dull, pedantic style that would not cause scandal in straitlaced academic quarters: "If I had not been a successful writer from my youth, very probably my subsequent philosophical and scientific works of that period would have been more elegantly presented."[19]

Certainly the journals and also the autobiography show that Eliade is a writer, pure and simple. He is a man who *has to* write, who *must* express his ideas, who *needs* to get them out. This exigence applies both to his scholarship and to his fiction. The following observation comes in the midst of the writing of the *Traité d'histoire des Religions* (*Patterns in Comparative Religion*): "It seems as if I have robbed myself if I let a whole day pass without having written a single line."[20] And he urges himself on to write, in spite of his obstacles and despairs.

More important, the journals reveal the agonizing conflict between the two vocations. The alternation between the diurnal and nocturnal worlds was certainly no easy or painless process in Eliade's case.

> I am incapable of *existing* simultaneously in two spiritual universes: that of literature and that of science. There lies my fundamental weakness: I cannot keep myself both awake and in the world of dreams or play. As soon as I "make literature," I find myself in another universe; I call it oneiric because it has another temporal structure and because my relations with the characters are of an imaginary and not a critical nature.[21]

The term "vocation" must be taken in its full sense here, not merely in the sense of occupation, but emphatically in that of calling or commitment. Eliade felt called upon and committed to be *both* a historian of religions (of a certain special kind) and a writer of fiction (in the Romanian tongue). *The two commitments were usually in conflict.* Eliade not only felt robbed when he did not write at all, he also felt robbed as a scholar when he indulged his literary side and robbed as a writer when he exhausted himself in scholarly work. Thus another alternation emerges, that of self-complaint and guilt for not fulfilling one or the other vocation.

At one moment Eliade is cautioning himself against the temptation to write novels (and in Romanian at that!), and soon thereafter he is lacerating himself for his failure to follow just that vocation.[22] Intensely at work on a play, he "abandons" several unfinished scholarly works so as not to interrupt his play-writing, even for a day or two.[23] Many years later he notes that for a decade he has sacrificed novel-writing, "the only literary genre that satisfies my talent," in order to provide "a new way of understanding *homo religiosus.*"[24] Always there is a conflict evoked by the earthly limitations of time, energy, mood, and circumstance, and by the alternative (if ultimately reconcilable) directions of the two souls within his breast. When he is "possessed" (and the word is used in its full sense here) with the urge to write fiction, he cannot concentrate on the history of religions; and when he is thoroughly involved in his scholarly work he cannot shift his mind to the creation of fiction.

It is noticeable, however, that by far the majority of his complaints and most of his *angst* about unfulfillment come from the non-consummation of his literary work, and that his negative remarks are almost entirely directed against scholarship as an annoying, frustrating obstacle to his true *métier*. For example, early in the *Fragments* he looks into the mirror of the future and shudders at the prospect of himself as an old man with "a shelf of learned books beside me: my work [*oeuvre*]. Is that really my destiny?"[25] The term "freedom" for him here always means "liberation from science," the completion of a scholarly task that leaves him free to do literature again, which is apparently his main, if not his first, love.[26] Looking back in 1950 at a decade of aborted novelistic enterprises, he wonders, "Could it be that I've lost my inspiration? That my epic vein has been exhausted? That's not my impression. But I have my wretched scholarly books to complete."[27] All kinds of petty tasks—research, article writing, lectures—prevent him from even doing that, let alone writing the novel (*Forbidden Forest*) which should be his primary endeavor.

His German translator, Gunther Spaltmann, gives Eliade a most terrible warning on the danger of losing his literary gift:

> He told me that I should devote myself henceforth to literature. I have
> lingered long enough in scholarship. And after reading the lines in
> my hand, he added: "You must hurry." If during the next few years
> I do not succeed in rebinding the threads woven in my "subcon-
> scious," I risk losing forever the gift of imagination. I will remain
> lucid, critical, philosophical to the end of my life.[28]

It was a prophecy that fortunately did not come true. Eliade proved
that he was able to combine both vocations without irremediably scant-
ing either. And at the time he was, as Spaltmann well knew, engaged
in a tremendous effort to write his major novel, *Forbidden Forest*. Yet,
despite Eliade's self-confidence and strong belief in his literary capacity,
he had many doubts and some scares. The simple fact, however, was
that he could not give up *either* of his commitments. He had to be *both*
a writer and a scholar. He had realized this long before when he was
a young university teacher in Bucharest.

> I asked myself if the passion, time and energy I had expended on my
> extra-literary researches would not eventually nullify my potentiality
> as a writer. I could not answer; but I knew that whatever the answer
> might be, there was nothing to be done. I could not abandon these
> aspects of my "opus" even as Goethe could never abandon his sci-
> entific researches.[29]

(Goethe has been Eliade's lifelong model.)

IV

There are two extreme interpretations of Eliade's double vocation—
both erroneous, in my judgment. One is that his fiction writing is a
violon d'Ingres, a French idiom (on the analogy of the great painter
Ingres' legendary pride in his fiddle-playing) that is defined as a "secondary talent or hobby in which a person takes more pride than in his
(her) chief profession."[30] The opposite extreme view is that Eliade is
un savant malgré lui, a historian of religions in spite of himself. Perhaps
the most emphatic statement of this viewpoint is contained in the
anonymous *Times Literary Supplement* review of the *Fragments*. The reviewer portrays Eliade as drifting into the history of religions almost
by accident at a time when he knew his real vocation to be that of a
novelist, and then finding to his permanent chagrin that while his
novels were a failure, his scholarly works were a great success. Thus,
impelled by circumstances and inspired by the prophetic and salvific
task of recuperating the patrimony of *homo religiosus* for modern man,
he transferred most of his talent and energy into the history of religions.
(One recalls the hero of Eliade's story "With the Gypsy Girls," who

knew himself *ab origine* to be an "artist," but who had in his earthly condition become a mere piano-teacher.)

To anyone who has had an opportunity to read Eliade's autobiography, or, for that matter, who has read the journals thoroughly, nothing could be further from the truth than this portrait. The scientific impulse, even in the common Anglo-American sense of the term "science," was just as evident at an early age as the story-telling one. In his early teens Eliade was an avid amateur scientist, an enthusiastic entomologist, botanist, geologist, and chemist, and his attic study in Bucharest was full of his scientific collections as well as of his growing humanities library. And on a far deeper level, there was always the example of Goethe. As far as the history of religions is concerned, Frazer was an early enthusiasm (and motivation for Eliade's learning to read English fluently), and quite early he became acquainted with the writings of Rafaele Pettazoni whom he sees as his seminal inspiration to become a historian of religions.[31] He is shown in the autobiography and in the journals as imbued with an enormous *libido sciendi* in this area, in his youth as in his maturity.

Why does the anonymous reviewer think that the young *lycée* graduate went to India to study Sanskrit and Indian religion and philosophy under Surandranath Dasgupta—simply to write the novels that came out of this decisive Indian experience? Undoubtedly, Eliade could have made a successful career as a writer in Romania. He was a prolific journalist, with abundant paid articles for various Romanian newspapers from an early age, and with many successful works of fiction and general non-fiction, not to speak of radio scripts and other writings, to his credit. Eliade's "failure" as a writer in pre World War Romania is a figment of the reviewer's imagination.[32]

He would have done better to describe Eliade as an all-around man of letters, on the old European model, a wide humanistic scholar and writer, as versus the narrow *Fachmensch* type that Eliade so deplores.[33] Undoubtedly, the reviewer is correct in seeing Eliade as a completely atypical university professor, and one may well wonder whether in academic life he does not at times feel, like Dick Diver in Fitzgerald's *Tender is the Night*, an unbridgeable gap between himself and colleagues made on a much simpler, conventional mode.

It is true, as I have said above, that practically all the complaints in the journals are against his scholarly work, deploring what this is doing to his literary productivity—that is where he seems to hurt the most. Yet we come across one exceptional and startling statement in which *literature* is seen as the incubus from which he must be liberated, while *scholarship* is now viewed as the liberating force. Remarking on Gide's and Sartre's attempt to avoid becoming merely "literary men" by stressing the socio-political dimension, he comments:

> My emancipation from literature by the history of religions and eth-
> nology corresponds to the same tendency: that is what is real for me—
> not literature. A critic who saw a penchant for scholarly learning in
> my scientific work would be gravely mistaken. It's a matter of some-
> thing else entirely; it's a matter of a world which seems more real to
> me, more alive than the characters of novels and short stories.[34]

Obviously, this statement contradicts many others, in which Eliade
asserts the greater truth and reality of the fictional over the historical.[35]
But though quite exceptional, it should not therefore be passed over
as anomalous and distracting from a clear summation of Eliade's work
and thought. It is quite relevant to his two-sided creativity, and should
provide a chastening corrective against seeing him as *wholly* devoted
to the "imaginary" as versus the "real" world. The temptation of pet-
tifogging objections against the hobgoblin of inconsistency should be
resisted, and the essential doubleness of Eliade's nisus and vision must
be integrally confronted.[36]

V

In Eliade's own understanding of his double vocation, two basic
stresses emerge. One emphasizes the analogy between myth, particularly archaic myths, and narrative fiction; another, the creative, revelatory character of the history of religions as a hermeneutic enterprise.
Thus envisioned, both fiction and scholarship partake of a cognitive
character, and both are produced by the creative imagination. This
view raises questions about what it is that literature brings knowledge,
about what is the relation between the "real" and the "imaginary,"
and about what "creativity" consists of in the history of religions.

In the startling passage just quoted and also in a journal entry a
fortnight before, in which he speaks approvingly of Gaston Bachelard's
remark on "the function of the *unreal*," applying it to his urge to write
fiction,[37] Eliade seems to use the term "real" in the common, everyday
sense of the actual, empirical, historical, as opposed to the merely
"imaginary." Yet Eliade has always seen myth as the imaginative
expression of the truly real, in the intentionality of those who live by
myths, and he has also seen modern fiction as one of the current modes
of myth. He has consistently seen myth as truer and deeper and more
revelatory of the real than history in the ordinary, empirical sense. And
this valuation has carried over to his view of his fiction. The Romania
and Bucharest of his stories, no matter how legendary, are truer, he
asserts, than the actual historical places of his experience.[38] Truer in
what sense? Obviously as regards possible, metaphysical, transcendent
reality.

In an entry a few years later, where he seems to put history and fiction on a par, he nevertheless extols the greater creative possibilities of the latter:

> The novel must tell us something, because narrative (that is, literary invention) enriches the world no more and no less than history, although on another level. We have more creative possibilities in imaginary universes than we do on the level of history. *The fact that something is happening, that all kinds of things are happening* [in narrative fiction] is just as significant for the fate of man as living in history or hoping to modify it.[39]

The accent here is on the *imaginary*, the *possible*, on the creation of imaginary, possible universes, and on the narrative mode of expression that is the essential medium of such creation. The imaginary and the possible are seen as just as real as the actual, historical world. And they are viewed as constituting an autonomous, parallel realm, and not existing merely as allegories of the empirical, historical world. Defending his short story, "With the Gypsy Girls," from what he considers wrong-headed critical interpretations, Eliade insists that far from being a "symbol" of anything in concrete reality, the story creates a completely *"new* universe, unprecedented, having its own laws," quite "independent of the geography and sociology of the Bucharest of 1930–1940."[40]

Yet, just as with myth and its exemplary models for human existence, so fiction too has a relation to everyday life, to which it provides meaning. And in stories such as "With the Gypsy Girls," "there is and there is not a 'real' world, that is a world in which everyday man lives or can live."[41] One thinks immediately of Kafka's fiction (e.g., *Metamorphosis*), with its wonderful combination of the familiar and extraordinary.[42] Note also Eliade's comparison of Joyce's *Ulysses* with the simple myths of Australian primitives, in which the most banal places and functions become freighted with value and meaning through the telling of the tale.[43]

The view that literature has a cognitive function and has to do with possible reality is to be found in classical Greek thought long before the advent of the German Romanticism, under which we are inclined to subsume it. Aristotle, in a famous passage of the *Poetics*, distinguishes poetry from history as describing what *might* happen, versus what *did* happen. The "might happen" lies in the category of "the possible as being probable or necessary," and this inherently involves *universal* statements, what a certain "kind of man will probably or necessarily say or do." Thus poetry is contrasted with history, which makes *singular* (factual) statements (e.g., that Alcibiades said or did this or that on a certain occasion). "Hence poetry is something more philosophical and of graver import than history," concludes Aristotle (and thereby truer, we may extrapolate). Nonetheless, he adds, the poet may take names, characters, and events from actual history and still be a poet, for actual historical events may also be viewed as probable and possible, and as such are appropriate material for poetry.[44]

Although the mimetic framework of Aristotle's aesthetics and its mental horizon may seem far removed from Eliade's approach, yet there are many points of congruence, particularly in the stress on the possible and universal, and on what we may call the deeper truth of poetry as compared with history. The *Poetics* provides a cachet both for Eliade's "fantastic" tales, with their anchorage in the possible, and for his "realistic" fiction, with its use of actual events and persons, including autobiographical materials.[45] It is also interesting to note that Eliade has seen his work in the history of religions as philosophical, concerned with man's situation in the universe, rather than scientific in the empirical sense. He views the history of religions much as Aristotle did poetry, as concerned with generic and universal structures.[46]

As noted above, narration is for Eliade the mode of expression *par excellence* of the possible, the universal, the meaningful, the valuable, the deeply true. It is this mode that connects literature, oral or written, with myth, he notes in his conversations with Claude Henri-Rocquet.

> It is well known that literature, oral or written, is the daughter of mythology and that it has inherited the latter's functions: to recount adventures, to relate what has occurred of *significance* in the world. . . . I believe that all narration, even that of a very ordinary fact, is an extension of the great stories told in the myths that explain how this world came to be and how our condition is what we know it to be today. I think that the interest in narration is part of our mode of being in the world. It responds to our need to understand [hear] what has happened, what men have done, what they can do: risks, adventures, trials of all sorts.[47]

We grasp the meaning and reality of the world and human existence—indeed, of our own lives—through these imaginary constructions. Seen from that perspective even fantastic literature, to which Eliade has made noteworthy contributions, far from being an escape from reality and history, may provide "a window into meaning."[48]

In discussing with Rocquet remarks in the journals about the potential contribution of history of religions to imaginative literature,[49] Eliade missed a chance to relate "story" and "history," which in French, the language of their conversation, is conveyed by the same word, *histoire*.

Obviously, if the narration of even the most ordinary event is of a mythological character, having to do with a world of meanings, then history must share with fiction in this essential characteristic. Does not the history of religions, like oral literature, deal with *"concrete spiritual life* as it takes place in culture?"[50] Does not it too deal with "risks, adventures, trials?"

Of course, Eliade, with his phenomenological, comparativist type of history of religions does not usually do history in the narrative mode. He does not usually narrate, but rather does systematic interpretations of narratives. Nevertheless, the monumental *History of Religious Ideas*,[51] which he is in the course of completing, does tell a story of spiritual adventures, crises, and responses on a worldwide scale, from the Old Stone Age to the Death of God. When he comes to do his final summary volume, freed from the albatross of scholarly documentation and problematics, we may hear a story that will be the crowning work of his career as a historian of religions—the tale of man's religious quest from the first traces of human habitation to the present critical nuclear age.

VI

Eliade's assertion of the cognitive aspect of literature has proved less of a stumbling block to his critics and interpreters than his insistence that creative imagination must play an essential role in the work of the history of religions. All kinds of objections, ranging from the serious to the trivial, have come from critics who see things differently than he does. A good example of such criticism may be taken from the *Times Literary Supplement* review that has served as our foil before in this paper.

After noting Eliade's frequent expressions of boredom with the tedious work involved in scholarly research, and noting the obvious fact that scholarship "is concerned with data and their analysis," the reviewer goes on to say:

> Whatever the object of inquiry, accuracy and a due respect for the sources, of whatever nature they may be, must be the foundation on which any theoretical construction, however imaginative, can validly be built. Professor's Eliade's weakness is that he is all too prone to bend his sources, however recalcitrant, to the exigencies of his creative imagination. . . . "Creative spontaneity" is one thing, accurate scholarship is quite another.

And, further on, the reviewer remarks, "Unfortunately, there *are* facts to be considered: you cannot just make them up."[52]

Certainly there may be objections in certain cases to the way in which Eliade puts together phenomena from widely separated eras, areas, and cultures, on the basis of documents of varying reliability and pertinence, as exemplary data for his "patterns," and it is legitimate for scholars who find such assemblages shaky or unconvincing to express their negative judgments. But, again, if the reviewer had read the *Fragments* thoroughly, he would have been aware that the reason Eliade was often so fatigued by his scholarly research, to the point of painful boredom, was precisely because it was so painstaking and exhaustive. And a perusal of the autobiographical writings reveals his absolute horror at proceeding without a thorough, first-hand knowledge of the relevant sources.[53] To my knowledge, there has been no serious challenge to his scholarship in his two major monographs in the history of religions, *Yoga* and *Shamanism,* whatever the disagreement among scholars as to his interpretations. And he certainly cannot be accused of inventing facts ("making them up") in his scholarly works, as is permissible with events and persons in fiction.

More important, the model of scientific knowledge thrust forth by the *Times Literary Supplement* reviewer, despite some suggestion of permissible subtleties and depths, seems distinctly positivistic: the data-hypothesis-verification syndrome. In a sense, the reviewer is quite right: Eliade is not at all interested in that kind of scholarship. He tells us in his "Autobiographical Fragment" that in his researches into archaic alchemy and metallurgy, he was not concerned with establishing some kind of empirical "pre-chemistry," but rather with the "metaphysical valorizations" and "soteriological techniques" that might be discerned in these archaic pursuits. So also in his work on ethnological and folkloric materials, he was not primarily interested in scientific description, but rather in abstracting the metaphysical meanings hidden in the documents, i.e., the views of man's place in the cosmos. This is a matter, properly speaking, of philosophy, not of science, he points out.

What Eliade seeks are general patterns of meaning, spiritual realities that are to be discerned in the facticity of historical and ethnological documents through the shaping imagination of the inquiring interpreter. Knowledge here is not a matter of photographic verisimilitude or logical analysis, but of *poiesis,* of a making and a shaping that in certain ways is analogous to that of the writer or artist. Eliade's "myth of the eternal return" or "Cosmic Tree" constructions cannot be verified simply by returning to an appraisal of the documentary materials, no matter how much he insists that they arise directly from them—he also insists repeatedly that they are *hidden, camouflaged, unrecognizable* for common, everyday vision. It requires the constructive imagination to see (or hear) them.

It is not without significance that Eliade reiterates in several places his enthusiastic appreciation for Jacob Bronowski's remark about the dependence of new scientific axioms on "a free play of the mind, an invention outside the logical processes . . . the central act of imagination in science and . . . in all respects like any similar act in literature."[54] Nor is it without interest how admiring he is of the creative, open, flexible spirit of contemporary mathematicians and physicists, so superior in his estimation to the "paltry" attitudes of nonscientific humanists in present-day academia.[55] This honorific stance of Eliade's is toward another kind of science than that envisioned by the *Times Literary Supplement* reviewer. It is the science of the worldmakers—of a Copernicus, a Newton, an Einstein. And it recalls the science of that grand intuitive spirit, Goethe, Eliade's intellectual hero.

There is a parallel to Eliade's approach in Northrop Frye's view of the imaginative (which he distinguishes sharply from the merely imaginary) as the constructive power out of which come all the human arts and sciences. Speaking of philosophy, history, science, religion, and law, he says, "When we think of their content, they're bodies of knowledge; when we think of their form they're myths, that is, imaginative verbal structures"; hence, literature is the central study as "the laboratory where myths themselves are studied and experimented with."[56] Admittedly, this strictly verbal emphasis does not account for music, the graphic and plastic arts, and mathematics, which for Frye is the purest example of the constructive imagination at work. Nevertheless, it might be very fruitful for an inquiry into the relation between "poetry" and "truth" to look back at some of the great theorists of the literary imagination, for example, Coleridge in the *Biographia Literaria*.

Certainly, the constructive function of the human mind, particularly of the imaginative faculty, in the attainment of knowledge is no new idea. (I am still convinced that it was Aristotle who said, "Imagination is the mother of the categories," although I cannot locate the passage.) Yet aside from natural scientists and mathematicians who, as Eliade notes, are more honest and braver in this regard than most humanists and social scientists, there is little open acknowledgment of the role of the imaginative in the world of learning. Academic scholarship too has its ritual, its prudishness, and, yes, its hypocrisy. It is not only the unlearned and the unwashed who dwell, blindered, in the cave.

Yet there is a distinct difference between science and scholarship, on the one hand, and literary and artistic production on the other. The relation of literature to reality, however that be conceived (assuming, against the formalists, that there is one), does not raise the same kind of problem of consensual agreement and verification or falsification that scholarship does. But this problem need not be solved in any crudely positivistic or analytical manner. In the case of Eliade, as in that of Gershom Scholem, growth in the fullness of meanings, a "polyvalence" that includes conflicting and even contradictory views, is the desideratum.[57] Fullness is all, we may say, echoing a motif of Gabriel Marcel, who also followed a dual vocation. Matei Calinescu has captured this note of "richness" remarkably well in what amounts to a prolegomenon to an Eliadean aesthetics of knowledge.[58]

For anyone who finds illuminating the notion that literature (art) and scholarship (science) are collaborators in the attainment of knowledge, Mircea Eliade provides an example *par excellence* of the co-working of the two modes. The "Autobiographical Fragment" provides Eliade's own account of this cooperation as the joint expression of a single, elementary intuition: the unrecognizability of miracle, the camouflage of the transcendent in history and, hence, the problem of the "fall" in history, the nostalgia for Paradise, the whole Eliadean *megillah*. If this view is to be accepted, then the conflictive emphasis earlier in this paper—the "two souls within one breast" motif—is transmuted by the eventual unity perceived in the joint *oeuvre* as a whole.

Eliade's account indicates "a real dependence of some literary writings on theoretical ones and vice versa." In the former case he records a *direct* as well as *unconscious* dependence, although, moved by the striking case of his novel *Şarpele*, he concludes "that theoretical activity cannot *consciously* and *voluntarily* influence literary activity." He also concludes "that the free act of literary creation can . . . reveal certain theoretical meanings."[59] These conclusions were confirmed later in the inception, development, and consummation of his major novel, *Forbidden Forest*.[60]

To respond critically to Eliade's view of his joint authorship, one would have to know the whole literary *oeuvre* (much of it still in Romanian), as well as the scholarly works that have become available in Western languages.[61] Such a critical response would also require some astute historical-biographical and literary-critical judgments. Eliade presents us with the type of generalized interpretation that is illuminating in such a matter: suggesting what might have been or could be the case, and inviting us to try our hands at a construction that will pull things together equally well. I must confess to a certain uneasiness, however, at having an author so self-conscious about the meaning and connections of his work, arising from the fear that the open, polyvalent realm of the imaginative—what W. K. Wimsatt calls "the polysemous ambiguity of poetry" and what Todorov sees as the both/and character of the fantastic—may be reduced to "naïve" mechanical allegory.[62]

Notes

1. *Fragments d'un journal.* Translated from the Romanian by Luc Badesco. Coll. "Du Monde entier." (Paris: Gallimard, 1973).

2. *No Souvenirs: Journal, 1957–69*. Translated from the French by Fred H. Johnson, Jr. (New York: Harper & Row, 1977).

3. *Şantier* (Bucuresti: Editura Cugetarea, 1935). See Eliade's comments on this "indirect novel" in his autobiography *Amintiri*. I am using Mac Linscott Ricketts' translation from the Romanian *Autobiography*, vol. I, 1907–1937, *Journey East, Journey West* (San Francisco: Harper and Row, 1981) (hereafter referred to as *Autobiography*), where the comments occur on pp. 295f. A French translation, *Memoire I, 1907–1937: Les Promesses de l'équinoxe*, was published by Gallimard (Paris) in 1980.

4. *Maitreyi*. Bucureşti: Editura Cultura Naţională, 1933. (French translation: *La Nuit Bengali*. Translated from the Romanian by Alain Guillermou. Lausanne: La Guilde du Livres, 1966).

5. *Autobiography*, pp. 239f.

6. Matei Calinescu, "Mircea Eliade's Journals," *Denver Quarterly* 12 (1977), p. 314; "The odyssey of the reluctant professor," *Times Literary Supplement*, 18 January, 1954, p. 50.

7. *Fragments*, p. 52.

8. Ibid., pp. 35f. See also pp. 10f., 24, 39f.

9. *No Souvenirs*, p. vii.

10. *L'Herne* numéro 33: *Mircea Eliade*, Les Cahiers de l'Herne (Paris: Editions de l'Herne, 1978), p. 287.

11. *No Souvenirs*, p. vii. Fragments from Eliade's Portuguese journal (1941–45) have been published in Romanian. Presumably much more is being held in reserve. See Douglas Allen and Dennis Doeing, *Mircea Ellade: An Annotated Bibliography* (New York and London: Garland Pub. Co., 1980), items #909 and #930.

12. *L'Epreuve du labyrinthe: Entretiens avec Claude-Henri Rocquet* (Paris: Belfond, 1978).

13. See Roy Pascal, *Design and Truth in Autobiography* (Cambridge: Harvard University Press, 1960), esp. ch. 5, "The Elusiveness of Truth." The fact is, however, that Eliade reveals his weaknesses as well as his strengths in his published journals, and makes no attempt to eliminate inconsistencies.

14. *Criterion* (Divinity School, University of Chicago), Summer, 1978, pp. 30–34. See also "Preface to the English Edition," *Forbidden Forest*, trans. Mac Linscott Ricketts and Mary Park Stevenson (Notre Dame: University of Notre Dame Press, 1978).

15. *Criterion*, p. 32. See also *No Souvenirs*, p. ixf.

16. *Criterion*, p. 33; *No Souvenirs*, p. ix.

17. *Criterion*, p. 33.

18. But see the discussion of *poiesis* in the history of religions in section VI, below. Also this statement by Eliade in his Introduction to *Two Tales of the Occult* (New York: Herder & Herder, 1970), p. xiii, indicates what he has in mind: "Actually, the historian of religions in the same way as the writer of fiction is constantly confronted with different structures of (sacred and mythological) space, different qualities of time, and more specifically by a considerable number of strange, unfamiliar, and enigmatic worlds of meaning."

19. *Autobiography*, pp. 308f.

20. *Fragments*, p. 36.

21. Ibid., p. 116.

22. Ibid., pp. 28, 42 ("my unfaithfulness to my *true* vocation, that of a Romanian writer.")

23. Ibid., p. 46.

24. *No Souvenirs*, p. 194.

25. *Fragments*, p. 18.

26. Ibid., pp. 41, 108.

27. Ibid., p. 135.

28. Ibid., p. 148.

29. *Autobiography*, pp. 299f.

30. Etienne & Simone Deak, *A Dictionary of Colorful French Slanguage and Colloquialism* (New York: Dutton, 1961), p. 204. Note Eliade's use of the term: "For me the writing of fiction . . . was more than a *'violon d'Ingres'* " (*Forbidden Forest*, p. v.).

31. *Fragments*, p. 103; *No Souvenirs*, p. 85.

32. Eliade's "Autobiographical Fragment" (English translation included in this volume) provides a convincing account of the alternation of emphases between the two modes of productivity during various phases of his career as to a large extent a response to external circumstances. In pre-World War II Romania he wrote for a market in which novels were more valued than "philosophy." During World War II he forswore new literary publication as a patriotic sacrifice. In his post-war Parisian exile he wrote for a market in which history of religions rated much higher than Romanian fiction. Again it is clearly evident that Eliade's dual productivity came from deep inner drives, neither of which could be denied. The double gift and drive were a given. Their consummation in incarnate existence varied with external socio-economic, historico-cultural circumstances. (I have used Mac Linscott Rickett's translation of this writing, in a handwritten, unpaginated manuscript.)

33. *No Souvenirs*, pp. 47, 49, 191f.

34. Ibid., p. 193.

35. See, e.g., ibid., pp. 51, 307f.

36. For a discussion of the apparent ambiguity and ambivalence in Eliade's views of the historical and transhistorical, see my paper, "Mircea Eliade: Attitudes toward History," *Religious Studies Review*, 6, 1 (January, 1980): pp. 13–16.

37. *No Souvenirs*, p. 190.

38. "The Bucharest of my novella *Mantuleasa Street*, although legendary, is truer than the city I went through for the last time in August 1942." (Ibid., p. 51) The novella referred to has been published in English as *The Old Man and the Bureaucrats*, trans. Mary Park Stevenson (Notre Dame: University of Notre Dame Press, 1979).

39. *No Souvenirs*, p. 205; bracketed phrase added.

40. Ibid., pp. 307f.

41. Ibid., p. 308.

42. See Tzvetan Todorov, *The Fantastic: A Structural Approach to a Literary Genre*, trans. Richard Howard, Cornell Paperbacks (Ithaca: Cornell University Press, 1975); see ch. 2, especially, for the inherently ambivalent character of fantastic literature.

43. *No Souvenirs*, pp. 180f.

44. *De Poetica*, ch. 9, 1451a36–1451b33, trans. Ingram Bywater, in Richard McKeon, *The Basic Works of Aristotle* (New York: Random House, 1941), p. 1464.

45. For Eliade's own description of the two kinds of fiction, see his "Autobiographical Fragment," sec. II, below. See also the discussion of his fantastic stories in *Two Tales of the Occult*, pp. ix–xii.

46. *Autobiographical Fragments*, sec. I.

47. *L'Epreuve du labyrinthe*, p. 190.

48. *No Souvenirs*, p. 279.

49. *L'Epreuve*, pp. 189f.

50. *No Souvenirs*, p. 225.

51. *A History of Religious Ideas.* vol. 1. *From the Stone Age to the Eleusinian Mysteries*, trans. Willard Trask (Chicago: University of Chicago Press, 1978); vol. 2, *From Gautama Buddha to the Triumph of Christianity*, and vol. 3, *From Mohammad to Contemporary Atheist Theologies* [will follow]. A summary volume of about 400 pages is projected, to be published after vol. 3 is completed.

52. *Times Literary Supplement*, 18 January 1954.

53. *Fragments*, p. 104; "Autobiography," I, IV, p. 80; "Autobiographical Fragment," sec. I.

54. *No Souvenirs*, pp. ixf; *Criterion*, p. 32; *Forbidden Forest*, p. vi.

55. *No Souvenirs*, p. 47.

56. *The Educated Imagination* (Bloomington: Indiana University Press, 1964), pp. 154f.; see also p. 127. I am indebted to Norman Girardot for bringing this work to my attention.

57. See David Biale, *Gershom Scholem: Kabbalah and Counter-History* (Cambridge and London: Harvard University Press, 1979); and my review, "Gershom Scholem Interpreted," *Midstream* (February, 1980): 56–58.

58. "Imagination and Meaning: Aesthetic Attitudes and Ideas in Mircea Eliade's Thought," *Journal of Religion*, 57 (June, 1977): 1–15.

59. "Autobiographical Fragment," sec. II.

60. See, e.g., *Fragments*, pp. 219f.

61. My own direct knowledge of Eliade's literary works includes *Maitreyi* and *Mademoiselle Christina* (in French), *Pe Strada Mântuleasa* (in French and English), and these English translations: *Forbidden Forest*, "The Snake," "Youth Without Youth," "Nights at Serampore," "The Secrets of Dr. Honigberger," "Twelve Thousand Head of Cattle," "A Great Man," "With the Gypsy Girls," and "The Bridge."

62. W. K. Wimsatt, *Hateful Contraries: Studies in Literature and Criticism* (Lexington: University of Kentucky, 1966), pp. 58, 61f.

Note on Translation: The translations from *Fragments d'un journal* cited above and from *L'Epreuve du labyrinthe* are my own. They are intended to be faithful, but not literal, adding or subtracting words where that seems best. The other translations are as listed. I have chosen to cite *No Souvenirs* in preference to the *Fragments* when they have duplicate entries to make the citations immediately available to the English-reading public.

Mac Linscott Ricketts

Mircea Eliade
and the Writing of
The Forbidden Forest

Mircea Eliade began the novel which he titled from the start, *Noaptea de Sânziene* (The Night of St. John), in Paris in the early summer of 1949, but he was not to complete it until five years later, in 1954, after many interruptions and many other significant accomplishments. The following year it was published in French translation, *Forêt Interdite* (trans. Alain Guillermou; Paris, Gallimard, 1955), and it was only in 1970–71 that Eliade saw the novel appear in the language in which he had written it, his native Romanian (*Noaptea de Sânziene* in two volumes; Paris, Ioan Cusa). In 1978 the University of Notre Dame Press published the English translation from the Romanian, *The Forbidden Forest* (trans. Mac Linscott Ricketts and Mary Park Stevenson), thus making available to the Anglo-American public this unique product of Eliade's imaginative genius.

While Eliade, who is known primarily as an historian of religions, has been rather reticent about discussing his literary writings, he was induced by his friend, Virgil Ierunca, then editor of a small Romanian emigré periodical, originating in Paris *Caiete de Dor,* to open his diary to his fellow "Romanians in exile" in 1955, and share with them the struggles he underwent in penning the then recently published *Forêt Interdite.*[1] Later, these journal excerpts (minus a few short passages) were included in a much larger body of selections published in French translation as *Fragments d'un journal* (trans. Luc Badesco, Paris, 1973).[2]

The novel, which in Romanian runs to 747 pages, cannot be briefly summarized. Suffice it here to say that on one level it is an epic of

Romania and the Romanians from 1936 to 1948, and on another level it is an "archetypal" myth of man's nostalgia for escape from time and history. It begins and ends on summer solstices, or Nights of St. John, the two dates being separated by twelve years, a "perfect cycle" or "Great Time"; and on both these magic nights there is a meeting of the hero and heroine in a mysterious forest. In between the two episodes we relive those tragic years of Romanian history through the lives of an assortment of Romanian "types"; but it is in the hero, Ştefan, above all that we see embodied the search for a way out of the labyrinth of human existence. And strangely enough, considering that the book is written by a scholar of religious studies, it is not "religion" which in the end seems to be Ştefan's salvation, but a kind of transcendental love for a girl—and death.

Like the narrative, the story of the writing of the novel begins on a summer solstice—or nearly so, at least. It was actually the 26th of June when Eliade "saw" the novel, and on the next day he wrote the first three pages, "in a state of grace," in the afternoon. However, a few days earlier, on June 21, he wrote of his peculiar feelings on that and every summer solstice when "something happens" to him; and he was reminded of a plot for a story that had obsessed him for several days a few years earlier when he was living in Portugal. It was the story of "the miracle of regeneration and eternal youth obtained on the Night of St. John." At that time he had felt as though he were living under some kind of spell, that "something was being revealed" to him, but he had set nothing down on paper. A little later (5 July), he was to recall that his first published novel, *Isabel şi apele diavolului* (1930), also centered on the summer solstice. Clearly, Eliade understands himself to be affected by this season with its universal mythology and mystery.

At the time he began to write *Noaptea de Sânziene* he was in the midst of composing one of his most significant scholarly studies, *Le Chamanisme* (E.T., *Shamanism, Archaic Techniques of Ecstasy*, trans. Willard Trask; 1964). When the idea for the novel came to him, en route home from an excursion to the Abbey of Royaumont outside Paris (a place which figures in the last chapter of the novel), his book on shamanism seemed suddenly ridiculous (*derizorie*) to him. Still, he attempted for awhile to work on both books simultaneously, but by July 3 he had given up the attempt and was devoting himself exclusively to the novel. As he has stated on several occasions, he finds it impossible to write fiction and "science" at the same time. For example, on 3 November 1949, he confesses:

> I am incapable of existing concurrently in two spiritual universes: that of literature and that of science. This is my fundamental weakness: I cannot remain awake and at the same time live in a state of dreaming,

of play. Once I begin "making literature" I find myself again in another universe; I call it oneiric, because it has another temporal structure and above all because my relationship with the characters is of an imaginary nature, rather than a critical one.

Eliade was to spend two months at Capri that summer, writing on the novel most of the time. He returned to Paris on September 12 with just over 300 pages of manuscript, some of it salvaged from an earlier, uncompleted novel called *Apocalips* (a book which featured Vădastra, one of the humorous characters in *Noaptea de Sânziene*). For the next two and a half months his journal indicates he was having difficulty making headway with the novel, although he was spending considerable time on it, rereading it, trying to perfect what he had already done. The inspiration was fading. On October 27, for example, there is a long soliloquy in the journal about how difficult he finds it to write if beforehand he has already "rehearsed" that part of the plot mentally. The spontaneity—what he had called in his youth "authenticity"—is gone. "I must divest myself of this remainder of immaturity," he declares. But within another six weeks he has put the novel aside to return to serious work on *Le chamanisme*. By this time he has pushed the total number of pages past 450 (cf. *Journal*, 23 November 1949), and he has begun to realize he must write more concisely.

He was not to resume work on the novel until a full year and a half had elapsed. In the interim his time had been given over mainly to study, writing, and lecturing in the field of the history of religions. It should be pointed out that Eliade's fame as a scholar was just beginning at this time. Aside from his dissertation on Yoga (later published in Paris in 1936) and several books in Romanian, he had published only two books in the history of religions: *Traité d'histoire des religions* (E.T., *Patterns in Comparative Religion*) and *Le Mythe de l'Eternel Retour* (English paperback title: *Cosmos and History*), both in Paris in 1949. He had lectured as a visiting scholar at the Sorbonne (1945 and 1947), and during this period (1950–51) he gave several lectures at universities and international gatherings of religion scholars in Europe. In the summer of 1950 he participated in his first Eranos Conference, an annual conclave of Jungian-oriented persons from various walks of life, at Ascona, Switzerland. Thanks to contacts made at this conference, in January 1951 he began receiving a monthly stipend from the Bollingen Foundation of New York,[3] the agency which eventually was to publish three of his works in English translation (*Myth of the Eternal Return, Yoga,* and *Shamanism*). This stipend was a godsend to Eliade, because prior to that time he had had no regular source of income since the end of the war, and finances were a continual cause of anxiety.

There had been little time to think about the novel, although apparently it was always in the back of his mind (cf. journal entry for 28 October 1950). Rather, his main concern was the book on shamanism, which he did not complete until the end of march, 1951; indexing and proofreading kept him preoccupied until the beginning of June. On the ninth of that month he again picked up the manuscript of *Noaptea de Sânziene,* but his first impressions on rereading it were bad:

> Impossible! Surprisingly artificial. I wonder how I could have *believed* in such pages. I shall have to start all over again (*Journal,* 9 June 1951).

The next several weeks were torture for Eliade as he tried to get back into the plot which had long since grown cold. The beginning of the novel was rewritten, all except passages relating to the comic character Vădastra, employing the techniques of "concentrated time" (as he calls it) and flashbacks. His aim was to reduce the volume of the text by about 50 percent. More than once he bitterly laments that he had allowed himself to be carried away by his "inspiration" of two years earlier. At the end of July, having reached p. 182 of the redraft, Eliade repents of ever having undertaken a new novel in 1949 instead of finishing the one he had begun several years previously (*Journal,* 31 July 1951).

One of the problems concerns the different kinds of time with which he has to deal in this novel: "fantastic time" at the beginning and the end, "psychological time" in some early episodes, and "historical time" in much of the novel, wherein the events of 1936–48 must somehow be integrated (5 March 1951). But having gained this insight into his problem, he has to lay the manuscript aside once more and prepare a lecture for the Eranos Conference.

In mid-September he resumes his work of trying to perfect the early part of the novel. He even estimates now that he can finish the whole book in five or six months of labor. To do this, he is prepared to postpone lectures at the University of Lund and at Rome, which he had promised for fall and winter (*Journal,* 17 September). He finds, on September 18, that instead of condensing he has actually increased the number of pages by about 100. Also, he seems displeased with the way Ştefan, the character who most resembles the author, is turning out. He calls him a "neuter," too much withdrawn into his inner world (18 and 25 September, from a typescript, omitted in published versions). On October 4 he is so discouraged and has such pressing commitments that he says he must break off work on the novel—and yet on the seventh he is still at it, very much engrossed in the new dimensions he is discovering in Biriş, one of Ştefan's friends, and with the problem of keeping his characters from becoming "common intellectuals." A week later he has interrupted work on the novel, obliged to fulfill other writing commitments.

About this time he reflects in his journal (undated, 1951) about the lack of success of the recently published French translation of his 1933 novel, *Maitreyi,* which had brought him overnight fame in Romania when he was still a young man.[4] But upon further consideration, Eliade realizes that if he is to make a reputation for himself as a writer in the West, it must be with a new work, specifically with *Noaptea de Sânziene,* not with one that is eighteen years old.

Hastily concluding his other promised pieces, he returns in a fever to the novel on 4 January 1952. Again he reworks the first chapters with which he remains dissatisfied. He wants at all costs to tell an engrossing *story,* to create a *narrative.* He has no use for those literary fashions which scorn plot, although he once had experimented with the interior monologue in *Lumina ce se stinge* (1930–34); still, brief passages of this type can be found in *Noaptea de Sânziene.* But even these interior monologues are more often recollections of events than soliloquies—he calls them "mental films." A major problem now, as earlier, is "Time": how to create the sensation of time's passage without employing the two thousand pages of Tolstoy's *War and Peace?*

By mid-January Eliade had finished reworking chapter seven, and he calculated that he had, "in a sense," written a new novel. He says he has been able to salvage only a few pages from each chapter written in 1949. "The novel must continually be reinvented" (*Journal,* 21 January, Romanian version only). Two more chapters, completing Part I, were done by February 2, but Eliade was still discontent with the "prologue," and in the next week he wrote and rewrote it four or five times.

> Tremendous difficulty with the "atmosphere": I had to avoid at all costs the faery or fantastic air of *Şarpele* [a novella of 1937], yet without sacrificing the element of the imponderable, the absurd, the "predestined," which was implied (more precisely, camouflaged) in "the car which ought to have disappeared at midnight," and which in any event I could not discard (9 February 1952).

Having finished Part I, and having many other pressing matters to attend to, Eliade worked no more on the novel during the remainder of the winter and spring. Friends to whom he sent copies of the first part to read had mixed reactions. Doubts plagued him.

June was spent vacationing at Ascona, at the Eranos Institute. Although he had planned to continue with *Noaptea de Sânziene* during that interlude, he found himself attracted by the Institute's library, and he became caught up in other activities related to his studies in the history of religions. (His main project now was the writing of *Le Yoga*.) Thus he was occupied until late fall, when in Paris at the end of November he dashed off a "fantastic" short story, "Douăsprezece mii de capte de vită" (Twelve Thousand Head of Cattle).[5] Immediately afterward (14 December 1952) he recommenced writing the novel he had scarcely touched for nine months. The first thing he did was to abandon the prologue on which he had expended so much effort and rework all the passages in which Ştefan and his wife Ioana appear, trying to give greater depth to Ioana. These revisions consumed all the time he could steal for "literature" over a three-week period.

At last, on December 21, he began Part II. He was to continue to work at it rather steadily throughout the winter, making corrections as he went along, trying to produce a finished manuscript he would not have to revise later. Sometimes he was gripped by moods of melancholy, perhaps because of the sad events about which he was then writing—events related to the historical fate of Romania in World War II and its aftermath. Guillermou began making the French translation of Part I that winter (for Eliade had decided to publish the novel in French), and Eliade was discouraged when he read the first chapter of it. "I have the impression that *Noaptea de Sânziene* loses one hundred percent in translation. More precisely, the translation illumines all too harshly the book's naivetés and imperfections" (19 February 1953).

By mid-April he had completed four of the seven chapters projected for the second part, and after a brief interruption he continued with chapter five in May. He wrote even during the time he was delivering a series of lectures at the Jung Institute and elsewhere in Switzerland. By June first he had begun chapter six, on which he worked for about three weeks during a vacation period at Ascona; then he laid the manuscript aside once more.

For almost a full year he was unable to "give himself to literature," being involved in conferences and especially his definitive study on Yoga. In the meantime the French translation of Part I was completed (June 1954). A great sadness comes over Eliade as he starts work, about the first of June, on the penultimate chapter of the novel which he had begun almost five years before. But this time he is, so to speak, in the "home stretch," and this time he will persevere to the end.

There are only two more journal entries pertaining directly to the writing of the novel, those for the 26th of June and the seventh of July, 1954. The former is an extremely important one and gives a key for interpreting the symbolism of the automobile and of Ştefan's mysterious love for Ileana. Indeed, without these notes it is unlikely that the reader of the novel would guess the full meaning of the symbolism.

The most astonishing thing of all revealed by the journal is that it was only while writing the final scenes that Eliade himself "understood" the symbolism which he then realized had been present from the start! The car, which he had taken to be a symbol of the eventual union of Ştefan and Ileana (cf. *Journal*, 9 February 1952, Romanian version only) which he had always planned as the climax of the book, now acquires a new significance.

> Now, today [26 June], I have understood that it is a matter of something else. Ştefan was obsessed by "the car which had to disappear at midnight," the car in which Ileana "ought to have come" to Băneasa in 1936. What seems strange in the meeting at Băneasa, stranger than his incomprehensible love for Ileana (incomprehensible because he continues to be in love with Ioana), is his obsession with her car. Now, everything is explained if Ileana's car, real at Royaumont twelve years later, is the cradle of their death. . . . Ileana shows herself to be that which she was from the beginning, an Angel of Death. . . .

Perhaps it is not an unprecedented experience for a writer of fiction to discover at the end of the writing of a long book that he himself has not understood its "true" symbolism, but for me, one who is not a writer, this journal entry is an astonishing confession. Moreover, this passage sheds much light on Eliade's view, expressed in many writings on the history of religions, that myths and symbols have "transhistorical meanings" of which individuals and cultures may be unaware.

Eleven days later, at 11:35 A.M. (Eliade records the exact time), 7 July, Eliade finished the last page. The final scenes were written "in a state of constant tension" and sadness, the author tells us, and for several days after finishing the book he seems to have remained in a daze (cf. 9 July).

Eliade, who has often written on the theme of the "coincidence of opposites," shows himself in the foregoing account of his writing of *Noaptea de Sânziene* to be in at least one sense an embodiment of this paradox. In him coexist two types of thinkers and writers: one, the scholarly historian of religions, interested in all manner of religious phenomena and passionate to search out the interrelations among these phenomena and to discover their "meanings"; and the other, a writer of fiction, an intellect of great imagination and inventiveness, a creator of *stories*. From early life these two "sides" of Eliade have been evident. In an "autobiographical fragment"[6] Eliade writes about how he discovered this truth about himself while he was in India:

> I would work for months with a passion and an indifference to overexertion which one can have only at age 21 or 22, and then suddenly I would become indifferent to the Sanskrit texts and my beloved Indian

philosophy. With an effort which I admire even now, after all these years, I would succeed nevertheless in continuing to work on my doctoral thesis—but not for more than a week or two longer. Then I *had* to drop everything and write fiction. I would write for as many as ten or fifteen hours per day, for a month or six weeks, and then I would return to the thesis. It was then that I realized I could not renounce either one or the other. Both activities were equally necessities for me: in the first place, necessary for my own inner equilibrium, for my spiritual integrity. At whatever risk, I had to continue them both.[7]

This pattern of alternation between "facts" and "fiction," between "reality" and imagination, which is so evident in the account of the composing of *Noaptea de Sânziene,* continues to the present day. Although Eliade at 75 (in 1982) feels he is racing against the clock to finish his three or four volume masterwork in the history of religions, *A History of Religious Ideas,*[8] a project which is the culmination of his life's work as a scholar, he still continues to interrupt this labor from time to time in order to write short stories or novellas.

However, an author who writes only sporadically, when he is "inspired" and when he can free himself from other matters of business, will find it very difficult to write novels of the length of *Noaptea de Sânziene.* This is one reason, surely, why *The Forbidden Forest* (to use the English title) was Eliade's last novel and why, since then, he has confined himself to shorter works, mostly of 50 to 100 pages each (some fifteen or sixteen short stories, *"littérature fantastique,"* have been attracting considerable attention in Romania, Germany, and France. I believe when they begin to be published in English translation they will be of some popularity here also.[9]

Indeed, it may be that in future generations, as Eliade has suggested in his autograph of my copy of *Noaptea de Sânziene,* it will be for this work (and his other fiction) that he will be remembered, more than for his erudite monographs. Progress in the study of religions will make Eliade's conclusions and perhaps even his methodology outdated; but his fiction, in which he has expressed his personal creed and "message," may remain a timeless source of inspiration. If Eliade ever succeeds in his lifelong ambition of conquering Time, it will be not through his works of history of religions—brilliant as they are—but through his fiction.

Notes

1. The article appeared in the December, 1955, issue of *Caiete de Dor* (No. 9), pp. 6–13 of the mimeographed publication.

2. An English translation was made of the latter half of this book: *No Souvenirs* (New York, Harper and Row, 1977), but the part containing the story of how the novel was written was not included.

3. Cf. *Journal*, 9 December 1950.

4. *La Nuit Bengali*, trans. Alain Guillermou (Paris: Gallimard, 1950).

5. Romanian and English versions printed on opposite pages in *Fantastic Tales*, ed. Eric Tappe (London: Dillon's, 1969).

6. "Fragment autobiografic," *Caiete de Dor*, 7 (July, 1953), p. 8. English translation below.

7. *Journal*, 9 December 1950.

8. Vol. I, E.T., University of Chicago Press, 1978; published originally in French as *Histoire des croyances et des idées religieuses* (Paris: Payot, vol. I, 1976; vol. II, 1978).

9. *The Old Man and the Bureaucrats*, a translation of Eliade's novella *Pe strada Mântuleasa* (1968) by Mary Park Stevenson, was published by the University of Notre Dame Press in 1979, and two others were published in *Tales of the Sacred and the Supernatural* (Philadelphia: Westminster Press, 1981).

Mircea Eliade

Autobiographical Fragment

I

The editors of *Caiete de Dor* have honored me by asking me how I reconcile those two fields of activity—literature on the one hand, science and philosophy on the other—and to what extent the scientific and philosophical occupations can coexist with literary creation, and to what extent they augment it or detract from it. That same question I have been asking myself, increasingly, for thirty years. I don't know if the answer I have found is entirely correct, but even if it is not, it has nevertheless a value: it is, as they say, "the author's viewpoint," a testimony about the inner meanings of a creation which, for the rest of the world, presents itself as independent, but which for the author is confounded with his own history.

From the outset I want to make one thing clear: the series of studies and researches which, apparently, could be considered "scientific," I consider rather to be "philosophical." This is because, even when I was involved with the history of science, and was trying to comprehend the meaning of Oriental alchemies and metalurgies, what interested me primarily were the metaphysical valorizations present in those traditional techniques rather than their possible "scientific discoveries." In the alchemical texts, for example, what interested me was what I believed to be peculiar to those soteriological techniques, not what might constitute the rudiments of a pre-chemistry. Alchemy was never a pre-chemistry, that is, an elementary "science" and an empirical practice; it could be so valorized only when, the spiritual horizon on which the traditional techniques having been darkened, man found himself on another horizon—that of the "laws of matter"—and, searching the old texts in the light of this new perspective, he found in them, naturally enough, the rudiments of "scientific observation" and "laboratory practice."

This is only one example, but it is by no means unique. I have written a number of works based on ethnology and folklore, but I do not believe I wrote them in order to add to the immense ethnographic and folkloric bibliography. Not that I hold those two disciplines in contempt; on the contrary I consider them among the most useful for the new ecumenical humanism our century is called to articulate. But I have never felt myself capable of composing a "purely scientific" work of ethnography or folklore. I am interested only in the spiritual documents which lie buried in those reams of books published by ethnologists, folklorists, and sociologists. In those hundreds of thousands of pages I believe there survives a world of myths and symbols which must be known and understood, if we are to be able to understand the situation of man in the Cosmos. Now, as we know very well, this situation constitutes already a metaphysics. Efforts at knowing and understanding are incorporated more properly in "philosophy" than "science," which, in this case, is preoccupied primarily with the rigorous collection of oral documents, with their classification according to "types" and "motifs," and finally with their historical and sociological interpretation.

But I shall have more to say later on the subject of traditional spirituality. For the time being, I wish to avoid a confusion which might be made with regard to the "typographical appearance" of my works: typographically, they present themselves as works of erudition; that is, they are highly specialized books, ordinarily. This state of affairs has two explanations: the first is of a personal nature; the other follows from the nature of the spiritual documents under investigation. Personally, I had—and still have—a horror of dilettantism, improvisation, "hearsay science," "books about—." This terror of being deceived, of being led into error by a charlatan or ignoramus, of building on the foundation of inaccurate assertions—I believe I felt it for the first time in the fourth class of lycée when, reading *Les grande initiés*, I took for granted all the fallacies of Schuré, assuming they were based on authentic sources. Much to my surprise, a little while after that, chancing to set eyes on a book by Oldenberg on Vedic India and Buddhism, I saw that Schuré had simply invented, quite arbitrarily, a good many of his stories about Rama, Krishna, and the Buddha. This lesson was for me decisive. From then on I endeavored always to go to the sources, to "see the text." I even wonder if my going to India at age 21 for doctoral studies is not explained by the doubt which, in time, I had come to have concerning even the works of Indianist "savants." I might very well have gone to Paris to study Sanskrit and Indian philosophy—but I had reached the point of doubting all Western interpretations and had decided to go to India, directly to the source.

Hence the need I felt to exhibit always the sources from which I started in order to arrive at a certain interpretation. Some of my works 1934–38 are marred by notes and references and an excessive bibliography which encumber the reading. I believe this mania is explained also by my "situation" in Romania at that time. It was my misfortune to have become, soon after returning from India, a "popular writer" due to the success of *Maitreyi*. A year before, I had been entrusted with a course on metaphysics and a seminar on the history of logic and metaphysics—and the university auditorium teemed with a youthful audience which was only to a limited extent interested in the problems I was discussing, but which, in any event, admired the author of *Maitreyi*. On the other hand, the necessities of life and the restlessness of youth made me publish, in newspapers and reviews of the time, a great many articles which did not have much to do with "science." So when I did publish truly "scientific" works—whether in reviews such as *Revista de Filozofie, Ricerche Religiose,* or *Religio,* or in books like *Alchimia Asiatică* (1935), *Yoga* (1936), *Cosmologie și alchimie babiloniană* (1937), or *Zalmoxis,* I (1938)—I took care to present sufficient documentation that they not be considered, by the malicious or the unadvised, simple "essays" of a "man of letters" or a "journalist." It would be interesting to recall, in connection with my "situation" in Romania after 1934, the reverberations of my nonliterary works among my former teachers and colleagues of that time. But concerning that I shall write on another occasion.

In addition to these reasons—dread of dilettantism, fear of not being taken seriously—a third motive explains the "typographically erudite format" of some works which, in spite of appearances, belong to philosophy and not to purely scientific scholarship. It is what I called a little while ago the nature of the spiritual documents with which I was dealing. Those documents appertained to India and the Orient in general, on the one hand, and to culture in an ethnographic state on the other. Now, these exotic cultures were, and are still, little known beyond circles of specialists. Since I was addressing myself to those circles only to the extent that they were able to verify the authenticity of the documents and the stringency of my interpretation of them, since the readers who mattered to me above all were "philosophers" (in the broad sense of the word), I felt obliged to present the whole dossier on the basis of which I had allowed myself certain conclusions—especially inasmuch as those conclusions were not exactly in accord with the interpretation generally given by ethnologists, Orientalists, and folklorists. If instead of "interpreting" exotic or popular legends, myths, and symbols I had "interpreted" texts of Plato or Kant, it would have been very easy to write books without notes and without bibliography; in any provincial library the reader would have had at hand, for possible verification, the works of Plato or Kant. But in proposing a certain hermeneutics on a theme from Romanian folklore or on an Oriental symbol, I was bound to exhibit, above all, the *facts* from which I set out. *Facts,* plural, because I did not claim by any means to adduce a "personal interpretation," such as a great poet or a great essayist has the right to do. It seemed to me that the interpretation I gave, although it was *new,* was not "personal": it did nothing except translate into intelligible terms one aspect of the archaic and traditional system of thought.

These, then, in brief, are the reasons for which these philosophical writings could pass sometimes, "typographically," for simple scholarly contributions to specialized problems (Oriental studies, the history of religions, ethnology, and folklore). You can easily prove that the opposite is the case: read them without notes and references and you will rediscover the philosophical problematics. Moreover, especially in these past few years spent in France, I have become convinced of the obstacles which the substratum of notes raises for the unforewarned reader, and my tendency today is to abandon the "dossier," contenting myself with a few references to earlier works. Since the "facts" which concern me are found already in three massive volumes—*Yoga, Traité d'Histoire des Religions,* and *Le Chamanisme*—I can permit myself now the freedom to write without erudite superstructure, as I would have done, for instance, if I had written about problems of Western logic or metaphysics.

There were some, however, who wondered what significance there could be for Romania and even for the West in such excursions into "exotic" and "archaic" philosophy. To this I replied, once, that what matters is not the *object* studied, but *how* it is studied; into this "how" there penetrates the way of being proper to the student and, therefore, also that which is specific to the culture to which he belongs. By "interpreting" documents so exotic as the Old Testament read directly in the Hebrew, Martin Luther established the most Germanic religious and philosophical tradition. Likewise, a great many Romanians in the nineteenth and twentieth centuries, when confronted with Romanian folkloric documents, interpreted them in the fashion of Paris or Berlin. The positions of Titu Maiorescu or Duiliu Zamfirescu on Romanian folk poetry represent only the opinions of Occidental savants at particular historical moments—opinions provisional and often contradictory—and they were borrowed *tale quale,* without any effort at personal reflection, by these "Romanian thinkers."

I might say even more. I might say that insofar as the "national character" and all the rest are concerned, I was closer to the sources of the Romanian folk genius studying the symbolism of the Temple of Barabudur, yoga, or Babylonian cosmology than were my colleagues in philosophy who were studying, for instance, Kant. Because there is no break in continuity between archaic Javanese or Mesopotamian symbolism and that which still subsists in Romanian folk creations. In order to understand folklore, and therefore to know how to valorize the "national character," the best path is through the study of archaic civilizations. In 1937 someone raised the question as to where my book on yoga could be situated in the history of Romanian culture, because, he added, it is true that Eminescu too was tempted by India but his interest was directed toward the Vedas, the Upanishads, and Buddhism, not toward a mystical technique as was my *Yoga*. In those days I never made any response to criticisms brought against me. (I told myself I had enough to do just writing the books without wasting any time defending them. If it were good, the book would defend itself, and if it were not, it would be futile for me to defend it). And yet, an answer to the bewilderment of my critic would have been easy to give. If it is absolutely necessary to "situate" it somewhere, *Yoga* must be situated among those Romanian books on the history of culture and the history of philosophy which have to do with what Lucian Blaga called the "revolution of the autochthonous foundation" (*revolta fondului autohton*), i.e., in the series inaugurated by Hasdeu's study, *Perit-au Dacii?* (Have the Dacians Vanished? published in *Foiţa de Istorie şi Literatură* between April and June, 1860) and continued by Vasile Pârvan and his pupils on the one hand, and by Simion Mehedinţi on the other. For just as one of the problems of modern Romanian culture was the persistence of the autochthonous, Getic substratum in ethnic and later syntheses, I tried to show in *Yoga* the persistence of the autochthonous pre-Aryan spirituality in the face of the Indo-European invaders. It was the same problem of the philosophy of culture treated in two different examples. But, being preoccupied primarily with external criteria, my critic sought for symmetries with the "India" of Eminescu. Now, this Eminescian India was more romantic and Schopenhauerian than Indian, properly speaking. If he had been sufficiently familiar with cultural philosophy, my critic would have noted immediately the solidarity of my monograph on yoga with, let us say, the "Getic tradition" in modern Romanian culture on the one hand and with that curious historical moment, on the other hand, which begins in 1934 and which has, among many other characteristic features, the identification of archaic, pre-Latin elements in the "Romanian character."

Other things might be said in connection with that controversy, but they would lead us too far. Suffice it to recall that in the year 1936 it seemed to me that, very soon, those nations which had had a glorious Middle Age and Renaissance would lose their primacy in Europe and that, on the contrary, the nations which had had only a "prehistory" and a "protohistory" rich in events and racial mixtures would be called to create the cultural values of tomorrow. I do not wish to dwell on this problem here, but it appeared to me that the spiritual dominance of the West was approaching its end and that, consequently, the dialogue with other, non-European cultures (and above all with Asia) would have to be resumed on another plane—that of equality and good will—on the part of the cultures of Eastern Europe. Thus, it seemed to me that the study of Oriental religions and archaic traditions not only was integrated perfectly into the horizon of Romanian folk spirituality, helping us to understand it "from the inside" rather than to describe its forms and structures sociologically, but it seemed to me also that such studies corresponded to an interest of the Occident which, one day not far distant, would have to communicate with other exotic cultures and would no longer know how. (In a series of articles I have shown how we arrived at this impass, and I shall not return to the matter here.)

Finally, what made me persist in such investigations was also the fear of letting ourselves be drawn into a cultural provincialism which, eventually, would have made us sterile. I was thinking in particular of the "great cultures," of the provincialism of Paris, or England, or Germany—which we Romanians had borrowed, considering it universal. A good part of the "cultural journalism" that was made in Romania—as also in Portugal or Greece—was made by commenting on the latest books from Paris. But during my student days I had had the good fortune to live for a time in Italy, and after that in India—and the Parisian provincialism in Romania had become unbearable for me. (Paris is a very great center of culture, but it must not be considered the navel of the earth, because then we fall into provincialism. Only in a provincial city do people believe the professors of pedagogy in the boys' lycée are the greatest philosophers of the time.) I said to myself that a small culture like ours—*small,* but by no means minor—was obliged to adopt things from as many sources as possible. That is why I did not follow the latest books on the French market: I learned about them from others. And one of the most amusing interpretations of my novels I have read was in Gheorghe Călinescu's *Istoria literaturii:* he speaks there of my "Gidism," although I discovered Gide only at age 30, while the many other literary "influences," which could have been identified with a little effort, are passed over. And this unexpected conclusion is from a literary critic who, in distinction from almost all his colleagues, knew several languages other than French. But he was, probably, like all contemporary Romanian writers, accustomed to finding French models.

II

As for the coexistence of those philosophical occupations with literary creation, matters seem to me less simple to explain in a few pages. All I know is that, from the first, I wrote them both. And from the first, the literature I produced was both "realistic" and "fantastic." I believe my first literary efforts to be published (in *Ziarul Ştiinţelor Populare*) were, "How I Found the Philosopher's Stone" and "Memories of an Outing." I wrote and published them in 1921–22 when I was fourteen to fifteen. The former was a "fantastic" sketch; the other a pseudo-autobiographical fragment (actually invented almost entirely). Soon afterward I published a great number of nonliterary articles, in particular on insect life—because for quite a long time I had believed I wanted to become a naturalist. But I did not cease for a moment to write—and even to publish—literary attempts. A good many of them, of course, remained unpublished. I recall two "fantastic" novels: the first took up two notebooks and was entitled, "The Journey of the Five Cockchafers in the Land of the Red Ants": it was a sort of satiric etymological novel, with allusions to my teachers and classmates in the fifth class at Lycée Spiru Haret. The second was in three or four copybooks and although it was modestly titled, "The Memoirs of the Lead Soldier," it was conceived so ambitiously that a hundred notebooks could not have contained it. I proposed, purely and simply, to present the history of the Cosmos from the appearance of the first galaxies to our own day. The lead from which the toy soldier whose memoirs I was writing would have been made in 1920—that lead remembered how it had been constituted in the very beginning, in a fragment of the solar system, then how the crust of the earth had cooled, how it had lain in a mine from whence it was dug by some Mesopotamians (but before it was dug, a great many cosmic catastrophes had occurred, then the first living creatures had appeared; there were earthquakes, floods, then all sorts of animals of the geological eras appeared, etc., etc.), how it had been used in an alloy—and from here on my story had no end, because I imagined that little piece of lead present at all the great historical events in the whole world: witness to the crucifixion of Christ, witness to the wars of Trajan and Decebal, and so on, until our day when, in the form of a lead soldier, it would find itself in the knapsack of a Boy Scout who was riding on a train destined to derail at Valea-Largă. A moment before the catastrophe the Scout is seized with panic and hides his head in his pack, thereby saving his life. And in that moment—how long!—of the derailment, the Boy Scout learns all that has ever happened to the lead soldier and decides to tell of it later.

This, approximately, was the plot of the novel. When I broke off writing it I had, I believed, arrived at the cooling of the earth's crust—but I had written other episodes too (with Decebal, with some Arabs, with the war of 1916, etc.), because I had had the inspiration to allow the lead soldier to remember in full his adventures and coexistences, thus leaping from the origin of the planetary system to the sufferings of Queen Tomiris. And I believe, moreover, that the appearance of Queen Tomiris on the horizon of my preoccupations contributed in large measure to my definitive abandonment of the "Memoirs of the Lead Soldier." Because, all of a sudden, I undertook to compose an opera on Tomiris. I composed it sitting at the piano, and since I had a poor musical memory and, besides, I did not know very well how to write it down, the melodies varied from one day to the next. Nevertheless, I succeeded in finishing the Prologue and the first scene of Act I (a dialogue between Tomiris and the high priest), and, gathering together my friends—Dinu Sighireanu, Haig Acterian, Mircea Mărculescu, and Vojen—I seated myself at the piano and performed my "opera" from one end to the other, trying to sing even the soprano part of the queen. I was in the fourth class then, but I remembered fragments from the Prologue until the end of lycée.

About that same time I collected "in volume" a part of my articles about insect life and presented them at Bibliotecă pentru toţi (Everyone's Library). The book was accepted, but fortunately it never appeared. When, many years later, I confessed to Mr. O., the director of publishing, that it must have been edited by Alcalay in 1923, he had a search made of the archives of Bibliotecă pentru toţi, but the manuscript was not there. As for the story, "Memoirs . . . ," something even more unexpected happened to it. In my first year on the staff of *Cuvântul*, in 1925–26, a likeable young man, Radu Capriel, came to see me, saying that he wanted at all costs to read my unpublished things. I gave him *The Novel of the Nearsighted Adolescent* which I had finished in the last class at the lycée and from which I had published excerpts in *Cuvântul* and *Universul Literar* (Perpessicius' review). But after he gave it back, he asked to read something else. Mostly as a joke I gave him "Memoirs of a Lead Soldier" which, to my astonishment, excited him—so much so, in fact, that he never returned the manuscript. I had forgotten about it until one day, on going to see General Condescu a little before his death, I met there, at the radio station, a woman who told me she had read all my books—even those I had not published, she added. I don't remember now her name. She was a brunette, and at that time young and good-looking. As I was leaving, she told me the manuscript of "Memoirs . . ." was at her place. I couldn't bear to ask her to give it back. . . .

Thus, insofar as I am aware, my literary efforts have been from the beginning and continuously since, both "fantastic" and "realistic." Among the latter I should number a series of sketches and novellas published between 1923 and 1928, and, above all, the two autobiographical novels: *The Novel of the Nearsighted Adolescent* and its sequel, *Gaudeamus,* containing memories of my student life. This latter was also my first novel of love, because at the time I wrote it I was in love. Like all students, I too, as I thought, was in love with two coeds at the same time. Several years later, in India, I wrote *Isabel şi apele diavolului* and *Lumina ce se stinge,* that is, two novels in which fantasy, autobiography, and "realism" were mingled in a more or less convincing way. I began *Isabel* in 1929 at Mrs. Perris' boarding house in Calcutta, and I finished it in Darjeeling, on the Sikkim border. *Lumina* I began a year later in Calcutta, and it was completed in Himalaya, in a little hut at Rishikesh. During the last year of my stay in India I began a large novel, *Petru şi Pavel,* which I later gave up, but fragments of which I utilized in *Întoarcerea din Rai.*

The difficulty of the "literature-science coexistence" I began to sense in India. I labored for months with a passion and an indifference to overwork which one can have only at twenty-one or twenty-two, and then, all of a sudden, I lost interest in my Sanskrit texts and my beloved Indian philosophy. With an effort I admire even now, after all these years, I succeeded in continuing to work at my doctoral thesis. But no longer than a week or two more. Then I *had* to drop everything and write fiction. I wrote as many as ten or fifteen hours per day, for a month or six weeks—and then I returned to my thesis. I realized then that I could not give up either one or the other. Both activities, equally, were necessary for my spiritual integrity. At any risk, I must continue them both.

The risks were, however, great, and they grew more serious the longer I lived. From a certain moment, time's tempo increased and I could no longer begin to do what I had done in the prime of my youth, even if I succeeded in working the same number of hours. Sometimes I felt threatened with not being able to finish any of what I had started. On the one hand, naturally, an ever-broader horizon was opening to me and I was attracted by problems for which, not having foreseen them, I had not prepared myself in previous years; and on the other hand, my "literary demon" constituted a continuous unknown quantity, ready to detach me at any moment from my work in progress. This fact explains why many of my books in the history of religions and philosophy appeared five or ten years after their inception. (And some of them have not yet been published: *La Mandragore*, begun in 1935, appeared fragmentarily between 1939 and 1942 in *Zalmoxis*; and from *Mitologiile morţii*, begun in 1938, nothing has yet appeared.)

Of course, the finishing and publishing of a book does not depend only upon the author. Circumstances, the publisher, and public—these too play an important role. If between 1933 and 1940 I published as many literary works as I did, it was not simply *my* fault. On the one hand, I was poor and Romanian publishers preferred the novel to books of philosophy; on the other hand, the majority of my friends were writers and they encouraged literature, trying to push my philosophical and scientific activity onto a secondary plane. Since the war, the opposite has happened, but I bear a share of the responsibility for that. I promised myself not to publish literature while Romania was at war, and from 1941 to 1945 I published nothing in Romania except philosophical essays and the book on Salazar. In those years I began two novels: *Viaţa Nouă*, the sequel to *Huliganii*, projected for a thousand pages, and *Apocalips*. I wrote several hundred pages on each, but because I knew they could not be published until after the war, I wrote them mostly for myself; thus I dropped them at the first sign of loss of interest, and returned to other things I had begun. During the years spent in Portugal I wrote the little book *Os Romenos, Latinos de Oriente*, the book about Salazar, *Ensayos luso-romenos* (studies and articles which appeared in the Portuguese press), *Comentarii la Legenda Mesterului Manole*, a good part of *Traité d'Histoire des Religions*, and the first chapters of *Le Mythe de l'éternel retour*. But on the literary plane, aside from a play, "Oameni şi pietre" (Men and Stones), and a few novellas, I finished nothing. I began another play, "1241," a "Portuguese Journal," and other smaller works. The decision I had made not to publish "literature" was somehow fatal to those works undertaken. And since my coming to France, literature has passed, as was expected, to a secondary level. In order to live, I have had to concentrate on an activity for which there is a "market": the history of religions, Indian studies, philosophy—which I do not in the least regret. Thus I have been able to finish and publish works begun long ago, and my theoretical output, left somewhat in the shade in my Romanian period, 1933–40, today balances the mass of my literary writings.

Seen from a certain point of view, however, the two groups of writings complement each other. This fact was observed long ago, and I remember that one of my students, Vojta, even wrote a book in 1934 showing how all my literary, philosophical, and scientific activity found its point of departure in *Isabel şi apele divolului*. That book [by Vojta] appeared only fragmentarily (in *Vremea* and other reviews) and, although it seemed to me to push the symmetries and correspondences too far, it was not devoid of ingenuity. There is, in any event, a real dependence of some literary writings on theoretical ones, and vice versa. Beginning with the most obvious examples, I might recall *Secretul doctorului Honigberger* which derives directly from *Yoga;* the play "Oameni si pietre" from the chapter on sacred stones in *Traité* and from an unpublished work, *Le Labyrinthe; Domnişoara Christina* from *Mitologiile morţii* and a course on death in Romanian folklore; "Iphigenia" from *Comentarii la Legenda Mesterului Manole;* another unpublished play, "Aventura spirituală" from *Mitologiile morţii;* and possibly others.

But even when the relationship is not as obvious, it is no less real. *Şarpele* may be considered the most revealing example. To begin with, a detail which seems to me important: I wrote the book in the course of ten nights, working between 11 and 3 or 4 A.M., in the spring of 1937. It *had* to appear on "Book Day," because otherwise the publisher, Ciornei, would not give me the 30,000 lei I needed to be able to spend the summer in the mountains. On the other hand, I was teaching a course at the university and, most importantly, I was proofreading the Hasdeu edition which the Royal Foundation *had* to publish on Book Day also. I was overworked, exhausted, and in order to stay awake I drank coffee; then, so I could sleep in the mornings I took sleeping powders. Every morning Ciornei sent a boy to pick up the 15 or 20 pages I had written during the night and take them directly to the printer. I did not reread a single page of the two hundred which comprise the book; nevertheless, *Şarpele* is one of my most successful writings. But there is something else: concerning the symbolism of the snake I had access to a considerable quantity of folkloric and ethnographic material, and yet I did not consult it. Perhaps, if I had taken pains, the symbolism of *Şarpele* would have been more coherent; but then, probably, the literary invention would have been disrupted. I don't know. What interests me is the fact that although I "attacked" a problem very dear to the historian of religions which I was, the writer in me refused any *conscious* collaboration with the scholar and interpreter of symbols; he insisted at all costs on remaining *free* to choose what pleased him and reject symbols and interpretations which the scholar and philosopher offered him ready-made.

The experience of *Şarpele* convinced me of two things: 1) that theoretical activity cannot *consciously* and *voluntarily* influence literary activity; and 2) that the free act of literary creation can, on the other hand, reveal certain theoretical meanings. Indeed, only after I read *Şarpele* in book form did I understand that in this book I had resolved, without knowing it, a problem which had preoccupied me for a long time (from *Soliloquii,* 1929–30) and which only in *Traité* did I expound theoretically—namely, the problem of the unrecognizability of miracle, the fact that the intrusion of the *sacred* into the world is always camouflaged in a set of "historical forms," manifestations which do not *apparently* differ in any way from millions of cosmic or historical manifestations (a *sacred* stone is not different, *apparently*, from any other stone, etc.). Much more might be said about the dialectic of *hierophanies*, but this is not the place for that.

Branching off from this "discovery" of *Şarpele* are two roads: one which leads, via *Traité* and *Le Chamanisme*, to my current writings, as yet unsystematized, about the "fall into History" (*Images et symboles*, etc.); the other, purely literary, which passes through *Nunta în Cer*, several novellas ("Un om mare," etc.), and arrives at the novel, as yet unfinished, *Noaptea de Sânziene*. Both roads lead eventually to the same problem: the unrecognizability of the transcendent camouflaged in History. This problem, which is closely linked to that of Time and History, is found already *in nuce* in *Isabel* (in the chapter, "Youth without Old Age"), in *Întoarcerea din Rai* (the coexistence of the two loves of Pavel Anicet and the "rupture of planes," which can be achieved only through death), and in *Nunta în Cer* (Ileana's two loves *in time*); and it constitutes also the central theme of *Noaptea de Sânziene*. The same problem, examined theoretically, is found in *Le mythe de l'éternel retour* and *Images et symboles* and will be taken up again in *La nostalgie du paradis* and *La chute dans l'Histoire*. [These last two books were never published (Tr.).] Summing up, I could say that all these works try to uncover the same central mystery of the rupture provoked by the appearance of Time and the "fall into History" which followed of necessity. Each of them is permeated, more or less explicitly, by the nostalgia for Paradise, for the reintegration of the primordial unity, for the "emergence from Time." Hence, an attempt to valorize Death as reintegration (*Întoarcerea din Rai*); hence, likewise, the nostalgia for eternity (*Isabel*), for the reversability of Time (*Nunta în Cer*), for the "sabotage of History" (*Noaptea de Sânziene*). Hence, finally, the motif of the "Philosopher's Stone," from my first literary text published at age fourteen to *Noaptea de Sânziene* and, above all, the motif of the "coexistence of two loves" which appears already in the university novel *Gaudeamus*, is defined with progressive precision in *Petru şi Pavel*, *Întoarcerea din Rai*, and *Nunta în Cer*, and becomes the theme of *Noaptea de Sânziene*. The motif of the "two loves" is also a way of abolishing the human condition and thus all that is connected with the "fall" and "History"—a way of obtaining a freedom which seems to be allowed, here on earth, only to saints: the rest of mankind can hope for it only, at best, in death (Pavel Anicet's conclusion).

I have not, up to now, made any reference to *Maitreyi* or *Huliganii*, although these novels had more success with the public and the critics.

My young friend Vojta found in *Maitreyi* traces of Tantrism (this reminds me that Professor Bachelard, when he read the French translation, *La nuit bengali,* spoke to me of a "mythologie de la volupté"). I don't know to what extent those observations are justified. I consider *Maitreyi,* as well as *Nunta în Cer,* to be novels of love; as such, their metaphysical significance seems beyond doubt (one of the first things I learned from Nae Ionescu was this: "love as an instrument of knowledge"). As for *Huliganii,* I must explain that the destinies of all the characters were to have been fulfilled only in the sequel, *Viaţa Nouă.* There, for example, Petru Anicet repeats Pavel's experience of the "two loves" (Nora-Stefania), but he opts for another solution: the acceptance of the "rupture" by the renunciation of Stefania (who somehow incarnates the "higher") and the reintegration of Nora, the frank and triumphant epiphany of a Magna Mater eminently pre-moral. In a certain sense, Petru Anicet accepts History. . . .

Of course, I do not wish to leave the impression that I write literature to "demonstrate" such and such a philosophical thesis. If I had done so, it is probable that my novels would have been, philosophically speaking, more consistent. In reality, as the experience of *Şarpele* amply demonstrates, I wrote literature for the pleasure (or the need) of *writing freely,* of inventing, of dreaming—of thinking, even, but without the stringency of systematic thought. It is probable that a whole series of marvels, mysteries, and problems which exude from my theoretical activity demanded full expression in the freedom of my literary activity. But this question exceeds the bounds of these notes.

III

I must add a few words with respect to what is called literary destiny. I belong to the most fortunate generation Romanian history has ever known. Neither before nor after our generation has Romania had the freedom, abundance, and opportunity we enjoyed—we who wrote between 1925 and 1940. The generation of Nicolaie Iorga had been almost entirely given over to the national and cultural propheticism which was necessary to prepare for the war for the integration of the nation. The generation of the front had been sacrificed that we might find a Greater Romania, free and rich. When we began to write in 1925 there was no "national cause" demanding our immediate attention. We were the first Romanians who could write something other than national history, Romanian philology, and cultural prophecy, without having the feeling we were betraying the cause of our people. We enjoyed a freedom won with much blood and renunciation, and I don't know if we were always conscious of those enormous sacrifices made by our forebears that we might go to India or the United States, that we could discuss Freud or André Gide at the Carol Foundation before

an audience of two thousand, that we could speak of cultural autonomy, of the primacy of the spiritual, of non-alignment, and so on. I
always remember with deep emotion a letter by Radu Dragnea (whom
I never knew personally) sent in 1927 when I had written numerous
articles for *Cuvântul* about the "young generation" in a twelve-article
series. Radu Dragnea saluted us, the "young," approximately as follows: "How fortunate for you, that you can dedicate yourselves to the
spiritual, but how fortunate for me that I have lived to see this marvel
in our Greater Romania." He was right: we were the first to harvest
the fruits of all those generations more or less sacrificed. The empires
of the Hapsburgs and the Tzars had fallen, and in those fifteen years
preceding the Stalin-Hitler pact we could breathe easily. I believe we
were the only Romanians to enjoy such a long respite. The generation
which arose in 1940, already troubled by political tensions which had
begun after 1934, went to Russia, and those who returned, returned
with the Russians right behind them. Culturally, it was a generation
completely sacrificed. We knew the one miracle possible in political
history: "neutrality," or, more precisely, the free dialogue between
persons of opposite political beliefs. I refer to the phenomenon of
"Criterion" when, at the Carol Foundation and under the oversight of
a university professor, Lenin was discussed by Communists such as
Bellu Silber and Lucreţia Pătrăşcanu, by Legionnaires like Mihail Po-
lihroniade and Alexandru Tell, by bourgeois like Mircea Vulcănescu
and Mihail Sebastian. And such a discussion was possible! Beginning
in 1934 the dialogue was broken off. That year I published *Întoarcerea
din Rai* (The Return from Paradise). The "Paradise" had lasted exactly
three years: in one way or another we all had the feeling that we had
been banished from an "atemporal Eden" and hurled brutally into
history—which happened in fact soon afterward.

I had the good fortune to belong to the only generation "non-con-
ditioned" historically, and I took advantage of that good fortune as
much as was possible. What Petru Comarnescu called my "experi-
mentalism" was nothing but a translation into a strident barbarism
(such as only he had the talent to invent) of my inner need to *know* as
much as possible and as rapidly as possible. Especially the latter: *as
rapidly as possible*—because I had long since sensed that *we would not
have much time*, that the freedom we were enjoying was provisional
and our security illusory, that very soon *History* would engulf us again.
Strange as it may seem, I was apprehensive of the historical cataclysm
as early as 1927. I wrote at the end of that year in *Cuvântul* a pathetic
column: "Anno Domini" which impressed, among others, Simion
Mehedinţi and Perpessicius. I evoked there the spectre of approaching
war and, addressing (as usual!) the "young generation," I said that

each of us must repeat to ourselves daily that *I am going to live only one more year* and try to *do everything* in this, the last year of our lives. While still in the university, I was obsessed with Time and History. It seemed to me that if the Romanian exhibits such an indifference toward Time, it is because he has never had time enough to *do anything*. History has loved him so much that it has never ceased to hold him in its embrace. It has hugged him tight for a thousand years, not giving him a chance to breathe. We, the privileged ones, knew the joy of breathing freely and, at least so far as I was concerned, I trembled at the thought of losing it someday. . . .

In addition to this good luck, which belonged to my generation, I personally had numerous other blessings upon which this is not the place to dwell. But I should like to note only this: by enjoying very young what is called "literary success," I did not long for it and I did nothing to sustain it. On the contrary, after the dangerous success of *Maitreyi,* I published a number of hard books (one of them unreadable: *Lumina ce se stinge*), in order to discourage admirers. Moreover, by leaving the country in 1940, I had the opportunity to follow, until 1945, the post-mortem fate which awaits a writer; I saw, for instance, how my prolonged absence from the Bucharestian literary scene ended by pushing me into the shadows—and this was a good lesson for me: I realized on what a literary *currency* depends: it depends primarily on a physical presence. The newspapers and reviews speak especially about those who are *there;* when you are no longer around, at the most they read your books, but you no longer participate in the "current scene." Now, precisely this latter situation suited me: to be read for the merits of the books, not for the "currency" my presence would give. For some years now I have considered myself a posthumous *Romanian* writer; only the author of books which appear in alien tongues has remained alive.

Paris, 24 March 1953

Notes

First published in *Caiete de Dor.*, no. 7 (Paris, July 1953), pp. 1–13.

Part III

Meaning and the Literary World

Because of its novelty and its action, the poetic image has an entity and a dynamism of its own; it is referable to a direct *ontology*.

Gaston Bachelard
Poetics of Space

Eugen Simion

The Mythical Dignity
of Narration

I discover in *Fragments d'un journal* (Gallimard, 1973) a statement which sets me thinking: "[The novel] is the only literary genre suited to my talent." A surprising confession! Mircea Eliade, who has published essays, journals, novellas, and who has behind him a great scientific *oeuvre*, regrets that he can no longer write novels, believing that only the novel can express him wholly: To discover the structure of the atom and have the feeling that only poetry could translate the interior world; to be reckoned an authority in a very demanding discipline and to think nostalgically about a *return* to literature of the imagination—this is a fact very hard to understand. The truth is that Mircea Eliade has never ignored novelistic work and, in the same journal, he advances a seductive hypothesis:

> I am more and more convinced of the *literary* value of the materials with which the historian of religion deals. If art—and above all literary art: poetry, the novel—knows a new Renaissance in our day, it is due to the rediscovery of the function of religious myths and symbols and of archaic behaviors. Actually, what I've been doing for more than fifteen years is not wholly alien to literature. My researches may even be considered someday as an attempt to rediscover the forgotten sources of literary imagination.

The above is doubly important for Eliade's thought: 1) because it conceives a Renaissance of literature through the rediscovery myths, and 2) because the work of the historian of religions is not alien to literature.

We shall return to the first idea later. Let us see now what implications the second one has. Mircea Eliade wishes to suggest that the immense treasury of facts he has extracted from archaic spirituality is not exterior to a literary scenario. Literature of today could find an important source in myths and, at the same time, the search for myths is itself a literary adventure. Is there not, perhaps, in this suggestion a discreet invitation to read his *scientific oeuvre* like a novel? Mircea Eliade does not push things this far, but he leaves us free to do so. What are these conflicting relations between *sacred* and *profane, mythical births* and *eternal returns,* if not elements of a vast initiatory narrative? Its characters are the myths: wanderers, masked men, characters lost and found again under their profane representations in modern society.

If I am not mistaken, Mircea Eliade defines myth somewhere as a *sacred event.* In the beginning there was, then, a *sacred event* and from it something (a sign) has remained. In most instances, what is preserved is figured by a "character" who continues to live in a world from which the sacred has been eliminated. To search for myths is to search for the meaning and scenarios of the *sacred event,* which is equivalent to a well-known definition, *"l'écriture d'une aventure,"* whereas the *new novel* inverts the saying: *"l'aventure d'une écriture."* But what of the *mythic novel?* Certainly: *a spiritual quest, l'écriture initiatique d'une aventure mythique.* Perhaps it becomes: *l'aventure mythique d'une écriture initiatique?* This is what is attempted by such prose writers as Michel Tournier in *Vendredi ou les limbes du Pacifique* or in the novel which brought him the Goncourt prize, *Le rois des aulnes.* Everything here is *symbol, sign;* adventure corresponds to another plane, individuals are *bearers of myths.*

The composition of the novel is an extended initiatory scenario: it is necessary to find out the *code* in order to understand *as* one ought and especially *what* one ought; otherwise one wanders in an ocean of gray sentences. What is called for in cases of this sort is an initiated reader and a special type of reading. Gilbert Durand calls it *lecture mytho-critique* and a pupil of his (Simone Vierne) who also draws upon the thought of Mircea Eliade terms it *lecture initiatique.* Its aim is to discover myths hidden in the text, starting from the idea that the *text* is more than a *textuality.* Vierne calls our attention to the fact that not only the mythic novel but all prose can be read this way, from Novalis' *Henrik von Ofterdingen* to George Sand's *Consuela,* Jules Verne's *Journey to the Center of the Earth,* etc.[1] In the deep structures of the imagination there exist always myths waiting to be revived through an adequate reading. Because, says Simone Vierne (somewhat affectatiously, be it said in passing): "To read is not only an intellectual exercise; it is to die a little—to self and to the profane world."

I should put it this way: to read is to be reborn a little, to relive sacred events, to live in the company of *myth-heroes*. But let us return to Mircea Eliade. We must distinguish in his vast work two categories of books: those which start from the sacred and move towards the profane (from *myth* to *scientific interpretation*) and others which start from *profane events* and go on to suggest the durability and continuity of *sacred events*. These latter are the works of fiction. A reading (not necessarily *initiatory, mythico-critical*) will readily show the connection between the two planes. One half of the *symbol* (in the ancient Greek sense of the word) seeks the other half, in his writings. The man of science has a nostalgia for the man of letters and, intentionally or unintentionally, one helps the other. Fiction does not leave him in his analysis of Australian myths (the management of ideas, narration); the science of the savant does not remain on the doorstep of the fantastic novella. But, curiously enough, Mircea Eliade declares that he lives separated into two compartments: "I am incapable of existing simul-taneously in two spiritual universes: that of literature and that of sci-ence" (*Fragments d'un journal,* p. 116). And further on: "This is my fundamental weakness: I cannot remain at the same time in a state of waking and a state of dreaming, of play. Once I begin to 'make liter-ature,' I find myself in another universe; I call it oneiric because it has another temporal structure and because my relationships with char-acters are of an imaginary rather than a critical nature."

I simply can't believe this. At least, not entirely. In the interior of the oneiric universe, are not the relations between things (individuals) investigated with an "awake" spirit? When are we closer to the truth—in the universe of lucidity, or in the oneiric universe? The truth is that a purely oneiric universe ceases to exist, from the moment it is tran-scribed into literature. "Imaginary nature" becomes in a work of art a "mediated," "critiqued" nature. The individual who tells his dreams has introduced them, already, into the structures of his lucidity. From Mircea Eliade's confession, I retain the idea that literature and the science of myths solicit, on his part, different requirements and in-struments. This fact is true. But this does not mean that in one of these hypotheses he is different, completely different, without any connec-tion with the other who remains at the base line. Psychologically speak-ing, absolute doubling is impossible, especially so in art where the universes are, as we know personally, *conjured up, confounded.*

It is, then, a literature (*Şarpele,* "Secretul doctorului Honigberger," "La ţigănci," and, above all, his last novel, *Noaptea de Sânziene*) full of rituals and myths, a literature with *text* and *subtext,* invaded by the obsessions of the mythologue. It is true that Mircea Eliade defends, in the formal sense, the purity of the epic genre. Even from his old essays (in *Oceanografie*) we deduce the idea that the novel ought to be, above all, a novel, that is, a free narrative, an unfolding of events, without, if possible, the intervention of the author (in the form of "analysis" and "psychology"). A curious thing: because a writer who has as his epic model Gide and who esteems Italo Svevo, Aldous Huxley, and Joyce ought not raise objections against the intrusion of the narrator into the text. Nevertheless, Mircea Eliade does it. Speaking of John dos Passos (*Manhattan Transfer*), he praises the "total absence of psychology, of analysis and explanation" (*Oceanografie*, 1934, p. 105). Because, as he maintains further on, there is such a thing as a knowledge which is "essential, real, direct, which has no need of psychology." Consequently, "the author need not speak to us about Mr. John Smith—but only let him act as he is, as the author sees him."

The foregoing proposition explains the refusal of Eliade to accept "psychology" and "analysis" into the novel. Closer to the meaning of his thought would be: no *psychologism*, no analysis which refers to abstractions (spiritual reflexes). But what, then? In *Fragments d'un journal* we find the idea again, more clearly stated. This idea (and others to which we shall refer later on) fixes Eliade's conception of the novel: the novel as he thinks it, and the novel as he writes it. From the outset it must be said that by *novel* Mircea Eliade means *prose* in general. The requirements of the novel are valid for epic as a whole. We read in a journal extract from 5 January 1952:

This evening I continue, with effort, Faulkner's *The Sound and the Fury*. From what I have read so far, this book seems his least successful. Dated technique: 1930; the influence of James Joyce, John dos Passos. What is the use of that long, absurd, uninteresting interior monologue of a neurotic on the verge of suicide? The pretentious facility of the interior monologue which gives one a false sense of authenticity! I know all too well the attractions, the pitfalls, the fraudulence of the interior monologue and the mental film: I utilized them in *Lumina ce se stinge* (also in the year 1930). But where can such a procedure lead? To the Kabbalistic universe of the latter Joyce: cipher, mystical solidarity among sounds, spaces and lights; to seminal multidimensional universes. Must write a long article entitled: "On the necessity of the *roman-roman*." Show the autonomous, glorious, and irreducible dimension of *narration*, a formula of myth and mythology readapted to the modern conciousness. Show that modern man, as well as man of archaic societies, cannot exist without myths, i.e., without exemplary "stories." The metaphysical dignity of narration, ignored, of course, by generations of realists and the psychologized who began by raising psychological analysis to the first rank, then spectral analysis, arriving finally at facile formulas for filming psycho-mental automatisms. The great lesson of several Anglo-Saxon writers (Thornton Wilder, Faulkner, in novellas, but also Graham Greene) in rehabilitating narration directly, showing how much metaphysics and theology can be revealed to us by narration as such, rather than commentaries or analysis of the author.

At the time he penned these programmatic sentences, Mircea Eliade was rereading with great satisfaction Balzac (*Le Père Goriot, La Fille aux yeux d'or*—"positively one of the most beautiful creations of the young Balzac") and he was working hard—exasperatingly hard—on the novel, *Noaptea de Sânziene*. The novelist is passing, we may say, through a "Balzac complex." He rediscovers him, enjoys him. The eighth or ninth reading of *Goriot* gives him, again, the feeling of being in the presence of an extraordinary work. His satisfaction takes the form of a cult. He travels about Paris, identifying Balzacian landscapes. How thrilled he is to discover that Gobseck had his *boutique* on the present rue Cujas. He visits Balzac's house, the famous house with two exits (to enable him to escape his creditors) on rue Raynouard no. 47 and observes with great attentiveness the objects inside. It is at this time that the thought of revolt against the excess of "spectral" analysis, which leads to the dissolution of the plot, arises in his consciousness.

The excerpt reproduced above says all, I believe, about what the modern novel is, and what it ought to be, according to Mircea Eliade. Here, as well as in the study of archaic spirituality, he is, methodologically speaking, opposed to the general current. When everyone is mad about *structuralism* and *psychoanalysis,* he proposes (and practices) a different method of investigation, being interested to the highest degree in *le côté spirituel.* In literature, he wants the novel to remain a *novel* in a period when the novel is becoming increasingly *anti-novel.* I imagine Jean Ricardou and other theoreticians of the "new novel" would be quite irritated at the above sentences, yearning for epical deeds and autonomous characters. We may say further that Mircea Eliade has read Jean Paul Sartre (*Les mots*) and he does not believe in the image the French author gives to childhood. He does not like Sartre in general. He is unenthusiastic about Günter Grass, another author *à la mode.*

Looking over these examples we could, however, form a mistaken idea about Mircea Eliade's taste in literature (and his conception of it). A conservative spirit, a *dix-neuvièmist,* he is *not* in his ideas about the novel, nor in the novels he writes. He is only a spirit who, living more than others in close association with great, eternal myths, considers that literature can be reborn only by assuming them. His deepest sentiment is that modern literature has been emptied of meaning, has lost its spiritual dimension. The solution is to return to myths, but not through a literature *about* myths, abstracted from the common life. To identify "the presence of the transcendent in human experience" is the first task of the modern creator. In the books he reads, the individual who lives in a desacralized world must find "a dimension of cosmic sacrality." And, again, under another form: the author must observe "the camouflage of mysteries in the events of immediate reality."[2] A reality, thus, of the sacred, a new life of myth in a literature dead from spiritual starvation! Mircea Eliade believes still in the power of literature (in a time when others foresee its disappearance), because he believes, ardently, in the need for spirituality on the part of modern man.

A possibility for rebirth through a new mythology is offered by fantastic literature. Mircea Eliade has noted this idea on a number of occasions, citing also several sources of the modern fantastic. One nuance must be kept in mind: the fantastic is an experience within a reality viewed historically. Not an evasion into the atemporal, but a total involvement in history. Life is a sum of myths and archetypes which are not seen. The creator of literature must offer the reader in a discreet way a code and an itinerary to enable him to understand and orient himself in the world of signs that surrounds him. A literature, therefore, formative (in spirit); a reader active and penetrating. The new novel presupposes a productive reading and a structured reader, directed by little centrifugal narrations. Mythological narration, as Eliade conceives it, proposes a reading at the plane of the *latent message:* recognition—myths in degraded forms, the reconstitution of an initiatory scenario in the banality of the events of life. Mircea Eliade is not the only one who puts the novel into relationship with myths. The structuralist Lévi-Strauss sees in the contemporary novel *"des résidues déformalisés du mythe."* In other words, the novel preserves the meaning of myths; however, the latter are disengaged from their formal structures. Eliade does not deny the process of the "deforming" of myths, but, as a visionary spirit, he connects the opportunity of modern literature with the possibility of its detecting beneath the degraded covering of profane events the presence of myth. "Deformed," myths continue to exist. The activity of the common man is, without his knowing it, freighted with old rituals. Archetypes preside over his monotonous existence. Without saying so directly, Mircea Eliade thinks, basically, of literature as a *redeeming force (forta recuperatoare).* It puts man again in connection with the great universe and gives him back his cosmic vocation. Through it, he recovers a dignified, tutelary ascendency and he binds again his nature to a grandiose *History,* the history of a man who is master over things, and, experiencing "sacred encounters," creates myths, being in continuous connection with the life of the cosmos.

From another philosophical direction and with other moral demands, Jean-Paul Sartre also considers that the essential function of literature is to give man the meaning of the totality of existence. The difference is that Mircea Eliade sees this fact as possible not through the exercise of thought, but through the *reinvention* (the discovery) *of myths*. Good literature is that which puts the reader in the situation of discovering an essential fact: *the dimension of the spirit*. A new birth is produced from the encounter. Man, reinvigorated by myths from within and without, can look around with pride. Mircea Eliade's prose from the last few decades leads into an encounter with this idea. "La ţigănci," *Pe strada Mântuleasa*, and *Noaptea de Sânziene* are full of "epiphanic realities," they have a mythical substratum without being overburdened with mythological erudition. Myths must be intensified in the narration. A good *mythic novel* is one which conceals myths with great intelligence in the reality of social relations. The meeting of a man and a woman, the abandoning of a car, the rediscovery of the vehicle after some time, the discreet and tenacious desire to *find again* the lost woman—this is the initiatory scenario of a novel which, on the surface of the text, stubbornly ignores the great symbols. In order for the "signs" from the depth of the narration to acquire a mythical "charge," they must be touched by our profound gaze. Then we will be surprised to discover that in every person there hides a *myth-hero*, in an ordinary *history* there exists a "myth-history," and in the themes running through the book a multitude of "mythemes" are concealed.

Fundamentally, Mircea Eliade does not renounce realism (as an epic method) and therein lies the modernity of his literature: it is not a literature which turns its back on ordinary existence; it only seeks in its subsoil a network of hidden symbols which, touched by the light of the imagination, puts us into a new relationship with objects.

Notes

First published in *Secolul* 20, 205–6 (1978), pp. 52–56.

1. Simone Vierne, "La littérature sous la lumière des mythes," *Cahiers de l'Herne*, p. 33.)

2. From *Fragments d'un journal*, p. 443.

Matei Calinescu

"The Function of the Unreal": Reflections on Mircea Eliade's Short Fiction

The fascinating relations between Mircea Eliade's philosophical and scholarly work in the field of religious anthropology and his rich literary *oeuvre* can hardly be presented in a few pages. The inherent difficulties of such a study are compounded by the fact that even now, after the publication in English translation of Eliade's major novel, *The Forbidden Forest*, only a fraction of this prolific author's fiction is available to the English reader. Of his numerous short stories and novellas only two, "Nights at Serampore" and "The Secret of Dr. Honigsberger," originally published in Romanian in 1940s, have appeared in book form as *Two Tales of the Occult* (1970). A more recent short story, "With the Gypsy Girls" (written in 1959), certainly one of Eliade's most brilliant achievements in short fiction, was printed not long ago in a distinguished small-circulation university periodical, *The Denver Quarterly* (1974).[1] As for Eliade's journal, which contains a great many enlightening reflections on the recurring themes of both his research and imaginative work, his American publisher decided rather arbitrarily to leave out about half of the French edition of *Fragments d'un journal* (1973), retaining only the second part that deals with the author's experiences after his moving from Europe to this country in 1957.[2]

As I have shown elsewhere,[3] the two apparently independent lines of activity that Eliade has pursued uninterruptedly since the late 1920s as a scholar and as a fiction writer have so many points in common and are so mutually illuminating, that they ought to be given equal attention by anyone who wishes to apprehend Eliade's personality as a whole. Earlier I proposed that Eliade's world view is fundamentally *aesthetic* (if we take the term "aesthetic" in a broad existential sense), and I argued that the concept of *imagination* provides us with a methodological key to the meaning of both his scholarly investigations and his literary productions. In a recent text, published as a preface to *No Souvenirs,* Eliade has once again emphasized the centrality in his work of the notion of imagination, of what I am tempted to call, by analogy but also by contrast with psychoanalytical jargon, "the imagination principle." When he embarked upon his double career, Eliade took it for granted—encouraged by certain romantic cultural traditions which were still alive in Romania—that there were no incompatibilities between highly specialized scientific-scholarly research and artistic activity. "At the time," he writes, introducing a quote from the scientist Jacob Bronowski, "I was unaware of any structural analogy between the scientific and the literary imagination. One can thus appreciate the enthusiasm with which I read, many years later, statements by renowned scientists, such as the following: 'The step by which a new axiom is adduced cannot itself be mechanized. It is a free play of the mind, an invention outside the logical processes. This is the central act of imagination in science and it is in all respects like any similar act in literature.' "[4]

Here I will try to describe in more detail the universe of Eliade's fiction, with particular emphasis on his novellas and short stories, in which, by means of his use of the "fantastic," the writer is confronted by the same problems (sacred-profane qualities of time and space, the "camouflage of myth" and the "unrecognizability of miracle," etc.) that, from a different perspective, and working with different materials, the historian of religions has repeatedly encountered over the years. I in no way want to imply—and this will become even clearer later—that Eliade-the-writer "treats" or "illustrates" motifs, rituals and symbols, ideas and beliefs, that Eliade-the-phenomenologist-of-religion has previously studied in their historical and transhistorical connections. Actually, the opposite seems to be true in his case. In his career, there have been instances in which the writer preceded the scholar, in the sense that the former's *free* imagination made discoveries and arrived at insights whose validity was later confirmed by the hermeneutician. So, if there is a tension between Eliade-the-writer and Eliade-the-religious-scholar, it can be found in a certain wariness of the first in his unavoidable relations with the latter, in the writer's unwillingness to utilize the theories or even the suggestions of the scholar. Fortunately, the scholar does not reciprocate. On the contrary, we may say, he follows the activities of the writer with subtle and discriminating trust, on the assumption that literary imagination can help him more in understanding the *inner* workings of religious imagination than erudition, historical criticism, and the practice of hermeneutics combined.

Eliade himself makes this important point in the "Autobiographical Fragment" found in this volume (first published in 1953).[5] Referring to his 1937 novella *Şarpele* (The Snake), a work in which some of the most original features of his postwar fiction, including *The Forbidden Forest*, are clearly anticipated, Eliade writes: "Concerning the symbolism of the snake I had at my disposal a considerable amount of folklore and ethnographic material, but I ignored it. Maybe if I had taken the trouble to consult it, the symbolism of my *Snake* would have been more coherent—but then, in all likelihood, the literary invention would have been hampered. I don't know. What seems to me worth while pointing out is this: although I had 'attacked' a subject so dear to the historian of religions that I was, the writer in me refused to *collaborate* with the scholar and the interpreter of symbols; the writer in me wanted to stay *free*, at any cost, and to be able to choose whatever he liked as well as to reject the symbols and the interpretations that he was offered, ready-made, by the erudite and the philosopher." And he goes on to say, quite emphatically: "The experience of *The Snake* has convinced me of two things: 1) that one's theoretical activity cannot influence consciously and deliberately one's literary activity; 2) that the free act of literary creation, on the contrary, can lead to theoretical discoveries. The fact of the matter is that only after having reread *The Snake* as a published book did I realize that in it I had resolved unwittingly a problem which had preoccupied me for a long time (ever since my *Soliloquii*, 1929–32) and which I managed to expound more systematically only in my *Traité*. That is the problem of the *unrecognizability of miracle*, deriving from the fact that the intervention of the *sacred* in the world is always camouflaged in a series of 'historical forms,' manifestations that *apparently* are in no way different from millions of other cosmic or historic manifestations (a *sacred* stone is not distinguished, on the plane of *appearances*, from any other stone, etc.)."[6]

A few general observations about the development of Eliade as a fiction writer will help us situate his novellas and short stories of the "fantastic" within the larger "geography" of his literary *oeuvre*. Although he had published quite extensively in various periodicals (articles, essays, polemics, extracts from his personal diary and, occasionally, excerpts from novels in progress), Eliade made his real literary debut in 1930, with *Isabel şi apele diavolului* (Isabel and the Devil's Waters), a novel clearly marked by his Indian discoveries and experiences. It is interesting to note that most of Eliade's fiction inspired by India was written and published while he was still in that country or during the first years after his return to Romania, that is, between 1930–1935. Significantly, his early Indian novels are all strongly autobiographical. To take the example of the most successful one, the vibrantly poetic love story *Maitreyi* (1933), which the French philosopher, Gaston Bachelard, once described to its author in terms of a "mythology of voluptuousness,"[7] the reader cannot avoid the feeling that he is confronted with the fictionalized account of an unmistakeably personal affair. *Maitreyi* is Eliade's *Werther*, a modernist version of young Goethe's sentimental novel. As in Goethe's case, it is difficult—and ultimately irrelevant—to distinguish with any degree of precision, on the basis of external available information, what in the book is fact and what fiction. This is all the more so in the case of *Maitreyi*, given that within the context of modernism, in which the novel clearly belongs, the grounds for the very distinction between fact and fiction tend to become blurred. From the point of view of modernist consciousness one is perfectly entitled to say that facts *are* fictions (adding that even etymologically facts are *facta*, things made, or even "contrived"), as well as that fictions *are* facts.[8]

The autobiographical bent of Eliade's early Indian-inspired literary work is even more perceptible in *Work in Progress* (*Şantier*, 1935). This book, which the author labels an "indirect novel," consists of a series of undisguised and in all likelihood *real* diary entries. In the preface to *Şantier* Eliade readily admits that the work is a journal, but goes on to argue that its being a journal in no way contradicts its fictional character. To understand this paradox one must be aware of two facts: first, at that time Eliade thought of himself primarily a novelist; and second, he was one of the outstanding representatives of the Romanian school of "authenticity," a sort of early modernist-"existentialist" group whose members were committed to a literature of unmediated self-inquiry and self-expression, and who made communication of personal experience the major goal of writing. Thus, in the preface to *Şantier* the author could state without being afraid of any possible misunderstanding: "A novelist, even when he writes for himself, will write a novel whenever he speaks of men and events, and not of theories or his own reveries . . . I can't help it, everything I relate becomes a page in a novel."[9] But even this broad view of the novel seems to him restrictive and a few paragraphs later he is willing to accept that not only men and events but also theories, reveries, soliloquies, and in short everything that can occur in life or imagination is part of a potential novel.

This group of early fictional-personal works about India, in which the author appears caught up in an insoluble conflict between asceticism and the "mythology of voluptuousness," presents certain remarkable differences from the later novellas with Indian subject-matter, namely, "The Secret of Dr. Honigberger" and "Nights at Serampore." The two latter works display a more impersonal and objective fantasy (and a richer one, for that matter); their deep themes are more philosophical (they deal with the major problem of the fully mature Eliade, that of the ambiguities of the sacred and the profane in their dialectical relationship); and, most noticeably, they are, unlike the rather loosely structured early works, *good stories*, efficiently and artfully conducted narratives. Between *Isabel* and *Nights at Serampore*, from 1930 to 1940, the author has gone all the way from the modernist obsession with self and from a certain experimentalist temptation (Eliade's early fiction, with the exception of *Maitreyi*, is deliberately "not constructed" in order to convey as directly as possible the immediacy of lived "experience") to the timeless art of story-telling. By 1940, we may say, Eliade had discovered the "ontological" signification of narration, of the fact of recounting stories.

A similar trend is observed in Eliade's fiction on Romanian themes: such massive and rather loosely constructed novels as *Intoarcerea din Rai* (The Return from Paradise, 1934), or *Huliganii* (The Hooligans, 1935) are, like their Indian-inspired counterparts, illustrations of the same quest for "authenticity"; true, the personal-autobiographical element is harder to trace, the author's attempt being now to portray not his own estranged self (projected against the background of an exotic culture) but the "collective self" of his generation of "angry young men," questioning and rejecting their society and cultural milieu with a nihilistic fury equaled only by their deep sense of metaphysical alienation. During the second half of the 1930s a noticeable change occurs, announced by the "tale of terror," *Mademoiselle Christina* (1936), a Romanian adaptation of the "gothic" genre, with ghosts, vampires, scenes of demonic possesion, and a combination of eroticism and cruelty (is not Sadism the correspondent of gothic imagination in the realm of sexuality?). But *Mademoiselle Christina* remains an exception in the universe of Eliade's fiction, an exercise in story-telling for its own sake, important only insofar as it represents the first encounter of the writer with the fantastic, in the form of a dramatic, powerful clash between two radically heterogeneous worlds. *Mademoiselle Christina's* subject-matter is largely conventional, what is remarkable about it is the ability of the author to use skilfully and often with unexpected effectiveness the set conventions of a genre of literature whose traditions go back to the late eighteenth-century interest in the aesthetics of terror. The real change in Eliade's fiction, a change which might be described in terms of a "coupure epistémologique" (with major consequences in the other fields of Eliade's activity), is marked by *The Snake* (1937).

The extensive role played in this novella by allusion, suggestion, metaphor, ambiguity, and other poetic devices, explains why it is so hard to summarize. *The Snake* also lacks a clearly articulated story-line, which only compounds the difficulty of speaking about it intelligently (or even intelligibly) to someone who has not already read it. Fortunately, a certain acquaintance with Eliade's theoretical work and its problematic will be sufficient for recognizing the broad significance of *The Snake* in the author's career. What is this novella about? The best way I can describe it is to say that it is about the contrast *and* the contact between "reality" and "miracle," the profane and the sacred, banality and myth. Now, the contrast between these two sets of categories is nothing new, the very distinction, both conceptually and linguistically, belongs to the realm of the most obvious truisms. The interest of Eliade's approach lies in his stressing the notion of *contact*, to the extent that he implies the contrast between the world of "reality" and that of miracle would become meaningless and even cease to exist were it not for their close contact, a contact which accounts, among other things, for the possibility of mistaking one for the other.

The sacred, as Eliade has often said, takes on the appearances of everyday banality, it disguises itself and makes itself unrecognizable. Seen from this vantage point, *The Snake* is fundamentally a praise of sexuality as a manifestation of the sacred, a sort of epithalamium in prose, which reminds one of certain powerful pages in D. H. Lawrence, a hymn to Eros, whose mythical and symbolic embodiments are discovered behind the tritest of middle-class social and moral conventions. Another attractive feature of *The Snake* as a literary work is that its central theme (miracle making itself unrecognizable) is paralleled on the level of literary structures and devices: here is a poem about timeless sacred erotic drives which masquerades as a novella of Romanian middle-class manners in the 1930s.

The beginning of *The Snake* is highly deceptive in regard to the true and secret intention of the piece. The reader is introduced to a typical petit-bourgeois family gathering (described "realistically," not without a touch of irony), the purpose of which is to have Dorina, a nice-looking but rather silly young woman, meet the man whom her parents would like her to marry. At the monastery of Căldăruşani, one of the favorite resorts of the Bucharest middle class, where Dorina's party had gone to enjoy the "idyllic" pleasures of nature, a man by the name of Andronic (Andros-man, Nike-victory), who has apparently got lost from his friends, joins the company. He looks like a fashionable sportsman and claims to be, among other things, an amateur pilot—a rather glamorous hobby for the mid-1930s. Once the group settles down in the monastery's guest rooms, Andronic suggests that they play a certain game in the woods nearby, and everybody welcomes the idea. It is already dusk when Andronic starts explaining the rules. Curiously, he does not say a word about either the game's purpose or what one has to do to win and, when he is asked, he answers that the fun consists precisely in not knowing these things until later. The game is played— the participants do what Andronic tells them, they walk away by themselves and hide in the darkness of the wood for a while, all of them under the strange erotic spell of a mid-summer night's dream. The women in the party, and particularly Dorina, are attracted to Andronic; the men, and particularly the captain (Dorina's intended husband) feel uneasy and jealous, but everybody is excited, although unable to define or understand the nature of this excitement. In the end, there is no winner in the game and Andronic does not explain the purpose of the whole incomprehensible but enchanting rigmarole: perhaps its hidden purpose, the reader begins to suspect, has been to confront the players with their own inner freedom, with their obscure dreams and desires, with their fundamental self.

The climactic point of the novella is reached in the scene at the monastery, late at night, in which Andronic reveals his magical powers by calling in and then "exorcising" the snake. One need not document at length the rich sexual symbolism of the snake to understand the question addressed to it by Andronic: "You have come to the wedding? . . . You felt that there was a wedding here?" (p. 204) Actually, Andronic *himself* had made his appearance "out of the blue" because he had sensed that a wedding was being prepared. Who is he, after all? No one else, perhaps, than the god of love, disguised successively as a "fashionable sportsman," an organizer of daffy *jeux de société*, a charlatan, a magician, a charmer of snakes.

Obviously, Dorina falls in love with him, and in the second part of the novella, in which the narrative dissolves, as it were, into a vast symbolic reverie, she flees her petty, bourgeois world to unite with Andronic on the edenic island in the middle of the lake. But Andronic is not a person—although he is seen as one. He is in fact an impersonal force, a principle, the manifestation of a sacred power. It would, then, be erroneous to consider him a more fortunate rival of the self-effacing, timid captain. Dorina's escape from the prison-house of middle-class conventions is certainly real, since for Eliade imagination *is* reality, but on the plane of the "immediate unreality" of quotidian life Dorina is probably going to marry the captain after all. Andronic's revelations are perhaps only an unexpected wedding gift. The ending of the piece is as ambiguous as the story in its entirety—ambiguity being for Eliade the essential trait of miracle and therefore the literary device best suited to dealing with it.[10]

The problem of miracle and the disguises through which it renders itself unrecognizable is central in Eliade's next novel, *Nunta în Cer* (Marriage in Heaven, 1938), in which the transitional period in the author's creative biography may be said to have come to an end. Unlike *The Snake, Marriage in Heaven* does not contain any externally "fantastic" elements; also, the apparent lack of a definite story-line in the earlier novella is in sharp contrast to the carefully (almost geometrically) worked out plot of the novel. *Marriage in Heaven* presents the reader with two love stories, as recounted by two men, Mavrodin and Hasnaş, who have met each other by chance at a hunting party and share reminiscences to fill the emptiness of a long, sleepless night in the hunting cabin. Mavrodin is an artist, a writer, a successful novelist, and what he narrates during the night coincides with the theme of his autobiographical book, based on his unique love affair with a mysterious woman, Ileana. This book, also entitled *Marriage in Heaven*, had been written in the hope of convincing Ileana to return to her abandoned lover. Why had she disappeared from his life without leaving the faintest trace? Why, given that the relation between the two had been all along both passionate and happy? Mavrodin knows the answer perfectly well. The breakup had been provoked by Ileana's desire to have a child and by his reluctance to become a father, although he was prepared, for her sake, to enter into what he regarded as the complete antipode of an artist's duty to his art, namely, a normal, "bourgeois," happy family life. A true artist, Mavrodin thought, could have only spiritual offspring. For him marriage was, as he put it, "an institution I had only veneration for, but from which I excluded artists and thinkers. . . . I liked . . . to think of the fate of the artist as comparable to the calling of a monk."[11] (p. 208) Ileana decides to have an abortion and then, without any more explanations, she vanishes from his life. In vain did Mavrodin look for her; he would encounter her once more, but then only as a character in the story of Hasnaş's love affair with Lena (in Romanian both Ileana and Lena are familiar derivations from Elena or "Helen"). Hasnaş represents a type opposite to that of the artist: he is a "bourgeois" whose life, devoid of any transcendental purpose, becomes meaningless if he does not have to raise a family— the only means of counteracting the irreversible passage of time. So, in his marriage with Lena, Hasnaş is increasingly obsessed with the thought that he must have a child. He is happy with his wife, but this happiness by itself seems to him gratuitous and almost unreal, and he fears that one day it may be lost, as everything is lost in the merciless world of Chronos.

For Mavrodin, the artist living in a different time, love is perfect only when it is fruitless and thus separated from the "normal" world, with all the worries brought about by unrepeatable time. Once he tells Ileana: "Our destiny is not fulfilled here on earth. We have known one another through love only. Love is our paradise, love without fruit."[12] For Hasnaş, on the contrary, fruitlessness is the sign of a terrible, unbearable unfulfillment. But Lena refuses to give him a child. The two men have loved the same woman, Ileana/Lena, and have both been "punished" for their failure to recognize the miracle that had come their way under different disguises. In the case of Mavrodin, what is censored is the artist's tendency to downgrade and reject the "normal" time-order and his subsequent blindness to the humble, everyday forms that miracle can choose to manifest itself through. In the case of Hasnaş the opposite blindness—to the *real* timeless quality of happiness—forms the object of "punishment." The deep theme of the novel is the ambiguity of miracle and the impossibility of recognizing it from one-sided perspectives. When recognition comes it is too late.

All this may sound high-flown and somewhat melodramatic. Let me therefore emphasize that for Eliade there is nothing particularly spectacular, dramatic, or "tragic" in one's nonrecognition of miracle. Returning to the two men in *Marriage in Heaven*, it should be pointed out that Mavrodin writes, *after* the disappearance of Ileana, his best and most successful book; whereas Hasnaş is happily remarried and has two sons he is very proud of. This point is important, and Hasnaş underlines it very clearly and memorably toward the end of the novel: "What I felt like telling you, while listening to your confession, was that such things are easily forgotten, and without much suffering. You come across such a love only once in a lifetime. You were quite right when you said that such an encounter is somehow of the order of miracle—that is why, perhaps, it takes on such a fluky appearance, and seems to consist of a series of utterly frivolous, insignificant events. We realize that it was a miracle only when it is too late, the realization comes always too late."[13]

Among the prewar works of Eliade, *Marriage in Heaven* is the one which anticipates most, in both theme and tone, his great postwar novel *The Forbidden Forest*, written between 1949–1955; while *The Snake* and the 1940 tales of the fantastic set in India are in many ways close anticipations of the rich production of novellas and short stories. *The Forbidden Forest* itself, which I do not intend to discuss here, is certainly an exception within the framework of Eliade's most recent fiction. It may be seen as a culmination of his passion for the novel and, more than that, as a *summa* of his whole literary activity. Thus, beyond *Marriage in Heaven*, *The Forbidden Forest* is linked to Eliade's early novels, and particularly to *The Return from Paradise* and *The Hooligans*, with which it shares a deep concern for contemporary *historical reality*. But in the early novels, the narrator was "existentially" committed to a generational point of view (speaking on behalf of the *young* generation in rebellion against the old), while the writer of *The Forbidden Forest* has become much more detached and attempts to make sense of the "nightmare of history" (World War II) from the broad perspective of the later Eliade's dialectic of the sacred and the profane, of fundamental Time versus historical time, as expounded in *The Myth of the Eternal Return* (1949). On the other hand, the use of mythical patterns and symbols, as well as the sense of *fantastic presence*, which pervades certain key sections of the book, relate *The Forbidden Forest* to the fantastic stories written by Eliade after *The Snake*, and more particularly in the postwar years.

The reason why Eliade has come to prefer the genre of short fiction to the novel is fairly clear if we think of his post-1945 involvement in numerous scholarly projects, most of which have been successfully carried out, as is apparent by the most cursory glance at his compelling bibliography in the field of religious anthropology. In his years as a "Wandering Scholar," Eliade has also been faced with the language problem. His scholarly work was written mostly in French, even before the war (his important 1936 essay on *Yoga*, for instance), but as a fiction writer Eliade has always considered himself "to be a Romanian author, belonging within the organic whole of Romanian literature."[14] To this day, his literary pieces and his journal are written only in Romanian— "the language of my dreams," as he candidly recognizes. This accounts for the fact that many of Eliade's literary works are published by small émigré presses and that sometimes they appear in translation long before the originals (thus, the French version of The *Forbidden Forest* was published in 1955, sixteen years before the original Romanian was brought out by Ioan Cuşa, also in Paris). The natural dialogue between an author and his public cannot take place under such circumstances, and this by itself may discourage any writer from undertaking ample literary projects.

The fact of the matter is that Eliade has continued to write literature, against all odds, mostly to satisfy a personal need. To explain this need, of which his situation as an exile made him painfully aware, he mentions Gaston Bachelard's notion of the "function of the unreal" in a revealing diary entry (20 June 1963): "I am working on the short story. I tell myself that what I am doing is absurd. . . . But I feel I must write it, for my moral health. How right G. Bachelard was when he spoke about 'the function of the unreal'; which, if not satisfied, leads to neurosis and sterility."[15]

The relationship between myth and a certain type of fantastic short story (the one Eliade has a marked preference for) is closer than the relationship between myth and the necessarily more elaborate constructions of character without which no properly called novel can exist. What myth and the short story have in common is a strong *narrative element*—they both appear as manifestations of a kind of primordial narrative imagination, they both create an almost immediate sense that all kinds of things are *happening*, that unsuspected meanings, relations, phenomena, events come into existence and that, although they are qualitatively different from what we call "history," they enrich the "world no more and no less than history," being "just as significant for the fate of man as the fact of living in history or hoping to modify it." (*No Souvenirs*, p. 205) The novel, certainly, can achieve similar effects, but usually through the *mediation* of highly individualized, imaginatively irreplaceable characters. In a novel—at least in a traditional one—the emphasis is less on *what* happens, on the fact that things happen, and more on *how*, and especially *to whom*, they happen: the *narrative force* of a novel is derived from the vigor of its characters. In a myth or in a fantastic tale what imports, what *constitutes* the myth or the tale (leaving aside the numerous differences between the two) is simply *what* happens. The *narrative force* is here constitutive and unmediated; it is *original* (at the origin), and not merely a consequence or a result.

It is impossible to discuss here individually and in detail the two dozen or so short stories and novellas written by Eliade in the postwar years. I have therefore chosen to illustrate the major themes, procedures, and problems that occur in this outstanding section of Eliade's *oeuvre* by taking a closer look at two novellas, which both their author and those familiar with his literary work consider among his best. They are *"La tigănci"* (With the Gypsy Girls) and *Pe strada Mântuleasa* (Mantuleasa Street). The first, written in 1959, is available in English translation, as I have mentioned; the second, finished in 1967, has been translated so far into German (*Auf der Mântuleasa Strasse*, Frankfurt-Main: Suhrkamp, 1972), Dutch (1975), and French (*Le vieil homme et l'officier*, Paris: Gallimard, 1977). [English: *The Old Man and The Bureaucrats*, Notre Dame: Notre Dame University Press, 1979. (Ed.)]

Both these stories belong to the genre of "fantastic literature" and to understand the particular use they make of the fantastic one should be aware of a number of larger issues involved in the subject. In trying to define the fantastic, some of the most perceptive studies of this literary genre start by considering the question: "What is *not* fantastic?" The answer seems obvious: the *everyday*, the sense of everyday reality, as conveyed by the literary means of "realistic" prose. But this contrast is in no way absolute. We might even say that, perhaps, from a methodological point of view, it has been more fruitful to distinguish the fantastic from a number of neighboring categories such as the "supernatural," the "marvelous" (as used in fairy tales), the "legendary" or the "mythical," as well as from the more modern variants of utopian-scientific fabulation (the kind of "marvelous" used in science fiction). When all these distinctions are taken into account, the fantastic still preserves its implications of duality (in the sense that it arises from the encounter between *two* radically different worlds, the "natural" and the "supernatural"), but this duality becomes much less clear-cut and, at least on the level of its perceptible manifestations, much more ambiguous. It is this ambiguity, this metalogical suggestion of "the unity of opposites," which accounts for certain psychologically-intellectually unsettling effects by which the fantastic can be recognized. In other words, the fantastic in a literary piece faces the reader with the possibility of what the Russian Formalist critic Boris Tomashevsky calls "double interpretation": the events presented by the writer can be seen to result from "natural" causes, but an equally valid point can be made in favor of a "supernatural" explanation. Tomashevsky quotes a statement made by the great Russian theologian and philosopher, Vladimir Solovyov, in a preface to Alexey Tolstoy's novella *The Vampire* (Solovyov's preface was published in 1899):

> The real interest and significance of the *fantastic* in literature is contained in the belief that everything that happens in the world, and especially everything that happens in the life of man—except that for which the cause is proximate and obvious—still depends on some other kind of causation. This other causation is more profound and universal, but to make up for that it is less clear. And this is the distinguishing characteristic of the genuinely fantastic; it is never, so to speak, in full view. Its presence must never compel belief in a mystic interpretation of a vital event; it must rather point, or *hint*, at it. In the really fantastic, the external, formal possibility of a simple explanation of ordinary and commonplace connections among the phenomena always remains. This external explanation, however, finally loses its internal probability. All the individual details must seem ordinary, and only their relation to the whole pattern must point to another cause."[16]

This broad definition of the fantastic applies perfectly to Eliade's stories if we deemphasize the notion of "causation," which occupies such a prominent place in Solovyov's formulation. With Eliade, as we shall see, the fantastic consists less in the confrontation between two kinds of causality and therefore between two conflicting possibilities of *explaining* the same unusual sequence of events; it consists more of a growing awareness that the world of *primordial Time* and the world of banal *linear time* can and do express themselves through a strikingly similar language. The problem is not one of causation but one of *recognition*. While in Solovyov's definition the fantastic is never "in full view" but only "hinted at," Eliade's effort is precisely to bring it *in full view*, to make it almost indistinguishable from what is *ordinarily* in full view. Certainly, the confrontation between two worlds is maintained, for without it the specific tension of the fantastic would disappear, but the relationship between them is changed. Traditionally, fantastic literature has derived its effects from a sense of menace posed by the sudden irruption of the incomprehensible (the supernatural) in the comprehensible flow of ordinary life.[17] Everyday reality is seen as reassuring and the obscure world of the supernatural (glimpsed at now and then but never in full view) is conceived of as dangerous, malevolent, destructive. With Eliade this relation is reversed: it is everyday reality which is essentially incomprehensible, meaningless and cruel. It is only when we recognize the presence of the *other* world (miracle, primordial time) that we are saved from meaninglessness. From the point of view of the writer, this *other* world must be created, and that is why, speaking about "With the Gypsy Girls," Eliade has insisted on the fact that his story attempts to *found* a world, to *present* a new universe, by which everyday life is delivered from its arbitrariness.

The problem I have just touched upon is so crucial for understanding Eliade's personality as a whole that it deserves to be dealt with at some length. The problem is, simply put, one of "existential alchemy": how does one transform everyday meaninglessness into something meaningful? To learn Eliade's answer to this grave question, let us take a look at his journal and find out how he comes to terms with his fundamental postwar life, that of an *exile*. In the entry dated 1 January 1960 (it is perhaps worth mentioning that the passage was written on the first day of a New Year and a new decade), Eliade notes:

> Every real existence reproduces the Odyssey. . . . I had known that for a long time. What I have just discovered is that the chance to become a new Ulysses is given to *any* exile *whatsoever* (precisely because he has been condemned by the gods, that is, by the "powers" which decide historical, earthly destinies). But to realize this, the exile must be capable of penetrating the hidden meaning of his wanderings, and of understanding them as a long series of initiation trials (willed by the gods) and so many obstacles on the path which brings him

back to the hearth (toward the center). That means: seeing signs, hidden meanings, symbols in the sufferings, the depressions, the dry periods in everyday life. Seeing them and reading them even *if they aren't there;* if one sees them, one can build a structure and read a message in the formless flow of things and the monotonous flux of historical facts.[18]

The above quoted passage is remarkable for several reasons. It brings into focus the main theme, the central "existential situation" around which Eliade's postwar career is built—exile. It connects this theme with the fate of Ulysses, taken as an expression of both mythical thought and poetic imagination. Then, it sets the theme in a wider perspective, that of "initiation trials" (one of Eliade's major subjects as a student of religion), a perspective in which, quite unexpectedly, the condemning gods of faded mythologies are no longer separated from the political "powers" of our day by an unbridgeable gap. Seen from such a vantage point, the wanderings and sufferings of any individual exile become meaningful: they are bearers of signs and symbols which one should learn how to read. Lastly, and more important, the passage contains the highly original idea that these signs and symbols should be seen and interpreted even *"if they aren't there."* This becomes clearer if we stress that Eliade's metaphysics of meaning hinges on the cardinal notions of *imagination* and *creativity.* The workings of imagination have nothing arbitrary about them and the meaning that is discovered or created through the imaginative process is always infinitely more rich and real than "the formless flow of things." Thus, for Eliade, to discover (in the sense of revealing that which is concealed, invisible, unrecognizable), is to create, and to create is to discover (or to uncover) reality.

This long parenthesis will help us understand, I hope, the thrust of Eliade's remarks concerning his story "With the Gypsy Girls." "Some day," he writes in his journal, on 3 March 1968, "I ought to write a critical commentary on the articles which have appeared on 'With the Gypsy Girls.' I have the impression that the essential has not been grasped: this story does not symbolize anything, it does not transform immediate reality by a cypher. The story *founds* a world. . . . It is the presentation of a *new* universe, unprecedented, having its own laws—it is this presentation which constitutes the act of creation. . . . In penetrating this universe. . . . something is revealed to you. The problem that poses itself for the critic is not to decipher the 'symbolism' of the story, but . . .to interpret the *message* hidden by the reality of the story (more precisely the new type of reality that the adventure of my hero, Gavrilescu, unveils)." And on 10 March 1968, Eliade adds in connection with the same story: "Such a literature as this founds its own universe;

just as myths unveil for us the foundation of worlds, of modes of being (animal, plant, man, etc.). . . . It is in this sense that one can speak of the extension of myth into literature: not only because certain myth-ological structures and figures return in the imaginary universes of literature, but especially because in both cases it is a matter of *creation,* that is of the creation (revelation) of certain worlds parallel to the daily universe in which we move. . . . As a myth, 'With the Gypsy Girls' (and other stories of the same genre) reveals unsuspected meanings, gives a meaning to everyday life."[19]

At the heart of "With the Gypsy Girls" is the figure of a failed musician, Gavrilescu, who lives in Bucharest during the 1930s and makes a precarious living as a piano teacher. Everyday, to get down-town to his pupils and then back home, he rides a streetcar which passes by the "gypsy girls' " a sort of bordello located in a beautiful, secluded garden. On a hot summer day, walking by the gypsy girls' by chance, Gavrilescu decides to enter. He pays the fee, is admitted, then met by three girls (the Parcae?), who entertain him in a quaint manner, engaging him in a silly guessing game in which he cannot help feeling that he is behaving like a fool. At the same time, during the whole episode, Gavrilescu remembers (with acuteness and a mix-ture of pain and happiness) Hildegard, the young woman he had been in love with years before in his student days in Germany but had abandoned. The scenes from the present and the past succeed them-selves in an incomprehensible pattern. As in a dream, everything is both clear and fuzzy, and certain details are both comical and charged with obscure ominous significance. After a few hours a befuddled Gavrilescu leaves the place to go about his ordinary business. But during the few hours he has spent at the gypsy girls' twelve full years have passed. Gavrilescu learns that his wife, Else, had left the country a few months after his strange disappearance, which had been widely reported in the papers. His apartment is now occupied by new tenants, his pupils are gone, etc. But Gavrilescu fails to understand. He thinks he might find out what had actually happened by going back to the gypsy girls'. There he is met by Hildegard, who was apparently waiting for him. They both get on a horse-cab and Hildegard tells the driver: "Drive us to the woods, and go the longest way . . . and slowly. We are in no hurry."[20] The reader understands that the two lovers are taken to the realm of the dead where there is no time, no hurry. The cab-driver is Charon.

Eliade's short story, although it contains nothing that is directly related to death or dying, can be understood adequately only in terms of a "mythology of death." The narrative starts "realistically" and it takes a while until the reader becomes aware of the strangeness of the world he is being presented with. Little by little, his *symbolic imagination* is drawn into action—certain words and images in the text seem to have a double meaning, certain gaps or discontinuities in the narrative are like missing pieces in a jigsaw puzzle, which one is tempted to "invent," although one can never be certain that such "inventions" are even remotely similar to the real missing pieces. The jigsaw puzzle analogy is apt, I think. Eliade's story should not be read as an allegory. Once one has finished reading "With the Gypsy Girls," one is sure that the story is "about" death; But this realization is not a "key" to the meaning of the story, and it does in no way clarify its fundamental obscurity. What the realization does is simply to confront the reader with the mystery of death: the *real* mystery, the *real* puzzle with missing pieces (forever lost). An allegory, when you manage to solve it (very much like a riddle), provides you with a clear-cut answer. "With the Gypsy Girls" does not purport to resolve an enigma but to *found* one: an enigma, a universe, a myth. The story sets out as a description of everyday reality and finishes as a mythical intimation of "real reality" which, camouflaged, had in fact manifested itself all through the story.

If "With the Gypsy Girls" can be seen as a mythology of death, then it would be proper to call *Mântuleasa Street*, perhaps Eliade's master-piece in the genre of novella, a mythology of myth itself. Indeed, the piece is built on the theme of the both explicit and implicit incompatibility between the world of *myth* and the anti-mythical world of ever-suspicious *political power*. The latter is described in its total—that is, totalitarian—embodiment. The story takes place in Romania, in the early 1950s, during the heyday of Stalinism, and one of the main characters representing the world of political power, the minister Anca Vogel, is a recognizable portrait of the historical figure of Ana Pauker, a devoted Stalinist who became the victim of a Stalinist purge in 1952. It is important to note that in dealing with fairly specific historical and political events Eliade does not take sides, as one might have expected from somebody who, after all, was forced into exile. The author's portrayal of communist officials, and specifically of Stalinist political police investigators (a rather horrendous species by any standards) is remarkably lacking in bitterness or polemicism. What Eliade is interested in, from his detached and serene point of view, is simply to describe the functioning of a certain "mentality," to reconstitute a certain "political" world view which is diametrically opposed to the world view characteristic of myth. The real hero of the story is an old man, Zaharia Fărâmă, a retired grammar school teacher, who does not seem to have much to do except for walking aimlessly around his old neighborhood and reminiscing and, when given the occasion, telling stories about his former pupils. The action starts with the teacher trying to get in touch with the new occupant of an apartment in a Mântuleasa Street building, a certain security police Major Borza, whose name reminded the old man of that of a former pupil of his, back in the days before World War I, when he was Director of Mântuleasa school. Zaharia Fărâmă had learnt by pure chance about Borza's moving in, from people chatting in the street. The old man's unexpected visit arouses the suspicions of both Borza and his colleague, Dumitrescu, who happened to be at Borza's at the time. Fărâmă's innocuous stories seem to have hidden political content or at least political implications. Borza denies having ever studied at Mântuleasa school but his colleague is not entirely convinced that he had not had some obscure dealings with the old teacher. To check into the matter and to test Borza's credibility, Fărâmă is arrested and subjected to lengthy interrogations. To the questions he is asked the old man answers—almost happy to be listened to—by telling stories and stories about these stories. An extremely complex and strangely fascinating narrative network is thus created, in which the credible and the incredible, the fantastic and the "historical" are indissolubly combined. The investigators—first Dumitrescu, then the higher-ranking Economu, then, finally, Anca Vogel herself—are baffled and puzzled by Fărâmă's inexhaustible tales. What in these tales is checkable is carefully checked out and some of the least plausible details they contain turn out to be perfectly accurate. The old teacher's rambling reminiscences—when carefully "decoded" by the specialized services of the security police—appear to hide certain important "revelations" concerning certain people working for the security police itself. Thus, it is learned that if Borza had indeed not studied at Mântuleasa school, he had lied in connection with other aspects of his past (he had concealed the fact that he had been employed by the secret police of the previous regime). So he is purged. Likewise, Fărâmă's mythical tales offer unsuspected "leads" through which other important members of the party apparatus are "unmasked": it is discovered that Economu had been involved in a conspiracy to defraud the socialist state (to prevent his arrest he commits suicide) and, finally, Anca Vogel herself is linked to that conspiracy and removed from her post.

But all these events which may be said to belong to the "historical" dimension of the novella, are kept in the background. The foreground is occupied by the intricate network of stories the old man tells about his former pupils and their friends. The reader thus gets to know the group of school-boy friends (Lixandru, Darvari, Iozi) who were interested in symbolism and magic, and who were exploring the basements and cellars of the houses in the Mântuleasa neighborhood to discover certain mysterious "signs." By "recognizing" these signs, one of them,

Iozi, had managed to cross the border between this world and the marvelous underground world, the "other world" of folk tales and myths. Among the boys' friends is a girl, Oana, a giantess, whose story is told and retold at great length—we learn about her parents and grandparents, about her childhood, about her puberty, about her flight to the mountains where, like a new Parsiphaë, she falls in love with a bull, about her finally meeting a human match, a giant man to whom she gets married, about her wedding, about her dreams. Oana is in fact a goddess who has made herself unrecognizable by assuming the appearance of a freak.

The old man with his endless wild tales is regarded by the police as a shrewd, unusually wily mystifier, as somebody who tries to hide something, something whose *full* knowledge should be of extreme importance for the police. On a purely *aesthetic* level, Fărâmă's tales are openly appreciated by the most sophisticated representatives of the police apparatus. Anca Vogel is not only delighted but thinks that Fărâmă's art of story-telling is by far superior to that of the regimented fiction writers of the regime. "They should learn from you," she tells the old man. In a sense, her downfall is a punishment for her "aestheticism": instead of relentlessly trying to decipher the "true" meaning of Fărâmă's artful lies, she has let herself get carried away by their curious imaginative power. She has thus made herself vulnerable to other policemen's "interpretations" of the "latent content" of the old teacher's ramblings. Had she not been trapped into aesthetic considerations, she might have come up with her own "interpretations," which she could have used against her enemies within the party. At least, she could have counterbalanced the danger to her of letting her political peers, all of them engaged in a ruthless competition for power, "interpret" the deceptive statements of Fărâmă.

This brings us to the real conflict on which Eliade's novella is built: that between the "logic of myth" and the "logic of power," or secular authoritarianism. The latter manifests itself more directly in totalitarian politics, but has something to do, in Eliade's view, with modernity in general, including the manifestations of the "scientific spirit," which so often oversteps its natural boundaries and boasts of being able to explain everything. Although *Mântuleasa Street* is a fully successful *literary* piece (that is, the reader can derive sufficient aesthetic gratification from its rich texture and from its wonderful display of narrative fantasy to dispense with its would-be theoretical implications), one can better grasp its significance within the context of Eliade's work when one realizes that it is, no matter how covertly, a *conte philosophique*. The philosophical questions that are involved in *Mântuleasa Street* revolve around one of the central themes of Eliade's thought—the nature and forms of *interpretation*. The stories told by Zaharia Fărâmă are ultimately nothing but interpretations of certain unusual facts or events, whose meaning is constituted by other stories, themselves interpretations of other unusual facts and events, and so on and so forth. Mythical thought, as illustrated in the naïve and attaching character of the old teacher, is simply that: an expansion of the story. Any particular story has a *hidden meaning*, and this meaning is another story. From this point of view, to interpret is to narrate, to unfold stories from other stories. This concept of interpretation is compatible with Eliade's deep-rooted belief in a vital, manifold, irreducible truth (synonymous with the sacred), which hides itself in the very process of revealing itself. Story-telling, recounting myths is then a cognitive activity—the cognitive activity *par excellence*.

Such a view of the hiddenness of the obvious and the obviousness of the hidden leads naturally to a "hermeneutics of trust." The opposite view—which in Eliade's novella is implicitly upheld by the representatives of the political police—belongs to what Paul Ricoeur has called the "hermeneutics of suspicion."[21] The three philosophical masters of suspicion, as Ricoeur identifies them in the introductory part of his *Freud and Philosophy*, are Freud, Nietzsche, and Marx—and the name of the latter is especially relevant to our discussion. But before reviewing the major implications of the notion that interpretation is basically an exercise of suspicion let me observe that Eliade has always been philosophically opposed to the doctrines of these three *maîtres à penser* of modernity, and in particular to their fundamental *reductionism*. Actually, suspicion and reductionism are closely linked intellectual attitudes, the two faces of the same metaphysical revolt against *diversity*: once suspicion pierces through the variegated veils of illusion, the diversity of apparent facts can be reduced to some ultimate determining force—sexuality and the conflict between the pleasure principle and the reality principle for Freud, the *will to power* and the conflict between master morality and *ressentiment* for Nietzsche, the economic mode of production and the conflict between the forces of production and the relations of production for Marx. Another common feature of the three major schools of suspicion consists in their strong bias in favor of *demythologization*. Their methods, assumptions, and goals differ widely but all three are bent on discovering the *profane* content of *mythical* (sacred) manifestations, as if the profane, ashamed to show itself openly, went to incredible lengths to put on "nobler" and more "mysterious" appearances. Eliade's whole effort goes in the opposite direction: instead of "demythologizing," we should, he thinks, "remythologize" the world; instead of exposing the *profane* elements contained in myth (note that the existence of such elements is never denied by Eliade), we should strive to recover the hidden *mythical* components of profane realities or events (whether they belong to the banality of history or to what Eliade calls, in *The Myth of the Eternal Return,* "the terror of history").[22]

Returning to *Mântuleasa Street,* let me now try to examine some of the implications of Eliade's opposition to the "hermeneutics of suspicion" as they can be inferred from the text, if we read the story as a *conte philosophique*—and paranthetically, is not Zaharia Fărâmă, *mutatis mutandis,* a new version of Candide, and is not Eliade's critique of Marxian sociological optimism comparable to Voltaire's critique of Leibniz's metaphysical optimism and its maxim *"Tout est pour le mieux dans le meilleur des mondes possibles"?*). Discussing abstract philosophical issues in relation to a piece of literature such as *Mântuleasa Street* is even less of an heresy if we remember that for Eliade myth, literary fiction, and philosophical imagination (even scientific imagination) have more points in common than we are usually ready to admit. Actually, I think that the real reasons why Eliade is critical of the "hermeneutics of suspicion" are expressed more clearly in a literary work such as *Mântuleasa Street* than in theoretical works. And this is so because of the very nature of these reasons, which are a matter of fundamental *value* choices rather than of intellectual argument. Ultimately, I would submit, Eliade rejects suspicion and the interpretative methods based on it (some of them extraordinarily subtle and sophisticated) simply because he finds the ethos of suspicion objectionable and is committed to an ethos of trust. The latter is illustrated in the sympathetic portrait of the old teacher who, even though he is arrested and constantly harrassed by the representatives of suspicion, is essentially invulnerable to their weapons and does not even seem to suffer too much while he is their prisoner: he is saved by the stories he keeps on telling, by his faith in myth, by virtue, I might add, of "the function of the unreal."

Suspicion, Eliade seems to suggest in *Mântuleasa Street,* should not be considered a "means to knowledge," and even when some kind of knowledge is attained through the exercise of suspicion, this is largely a matter of chance, if the meager "truth" that is eventually reached is not simply "fabricated" in the process of searching for it.[23] But this is not Eliade's major objection to the philosophy of suspicion. What he dislikes most about this philosophy is its *authoritarian* implication, the strange *fanaticism* that goes with it, the dictatorial self-assurance that many of its proponents display (even when they are truly great and original thinkers). To this authoritarian bias Eliade opposes the value of intellectual and moral *tolerance* (acceptance and praise of diversity, recognition of the validity of widely different approaches to the same questions, open-mindedness, and even skepticism—which should not be confused with suspicion—in the face of stubbornly dogmatic beliefs and attitudes).

Such a tolerance comes from Eliade's deep conviction that myths and stories present us not with cyphers and codes to be cracked but with the actual processes by which new worlds of meaning are created. Myths and stories teach us this important lesson: to grasp the meanings of things (all the more so when these meanings "aren't there"), we should trust what myths and stories tell us, we should recognize their exemplarity. *All myths and stories are exemplary:* this is, I think, the constitutive principle of Eliade's ethics of tolerance as well as the starting point of his critique of suspicion. But even this critique, as the reader of *Mântuleasa Street* will not fail to realize, is pervaded with the spirit of tolerance: if the representatives of suspicion have no use for the "function of the unreal" (except for the opportunity that myth gives them to exert their decoding aggressiveness), the "function of the unreal," the great motive force of story-telling, generously and wisely fictionalizes them and, in telling their story, *understands* them.

Notes

Parts of this article have appeared in *Southeastern Europe* 7 (1980), pp. 62–73, and in *The Notre Dame Journal of English* 13 (1980), pp. 74–78.

1. *The Denver Quarterly,* vol. 8 (1973–74), No. 2, pp. 13–58. The translation is by William Ames Coates, who also did the translation of *Two Tales of the Occult* (New York: Herder and Herder, 1970). Republished in *Tales of the Sacred and the Supernatural* (Philadelphia: Westminster Press, 1981). [Ed.]

2. Cf. *Fragments d'un journal,* translated from the Romanian by Luc Badesco (Paris: Gallimard, 1973), which covers the period 1945–1969, whereas the American edition, *No Souvenirs: Journal, 1957–1969,* trans. Fred H. Johnson, Jr. (New York: Harper & Row, 1977), covers the second half of that span only.

3. See my article "Imagination and Meaning: Aesthetic Attitudes and Ideas in Mircea Eliade's Thought," in the *Journal of Religion* 57 (January 1977), pp. 1–15. For further discussion of Mircea Eliade's literary works, see the third section of *Myths and Symbols: Studies in Honor of Mircea Eliade,* ed. by Joseph M. Kitagawa and Charles H. Long (Chicago: University of Chicago Press, 1969), pp. 327–414, and especially the essay by Virgil Ierunca, "The Literary Work of Mircea Eliade," pp. 343–364. In French, the recent issue of *L'Herne* devoted to Eliade (Paris: Editions de l'Herne, 1978), offers nine essays on Eliade as a writer in the section entitled "Les voies du fantastique," pp. 315–390. The most helpful recent studies of Eliade's literary work in Romanian are: Sorin Alexandrescu, "Dialectica fantasticului," Introduction to Mircea Eliade, *La ţigănci*

şi alte povestiri (Bucharest: Editura pentru literatura, 1969), pp. V–L; Ion Negoitescu, "Mircea Eliade sau de la fantastic la oniric," in *Viaţa româneasca*, 23 (February 1970), pp. 71–77; Sanda Stolojan, "Mircea Eliade şi *Noaptea de Sânziene*," in *Ethos* (Paris), I, 1973, pp. 232–237; Eugen Simion, "Mircea Eliade," in his *Scriitori români de azi*, Vol. 2 (Bucharest: Editura Cartea Românească, 1976), pp. 319–336. N. Steinhardt, "Fantasticul lui Mircea Eliade," in *Steaua*, 28:4 (1977), p. 1820.

4. *No Souvenirs*, pp. ix–x.

5. "Fragment autobiografic," in *Caiete de Dor* (Paris), No. 7, July 1953. [English translation published in this volume. Ed.]

6. "Fragment autobiografic" (typescript), pp. 9–10.

7. Ibid., p. 11. Bachelard had read A. Guillermou's translation of the novel, entitled *La Nuit Bengali* (Paris: Gallimard, 1950).

8. We may note, however, that unlike Goethe's Lotte, Eliade's heroine has found it necessary to publish her own version of the story. See, Maitreyi Devi, *It Does Not Die* (Thompson, Connecticut: InterCulture Associates, 1976). This is a translation, by the author herself, of the original Bengali *Na Hanyaté*, published in 1974. The young Eliade appears under the name Mircea Euclid (an allusion to the "esprit de geometrie" represented by the West?). The book will certainly interest a future biographer of Eliade (among other things, it reproduces—how faithfully?—three letters sent by Eliade from the Svarga Ashram in Risikesh, in November and December of 1930, pp. 250–254).

9. *Şantier* (Bucharest: Editura Cugetarea, 1935), p. 7.

10. The following passage about *The Snake* (the entry of June 24, 1963, *No Souvenirs*, p. 191) is an important statement of Eliade's conception of the fantastic: "A young student of social thought, Botinovici, came to see me. He had read *Andronic and the Snake* in the German translation and had been enthusiastic. He would like to read more of my 'literary' works, but I didn't encourage him. Nevertheless, we spoke about my conception of the fantastic in literature. I reminded him that this conception has its roots in my theory of 'the incognizability of miracles'—or in my theory that, after the Incarnation, the transcendent is camouflaged in the world or in history and thus becomes 'incognizable.' In *The Snake* a banal atmosphere and mediocre characters are gradually transfigured. But what came from 'beyond,' as well as all the paradisiac images of the end of the story, were already there from the beginning, but camouflaged by the banality of everyday life and, as such, unrecognizable." Eliade's student had read Günther Spaltmann's version of the novella: *Andronic und die Schlange* (Munich: Nymphenbürger Verlagshandlung, 1949).

11. *Maitreyi, Nunta în Cer* (Bucharest: Editura pentru literatura, 1969), p. 208.

12. Ibid., p. 210.

13. Ibid., p. 310.

14. *No Souvenirs*, p. xi. The dilemmas of a writer separated from his "natural" public have haunted Eliade ever since his self-exile. Thus, on July 20, 1946 (*Fragments d'un journal*, p. 28), he notes: "Ce dont je dois me garder: la tentation de la littérature. Il serait absurde de me laisser entraîner à écrire un roman en roumain, donc pour des lecteurs 'de demain.' "

15. *No Souvenirs*, p. 190.

16. Quoted from *Russian Formalist Criticism: Four Essays*, ed. by Lee T. Lemon and Marion J. Reis (Lincoln, Nebraska: University of Nebraska Press, 1965), pp. 83–84. Tomashevsky considers Solovyov's "a satisfactorily precise formulation of the technique of the fantastic narrative viewed from the norm of realistic motivation." Interestingly, Solovyov's definition, formulated from philosophical, and specifically theological point of view, has been appealing to Formalist critics, from Tomashevsky to Tzvetan Todorov who, in his *Introduction à la littérature fantastique* (Paris: Editions du Seuil), restates it and illustrates it by a large number of examples but does not essentially improve on it.

17. For this view of the fantastic in literature, see Roger Caillois, "De la féerie à la science-fiction," an Introduction to his *Anthologie du fantastique* (Paris: Club français du livre, 1958). Also, my essay "Conceptul de fantastic," in *Eseuri despre literatura moderna* (Bucharest: Editura Eminescu, 1970), pp. 165–174.

18. *No Souvenirs*, pp. 84–85.

19. Ibid., pp. 307–308.

20. "With the Gypsy Girls," p. 58.

21. *Freud and Philosophy: An Essay on Interpretation*, trans. Denis Savage (New Haven, Connecticut: Yale University Press, 1970), pp. 32 ff.

22. Eliade speaks of the need for a "demythologization in reverse," which is, up to a point, accomplished by certain modern critics who are interested in identifying mythical archetypes in literary works. These critics, according to Eliade, are engaged in a highly significant activity of remythologization. On September 1, 1964, Eliade notes in his journal (*No Souvenirs*, pp. 229–230): "If Freud is right (what is *essential* is unconscious), the current tendency of literary critics to decipher initiatic scenarios, myth and ritual patterns in novels, short stories, plays—this tendency has a deeper meaning. Therefore it is necessary to apply demythologization in reverse. Freud, like Marx, taught us to find the 'profane' in the 'sacred.' In the case I am considering here, it is in 'the profane' (the narrative novel, everyday characters, common adventures) that the critics are finding the 'sacred,' implicit and camouflaged. And that is precisely what is significant in the situation of modern man: he satisfies his nonexistent religious life (nonexistent on the conscious level) by the imaginary universes of literature and art. And it is just as significant for literary critics who find religious significance in profane works."

23. How the method of what might be termed "police psychoanalysis" really works is shown at some length in chapter 9 of *Pe Strada Mântuleasa* (Paris: Caietele Inorogului, 1968), pp. 114–124. An interesting comparison between certain psychoanalytical procedures and the police methods used in totalitarian countries is broached by Michael Polanyi in *Personal Knowledge: Towards a Post-Critical Philosophy* (Chicago: The University of Chicago Press, 1958). A modern dictatorship "creates a situation in which any dissenter must in fact become its mortal enemy, and this justifies unlimited suspicion. When all open dissent is eliminated, disaffection can manifest itself only in trifles, and hence the secret police must be allowed to construe trifles as potential conspiratorial acts. The presuppositions of such investigations become analogous to those governing the Freudian analysis of a neurotic. On the assumption of an Oedipus

complex, the patient's every word and action, whether uttered or unspoken, done or undone (and events in which he became involved by accident), can be interpreted as expressing his hidden hostility to his father. Similarly, once you assume that any trifles may be interpreted as a sign of disaffection which, in its turn, may be construed into an act of high treason, the method of fact-finding practised in Stalin's prisons will appear to have been altogether appropriate to the purpose" (p. 241).

Mircea Eliade

"Good-bye!"

If I should decide some day to write a play, this is how I'd do it:

An actor appears from behind the curtain and, approaching the foot of the stage, shouts: "Good-bye!" He turns slowly, looking around the hall as if searching for someone, and shouts a second time, "Good-bye!" Then, after a long, unbearable pause, he adds, "This was all I had to say, 'Good-bye!' " Skillfully, with emotion (because he is an actor), he raises his arms in the air or makes another gesture of farewell, and discreetly, but sadly (leaving us to understand that there is no other solution), he departs slowly and disappears behind the curtain.

Of course, the public will not understand. They will think this is part of the play, and they will wait to see what will happen next. Some will turn around toward the back of the theater and will begin to talk among themselves, waiting. In vain. The curtain will not be raised. But they will begin to hear noises on stage, behind the curtain, and soon they will hear voices: a woman's cry, then other voices, as if several men were reciting together the same text consisting of short, somewhat threatening propositions. At the rear of the theater the spectators, the majority of them students, will begin to laugh. Some will rise to their feet, hoping in this way to be able to see what is happening. But the others will protest and will shout: "Sit down, sit down!" And then, all at once, the people on the front row will start to applaud, and after them, the whole audience—volleys of applause, cheers; and the students will stamp their feet rhythmically.

Then, from a corner which I have not yet specified, someone, a middle-aged man with a pale, melancholy face, will step toward the stage. The applause will cease for a moment, then will commence anew, like a storm, until the man will raise his arms above him and, before a full silence has come, he will begin. (For that reason, his first words will not be heard. The spectators will ask one another, "What did he say? What did he say?")

"In the name of the director and also in the name of my colleagues, please, I beg you, be quiet. It's very hard to explain why—and whether or not you believe me, I tried to get out of it. 'Send someone else, Mr. Director,' I said—I implored him, even. 'Choose someone who knows how to speak directly: Darius, for instance, or Melania. You know,' I said to the director, 'you know me very well. You know I'm not good at anything except indirect discourse. Ask me to explain why now, at the beginning of autumn, the sun moves toward the south, and I'll find ten, a hundred, a thousand sundry and seductive allusions and images and allegories. But why, *me, of all people, now, when we haven't yet gotten past the first scene?'* "

"Louder! Speak louder!" someone shouted from the back of the theater.

"It's going to be difficult, because of my monologue . . . I can tell you, because of my monologue in Act II, I refused an engagement in the provinces, in a very prestigious role."

"Louder!" they shouted again.

"I said, it's going to be hard, because the monologue I'm going to speak must be uttered almost in *sotto voce*. I'll creep in among the barrels, and I'll speak a monologue—but you won't hear it. And you won't be able to see anything worth seeing, because there'll be a curtain between us."

"Speak louder, sir!" shouted a woman, rising to her feet (an elderly woman).

A few people broke into laughter, while others applauded. But a "Sssh!" was heard again sharply, and an unnatural silence fell upon the auditorium. It was broken, however, a few moments later by a loud voice coming from behind the curtain. It seemed to be commanding someone, because cheers were heard from a distance, but there was also the sound of sobbing very close to the curtain. Undoubtedly it was the crying of a woman. The actor turned his head in surprise.

"How time passes here with you!" he exclaimed. "It seems to fly! We've reached Scene III already—perhaps the most mysterious one. At any rate, it's the most tragic. Believe me, it's hard to explain—very hard. How shall I begin? I know what the director would want. He'd want me to say, politely but with much sympathy, that we began the show at 8:30, as we agreed, and that you should be understanding, please, and not make too much noise. It's true, this curtain is old: and so it's hard and it deadens the sound. But if you laugh too loudly or applaud or stamp on the floor, they'll hear it behind the curtain. And there are scenes of great subtlety, monologues uttered almost in a whisper, and imperceptible dialogues. Why is it we answered immediately when a stranger, or someone very far off addressed us? We answer when we think it proper. We have time. I repeat: apparently, the show must close at 11:35, but actually, *we have time*. We're in no hurry."

It was certain that he wanted to smile, but he changed his mind and passed his hand over his lips and stroked his chin. Just then the curtain rustled a moment from one end to the other, as if blown by the wind, and a muffled noise, impossible to identify, was heard.

"Someone has fallen!" exclaimed a young man in the first row, and he started to get to his feet.

"You see, this is just what I meant," the actor continued. "We don't understand each other. At first I thought that the fault was the curtain, that the curtain separates us, that by virtue of the simple fact that you make up the public while we are the actors, a gulf is fixed between us. But that isn't the case. Whatever one may say, on both sides of the curtain, we're all human beings. *But it's because of Time. We* have time, *we* don't hurry—and so, all that we say *among ourselves*, is simply . . ."

He hesitated again, and put his hand to his chin.

"As a matter of fact, it's not so simple," he added. "But we don't understand each other. You can't understand us, although, apparently, we speak the same language. Who among you didn't understand that simple, pathetic, if not even tragic word, 'Good-bye'? And yet, a little while ago when my fellow actor explained to you that *this was all*, that *this was all we have to say*, you burst out laughing, you began to applaud, you stamped your feet. But, once more, on behalf of the director and the actors, I beg of you: be quiet. Or, if you don't have the patience to wait till the end of the performance at 11:35, you may leave, you may go back to your homes. I'm sure you have many other things to do!"

He bowed, as though he were about to withdraw. But suddenly the spectators on the front row stood up. One of them began to shout, "We are not an ordinary audience!" He had a very serious voice and he seemed excited, but his words were scarcely heard. His neighbors on the front row, however, supported him.

"We aren't an ordinary audience!" they repeated. "We've studied, we've prepared ourselves."

"All summer long," continued the others, "we read difficult books."

"We've been studying," their neighbors added. "We're well prepared."

"*Prepared to understand!*" the man with the serious voice burst out again. "We waited for autumn—*we waited for autumn . . .*" he repeated in a choked voice, but he was not able to go on.

"Now summer's passed," his neighbor began.

"But we're not sorry," continued the others. "We said, 'It's nothing! It's nothing! In the fall the theater will open again.' "

"The theater!" cried several students enthusiastically, suddenly rising to their feet. "*Life, ideas, imagination!*"

When we read the title on the first billboard, *we understood!*" a young woman declared with fervor.

"We understood!" many more repeated, standing up.

The actor listened sympathetically, but with his mind on other things, shaking his head from time to time. He lifted both arms, and even before they had become silent, he began:

"This is exactly as I had forseen. I said to the director, 'Scene V! We have to prepare for Scene V because they'll be prepared too. They've had the whole summer to get ready. Perhaps they will have learned Sanskrit. At any rate, they've studied anthropology, myths, structures. Especially at the premiere, we'll have a learned audience, probably with a lot of students. We'll have to raise the curtain!' "

It had become so quiet again in the theater that the last words were heard almost in their entirety. "Now it will really begin," someone whispered. "This is the beginning." (Of course not everyone had heard. "What does he mean?" a young woman asked in a whisper, but insistently. "It's a difficult text," her companion explained. "A poetic text, full of enigmatic allusions.")

The actor remained in the center of the stage with a lost look, as though he wondered what he were doing there.

"*For God's sake!*" they heard clearly from back of the curtain.

Almost no one dared to breathe. Slowly, and seemingly reluctantly, the actor began to finger the curtain. He found the edge he was looking for and began to draw the curtain after him.

"Scene V," he resumed. "From a certain point of view."

But no one was listening any more. Although the curtain had been pulled back less than half-way, the essential was there: a beautiful young woman, with her hair falling to her shoulders, holding her hands behind her back—and everyone very quickly understood that she was holding them thay way because they were tied behind her back. In front of her a man past middle-age was standing, frowning, with his eyes fixed on the ground. But no sooner had the spectators begun to see—to understand that he was frowning, that he did not dare lift his eyes—than the old man disappeared. He took only a few steps and disappeared behind the curtain. The girl seemed to have awakened from a dream. She looked around her, and little by little her face lighted up. "Is she smiling?" some asked themselves. But before it was possible to reply, the curtain, which the actor was holding up with a great effort, fell down suddenly, and the whole audience sighed in disappointment.

"Please, don't applaud," the actor began, approaching the foot of the stage, "because Scene V is not yet finished. As I told you, and as the director said . . ."

"Louder!" several students in the rear called out.

The actor raised his hands in exasperation. "Quiet, please, please!" he whispered. "Be willing to make this sacrifice. It won't last long, but for us it's a scene of major importance. Think about your childhood. Remember the friends you've lost."

At that moment a prolonged howl broke out behind the curtain. The actor turned his head, obviously moved. Several voices were heard, then were drowned out again in the shouting. But all at once, unexpectedly, the spectators lost patience and began to clap and stamp their feet. In vain did the actor implore them to stop, with both arms raised in the air. The students let themselves go. Then, from behind the curtain, the girl emerged, obviously angry.

"What's going on here?" she asked in a voice that was harsh and unexpectedly coarse, almost vulgar. "Perhaps you've forgotten you're at the theater. If you don't understand, all you have to do is to leave quietly. Go on home, and the price of your ticket will be refunded."

"But we *do* understand," a young man spoke up, calmly, and yet defensively. "Up to now we've understood very well. It's the mystery of the Father. But we want to see what happens next. Why have you dropped the curtain?"

The girl gave him a deep, intense look, as if she did not understand him. "Who has lowered the curtain?" she asked.

"Your colleague," the young man replied, all at once intimidated.

"I don't understand what you mean," the girl continued. "We take no notice of the curtain. Moreover, this is the great innovation of the play: we perform as if a curtain didn't exist. The author has kept the divisions of scenes and acts, but he has left out the curtain. And it's clear why he resorted to this procedure: it's closer to reality, to life. Life knows its scenes, and it can be said to be divided into acts, but the curtain falls only a single time. If you don't understand at least that much . . ."

She shrugged her shoulders and added nothing more.

"And yet," the young man began again, taking courage, "yet, *someone has lowered the curtain*. A little while ago. The curtain right behind you. And no one could have lowered it except the one who raised it, namely, your colleague!" He pointed to him with his finger.

"He's right!" many people burst out. "We saw it too! We saw when he let go of it."

The girl turned toward the actor and looked at him questioningly, in exasperation.

"I told them," he began, with a great sadness in his voice. "I told them they didn't understand. All their preparation in the summer, all their study—for nothing! *No matter what I do, they don't understand!*"

"Or maybe they *do* understand," the girl murmured, "but they've got it backward."

"Louder! For God's sake, speak louder!" the students shouted.

The girl shook the locks from her shoulders, clasped her hands behind her back, and taking a step toward the foot of the stage, began: "Like my fellow actor, I also tried to back out of this job. 'I'm no good at that sort of thing, Mr. Director,' I said. 'You want me to explain— but *how can I explain to them?* If you'd let me dance, it would be easy.' But I know," she added, lowering her voice, "that the author doesn't want this. He says he's a professor, and he's afraid it would be misunderstood."

"Louder, Miss!" several shouted.

"Finally," the girl resumed, "I beseeched him, I implored him: 'Pick someone else, Mr. Director. Pick a man—if possible, a man with deep religious sentiments: Darius, for instance. Someone they'll listen to, *someone they'll hear!*'" she shouted as loudly as she could.

"That's the way! That's the way!" the students from the back of the hall encouraged her.

"*Pick the Son of God, begotten, not made!*" she shouted with all her might. But she put her hand to her forehead quickly, and then, very pale, she looked all around. "I beg your pardon," she whispered. "I shouldn't have said that. That was from Scene XI."

"Yes and no," someone corrected her. "First it was in the Nicene Creed."

"What's he saying? What's he saying?" many voices asked.

" 'I believe in one God,' etc., '*begotten, not made,*' " the man in the front row repeated (a youngish man, intelligent, erudite, good-humored).

"So, what difference does it make?" someone asked.

"It makes a difference because the young lady claims it's from Scene XI. But if that's so, it's plagiarism."

"Perhaps it's a quotation."

"It depends on the context," said a student.

"And it depends, especially on how it's spoken," his neighbor added.

"Tell us how it's spoken," the students shouted.

The girl put her hands to her temples again. The audience could clearly see she was upset. Perhaps for that reason they suddenly became quiet.

"It's very hard to explain," she began, trying to smile, "to tell you how I speak it. Because, to begin with, you have to know my mood. But in order to understand my mood, you have to know my past, my social origins, the problems which have molded me from tender childhood. Because, ever since childhood I've felt an attraction for everything I didn't understand. Until one day—yes, I remember it very well; it wasn't long ago, a summer day—in fact, a day last summer. I was going down the street and I saw an announcement for a play, '*Goodbye!*' I was deeply moved. I understood. Someone, whom I did not know, but for whom I was waiting, whom I loved already, perhaps without realizing it, someone who could play a decisive role in my life, who could make me happy . . . Oh! I express myself badly. It wasn't a matter of happiness, of what *we* call happiness; it was something more noble and much more profound. In short, that someone whom I still had not begun to know, although I was waiting for him and maybe even searching for him, that man spoke to me—*to me*, a stranger who had stopped in front of the playbill with eyes full of tears (because the title was printed in huge letters which made you ill, which smothered you to look at them)—he said to me: 'Good-bye!' I understood, and I began to cry, right there, in front of the advertisement. I understood that there was no longer any hope, that I should never meet him, because he has taken leave of us. He had just enough time to say to us—to say to me, above all to *me*—to say, 'Good-bye!'

"I was crying in front of the billboard when a man approached me. I recognized him immediately: it was the director. He asked me if I would play the role of Melania. He pointed it out to me on the billboard. Melania was indeed playing, because he had called her that: Melania. I hesitated. 'I know what you're thinking,' the director said to me, 'but I don't mean an understudy. I'm proposing the role of Melania to you. It's a difficult role, but full of surprises.' I still hesitated. 'I'm a dancer,' I said. 'I express myself through the dance.' He looked at me in surprise, and, as I thought, disappointment. 'Then it will be hard,' he added. 'It will be hard because of the professor.' But, of course, I didn't understand. And now that I stop to think of it, I wonder who did know. *Did* you know, tell me honestly, *did* you know?"

It became suddenly quiet in the theater. But the silence was heavy, embarrassed—almost guilty.

At length a timid voice spoke up. "What should we have known?"

"Why it will be hard because of the professor."

"We didn't know," a great many admitted (but almost no one dared to look up).

"Of course! Outside of the director, no one knew."

"But the director, how did he know?" asked a man in the front row.

The girl looked at him in amazement. "Everyone knows that the director's great passion is the History of Religions."

Again, a silence fell upon the hall: this time a serious, thoughtful silence.

"Not the whole history of religions," Melania went on, "but the essential parts of it: India, for instance, and Tibet and Japan. Didn't you realize it when you saw how he interpreted Scene V: not as a symbol, as the author intended, but as an immediate reality, *hic et nunc*, as Mahāyāna, for example, understands it, when it affirms that *nirvāna* and *samsāra* are identical."

"I didn't see anything!" shouted an older woman, suddenly rising to her feet. "Nothing! Absolutely nothing! And I've even studied Mahāyāna, and I can tell when it's *nirvāna* and when it's not *nirvāna!*"

"We've studied it too!" shouted many more students. "We've studied it in the original!"

"Where's the director?" the woman demanded. "Let the director come and talk with us. You think we're too ignorant!"

"The director?" asked someone from the back of the hall. "I'm the director this evening." He headed toward the stage, taking his time.

"But what can I explain? And above all *when?*" he added, looking at his watch (a silver chronometer). "The intermission is over. In three or four minutes we begin Act II, and right after that I shall ask you to become quiet again. Act II is pre-eminently an internal act, if you understand what I mean."

"We understand," a good many voices replied. . . .

"Long, oppressive silences, broken by monlogues. Some of the monologues are truly sublime, but what's the use if no one hears them? In *sotto voce?*—To say the least! In fact, they're more like meditations. And, as the author has called to my attention, even some of the most famous hermits fall asleep during their meditation time. And then they don't know anything. I mean, they no longer know what's happening to them: do they return to non-being, become lost in the unconscious, meet face to face with God?"

He leaned against the front of the stage as he was uttering these questions, looking at first one, then another corner of the theater, as if waiting for a reply. But no one dared to answer.

"In a certain sense," the director resumed, "the mystery is impenetrable. But, do you realize what this means for a stage director? How to *show* the silences—long, arid silences which run through the History of Religions, which, in fact, make up in large measure the History of Religions—as well as History in general."

"Silences? Pure and simple silences?" someone asked.

"When nothing of importance is said," the director continued. "When men lived as they understood their first ancestors had lived, hundreds and thousands of years before; times when neither a god nor an idea was invented, and everything was repeated, and when *silence, especially, was repeated*. How to present a *sterile silence*, when no one says anything new, because no one feels the need of it, or he hasn't time to say anything new, significant, or fertile? In the manuscript which he gave me recently, the professor suggested this setting: barrels and a gallows."

"Barrels and what else?" asked a young person.

"Barrels and a *gal-lows*. But it seemed too *direct* to me, and at the same time too *symbolic*, if you understand what I mean."

"We understand," was heard from all over the hall suddenly.

"That is, for centuries, or even for millennia, nothing happened in the world of the spirit, nothing was *created*, but History went on. People drank and made merry in order to forget, while the masters hanged people in order to remain masters. It's too oppressive an image. Of course, the terror of History is one of the professor's obsessions. If you've read *The Myth of the Eternal Return* you'll remember that . . ."

"Barrels," several repeated, brooding. "Barrels for wine . . ."

"More annoying is the fact that the professor is continually changing the order of the scenes. For instance, what was Scene III the day before yesterday, today has become Scene V—a Scene in which, according to the author's notations, you also participated. Of course, I understand his point of view too: he's a professor, and as such he keeps abreast of the latest discoveries and publications, because, as he openly admits, he doesn't want to play false with historical truth."

"And, in spite of all that," the older woman burst out again, "what he calls Mahāyāna is *not* Mahāyāna!"

The director looked at her in amazement. "But how do you know what he says about Mahāyāna?"

"From what you showed us just a few minutes ago, when the woman stood with her hands tied behind her back, while an old man . . . But, you all remember," she added, addressing herself directly to the audience.

"We remember very well!" was heard from innumerable voices all over the hall.

"It's true that this isn't Mahāyāna," the director admitted. "Scene V, formerly Scene III, presents the existential condition of post-Vedic India, therefore at least a thousand years before Mahāyāna, but no less exemplary. I thought it was very clear."

"The mystery of the Father!" shouted the young man. (It could easily be seen by his voice and his whole manner that he was an intellectual.)

"I should say, rather, that it is the mystery of the discovery of the Spirit, of Being; the mystery of the discovery of *Ātman*. The angry man with his gaze fixed on the ground, represents the *old world*, in our case, Vedic polytheism, the ideology and practice of the sacrifice, etc. He's angry because he feels that History has taken him out of circulation. And you saw him: he disappeared after a few moments—after exactly five seconds, corresponding to the five centuries which separate the last Vedic creation from the first *Upanishad*."

The audience listened, enthralled. "The *Upanishads!*" was heard from all sides at once. "We've read *them!* How sublime!"

"The girl with her hands tied behind her back, Melania, represents the Spirit, more specifically *Ātman*, the Spirit which seems to be awakening from a dream. One should realize that she only *seems* to be bound. When she is fully awake, Melania—that is, the spirit, *Ātman*, can never be 'bound,' that is, enslaved, by matter."

"But what about Mahāyāna?" the woman asked, with a trace of regret in her voice. "When does Mahāyāna begin?"

The director consulted his watch again. He closed his eyes momentarily, as if he were making rapid calculations in his mind. "It depends upon the temporal perspective in which we are situated," he replied. "For us—I mean, the actors who are participating in the mystery—Mahāyāna took place exactly a minute and a half ago. For you, the public, Mahāyāna could happen at any time whatsoever, depending on the personal perspective of each one of you."

"Then, we can hope?" asked the woman.

"I believe so," the director said encouragingly.

(But many smiled skeptically. It seemed to them that the director had not spoken with complete conviction.)

"Actually, if I have understood correctly . . ." someone began.

But the director signaled with his hand as though he wanted to add something else. Actually, in the succeeding moment, they began to hear the cheering again, this time more subdued and farther off. The director listened, straining his ears to hear and slowly nodding his head. Soon the echo of the cheers died away, and the director looked at his watch with considerable satisfaction.

"And that was an interesting scene," he began, "although an extremely hard one to perform. Because the text calls for interior monologues, therefore, meditations; and *at the same time* cheering. To be sure, this time the howling is more moderate, and the exact time must not exceed eight seconds. I hasten to add that this time it's not a matter of centuries. The seconds don't represent centuries, but historic personages. But here the great difficulty begins, because since the text is extremely obscure, you can never be sure which historic personage is meant. You understand, I presume, that I'm referring to the iconoclastic and anti-iconoclastic struggle and at the same time to the irruption of Islam into history."

"Basically, if I have understood correctly," someone spoke up, "we have to do with a play inspired by the History of Religions."

"Not inspired," the director interrupted him, ambling back toward the middle of the theater. "One might say that just underscoring the title, 'Good-bye!' sums up and at the same time explains the whole History of Religions. Besides, it is just what we should have expected, since the author—perhaps it is well that I remind some of you—is an historian of religions. And what can a writer write about, except *what he knows,* or more precisely, *what he is,* his vocation or his profession. A poet writes poetry, a philosopher writes about philosophy. What will a professor of History of Religions write about, especially when he has decided to write for the theater?"

"If I understand correctly," said someone on the first row, "this is something r v, something which hasn't been tried before."

"It hasn't been tried from the perspective in which the author is situated," the director corrected him. "As you've been able to see already, the author disregards the curtain. It's easy to see why he disregards it. In his view—the view which is a result of his studies in the History of Religions—the curtain can fall but a *single time.*"

"When we die," someone murmured, perhaps mostly to himself. But the director heard him, and shook his head in disappointment.

"Oh, no, no, no!" he exclaimed. "Then we don't understand each other. We don't understand each other at all!"

At once the crowd began to murmur.

"What happens to us, to human beings," the director went on, "can't constitute the subject of a play in which the whole History of Religions is condensed, even distilled. As one of you put it so well a little while ago, we have to do with something new, with something which hasn't been tried before. Naturally, owing to the mode of being of this novelty, you're not able to grasp it. Do you understand what I mean?"

The great majority shook their heads, some with considerable seriousness.

"By refusing to make use of the curtain, the author *presupposes* it and at the same time ignores it." The director looked all around the theater, encouraging inquires. But no one dared to interrupt his explanation by posing questions.

"In other words," he continued, "the curtain is and it is not; or, more precisely, it *exists* and at the same time it does *not exist.* By the very fact that it exists for you, the spectators, it ceases to exist for us, the actors. Do you understand?"

"I don't understand!" the older woman called out, rising to her feet again. "And I don't understand why you're stalling so much; why don't you show us Mahāyāna?"

The director frowned. "I told you. It depends on your personal preparation."

"But I *am* prepared!" the lady exclaimed. "And I believe there are others, too, like myself," she added, speaking to the audience.

"Of course we're prepared!" shouted quite a few voices.

"I get the impression that you think we're a bunch of ignoramuses!" the lady continued. "You're afraid the text is too difficult for us, and for that reason you don't raise the curtain. You think that only you, the 'initiates,' the actors, are in a position to understand the play."

The last words were drowned out by a chorus of loud cries. They were so close that the curtain began to quiver. The director frowned and looked at his watch. Many of the audience rose to their feet, hoping, probably, to see something. "Curtain! Curtain!" the students began to shout.

But before the tumult grew any louder, an actor appeared running from left stage. He was dressed curiously, without taste, because on top of his period costume which he had only partially begun to take off, he had put on, surely in great haste, some old pajamas. But he was still wearing make-up, and the spectators recognized him easily: he was Darius.

"On behalf of the director, but also on behalf of us, the actors," he began, "I beg you, I implore you, be quiet! We're nearing the end of Act II, possibly the most important part for many of us, especially for the young people. If you only knew what sacrifices we made when we decided to play 'Good-bye!'—Especially the youngest of us. What haven't we given up!—to the critics, to the public. We have the right to ask at least this much of you: be quiet! We don't have much time . . ."

"Eleven minutes," the director specified from the middle of the theater.

"For you, that isn't very much," Darius continued. "How many times do you not waste eleven minutes? But for us, these minutes are decisive, essential ones. Actually, this is what we live for—we actors, especially the younger actors—to be able to play, once or twice in a lifetime, such a play as this."

A part of the audience listened sympathetically, but a few remained unconvinced.

"Raise the curtain!" the man in the front row demanded.

"Raise it at least half-way!" several cried.

Melania and the first actor hurried to Darius' side, and together they began to make signs to the audience with their hands. Probably the majority of the spectators did not understand, and the theater became silent again.

"It can't be!" the actors began, speaking sometimes together, sometimes by turns. "It can't be, because it's contrary to historic truth. For you, the spectators, the curtain *was lowered before you came;* it was lowered this afternoon at 4:30. Because *this* is the historic truth. You're living in the twentieth century, in 1964 to be exact, and *you cannot go back in Time. We* can, because we are actors; that is, we participate in the mystery; we're reliving, in condensed form, the entire history of religions."

"We can do the same thing too!" many shouted.

"It only seems to you that you can do it! It's an illusion. When you try to live in the Middle Ages, you try to do it in a *real* way, that is, in the historically concrete, not as we actors do, who are play-acting; because, precisely for the reason that we are actors, we are liberated from our historical context. But you can't be liberated, because you don't know how—or perhaps you don't wish—to play. You are responsible persons; that is, you assume your historic moment in full consciousness. You can live *only* in 1964."

"So, what does that matter? What does that matter?" voices began to be heard on all sides.

The three looked at one another, hesitating. "How can we explain it to them, Mr. Director?" Darius asked. "Where do we begin and how do we explain it? If there were more of us, maybe they'd understand."

"You have only six minutes left," the director warned. "You'll have to hurry."

The three took courage. From behind the curtain there began to emerge small groups of actors, actresses, and extras, dressed in all sorts of costumes, some of them rather eccentric. (For example, they had old-style helmets, but also carried pistols.) Melania looked at them warmly.

"You heard them," she began, pointing with her arm. "All summer we practiced crying out in unison. And after each repetition, all eyes were in tears. Each voice represents something: an era, a symbol, a prophet. Never have cries been heard that were more meaningful, more laden with messages, and yet so perfectly timed. Don't judge on the basis of what you heard tonight in this hall. The cries, like the interior monologues, are addressed to us, the actors."

"All right, I understand that," the man on the front row interrupted. "But why did you lower the curtain at 4:30?"

"Because *this corresponds to the historic truth,*" shouted Melania, no longer smiling to hide her exasperation. "As we've told you so many times, 'Good-bye!' is an historical play: that is, it recapitulates the entire History of Religions."

"Think of Nietzsche!" shouted the director from the middle of the hall. "When did he first proclaim the death of God? About 1880 or '82. Figure it out."

"And this means . . .?" asked a distinguished young lady, rising to her feet.

" 'This means,' " the director continued, "that for you, who participate in the modern elite society of the West, God died more than eighty years ago. In the author's conception, the curtain fell a single time—you understand when. Not when a man dies, because men don't constitute the subject of the History of Religions. But when God died— or *a* god, however you want to take it. At any rate, as far as your God is concerned, his death was already proclaimed—and therefore the curtain was lowered—*before* you entered the theater."

The lady remained on her feet, undecided, somewhat confused. "Then why didn't you tell us?" she asked.

"But you *were* reminded, very well," Melania said in a low voice. However, almost no one heard her, and the students began shouting again.

"Louder, Miss, louder!"

The director looked at his watch and his face suddenly brightened. "We're in the intermission," he said to Melania. "You may speak as loudly as you wish."

A few moments later several actors appeared from behind the curtain. One of them who looked very tired, almost exhausted, approached the front of the stage.

"*I* told you," he began. "I came out here, in front of you, and I cried, 'Good-bye!' I even shouted it three times."

"But why! Why?" the man in the front row asked at once, obviously irritated.

"You have to realize that this is the only detail which doesn't correspond with historic truth," the director interjected. "Because we have absolutely no evidence that before he died, God bade farewell to mankind. Not one among all those who proclaimed and demonstrated the death of God claimed that he had heard him say, 'Good-bye!' Actually, this constitutes part of the fate of Western civilization, that whether he died a natural death, or whether we killed him, he didn't say anything to us when he died—not even a single word. As if we, his creatures, didn't exist! And perhaps this explains the resentment and bitterness of modern Western man. Because, as anyone would agree, it's sad that someone in whom you've believed, to whom you've prayed, *on whom you've relied*, dies without saying so much as a word to you. Even if Nietzsche's explanation is correct, even if we mortal men have killed God, it's sad nevertheless that he didn't say anything before departing from us."

"That's very true," was heard from all sides.

"But the author is of another opinion," the director began again. "He believes that certain people, undoubtedly children, and also a few women, heard him when he whispered 'Good-bye.' And with that word, the History of Religions was closed, at least for us in the Western world. So, 'Good-bye!' became the title of the play. The play in which, I repeat, the whole History of Religions is recapitulated."

"But what about the cheers, the interior monologues, the barrels?" asked the young man who had spoken about the mystery of the Father.

"Ah!" said the director, shrugging his shoulders. "This is something else again. These things happened long ago, and therefore those of us who are actors can play them, because we're *acting*, and so we let ourselves really believe, really pray, really curse."

"But what about Mahāyāna?" asked the older lady.

"I told you! It depends on your personal preparation. But this has nothing to do with the death of God as a well-documented historical fact. And it has nothing to do with the mystery of his disappearance without telling us farewell—or, if we accept the hypotheses of the author, leaving with a 'Good-bye' to just a few women and children."

"But why *three times?*" a woman asked. "Why did he say 'Good-bye' three times?"

"Why three times?" the director repeated, puzzled. "Why three times? I never thought of that before."

"And yet it seems to be important," the woman went on.

"It's a symbolic number," someone said. "Consequently, it's quite important."

"Probably the symbol 'three' is the key to the whole play!"

"At any rate, it's *one* key."

"It's strange I hadn't thought about it before," the director admitted. "Have any of you thought about it?" the director inquired speaking to the actors and extras.

They all shook their heads; they seemed equally puzzled.

"And yet it *is* important, even very important," several students repeated.

"The whole theological mystery of the Trinity is reducible to this: to the symbolic, theological, and sacramental meaning of the number three."

"Now that you've brought it up," the director said, "I realize that it's quite important. But I've never thought about it. Let's ask the author himself," he added, turning to me all of a sudden.

For several minutes I had been expecting this, and I had crouched down in my seat. If I had suspected it would go this far, I should have left ten minutes before, as soon as they had begun to discuss the death of God. (It would have been thought that I was leaving the hall as a sign of protest.)

"Why three times, Mr. Professor?" the director asked me with a smile. It was obvious that he was curious, that he was seriously interested in the problem.

"Ah," I began, confusedly. "It's hard to say . . ."

"Louder!" the people cried out from many parts of the hall suddenly.

"It would be better if you stood up," the director suggested. "And you may speak as long as you want. We have plenty of time; we're in the intermission."

I heard as in a dream: "What's he saying? What's he saying?"

"It's hard for me to say," I repeated, rising to my feet and looking perplexedly at the actors gathered in front of the curtain. (Fortunately, I knew them all.)

"Of course it's hard," the man in the front row interrupted me. He too got to his feet. "It's hard because it's symbolic. But in the case of a specialist like you . . ."

"Of course," I began again, "it is symbolic. But this time, what can I say? This time, I admit, I haven't set out from a precise idea—from a precise symbol, I mean. I thought like this, *in general*—I thought that if I, for instance, wanted to bid farewell to someone, I'd repeat the word several times. 'Good-bye!' I'd say. 'Good-bye!' "

I stopped speaking and tried to smile.

"But this time you said 'Good-bye!' only twice," someone near me observed.

"Only twice?" I exclaimed in surprise. "Then I made a mistake. If I wanted to bid farewell to someone, I'd repeat 'Good-bye!' at least three times."

"But that's not the way the problem is put," the man on the front row interrupted. "We weren't discussing what *you* do, but what God did—or the representative of God—in your play. Why does he say 'Good-bye!' three times?"

"It's certainly symbolic," I heard on all sides.

"Yes, we know that. But what does it symbolize? How should we interpret it?"

I sought desparately for an interpretation. But I couldn't keep from listening to the whispers around me.

"It's the most interesting part, and he doesn't even know what it symbolizes."

"In fact, it's the only thing that's original."

"But if he doesn't understand it himself . . .?"

"How should we interpret it?" I heard from the group of students in the rear, who had by now gotten to their feet.

I approached the director. "I know now why I didn't want to write for the theater," I whispered to him. "I'm bashful. I don't know how to speak in public. The public intimidates me. Especially the learned public, the public of today. They know so many things, they've studied, they've reflected. Symbols, deep meanings . . . I know why I didn't want to write this play."

The director looked at me and smiled. "If you don't want to, don't write it."

I breathed more easily. "Then I won't write it," I said.

He continued to smile, but I could tell he was disappointed.

Notes

Good-bye! was first published as "Adio!" in Mircea Eliade, *Nuvele* (Madrid: Colecţia Destin, 1963); also in Mircea Eliade, *La ţigănci şi alte povestiri* (Bucureşti: Editura Pentru Literature, 1969), and in *idem.*, *In curte la Dionis* (Bucureşti, Cartea românească, 1981).

Part IV

Oceanographic Fragments

The starting point for (the) post-philosophic tradition of philosophizing is the awareness that the traditional forms of philosophic discourse have been broken. What remain as leading possibilities are mutilated, incomplete discourse (the aphorism, the note or jotting) or discourse that has risked metamorphosis into other forms (the parable, the poem, the philosophical tale, the critical exegesis).

Susan Sontag
"Introduction" from
E. M. Cioran's *The Temptation to Exist*

About Miracle and Event (from *Oceanografie*)

Those who contest the existence of miracle forget that miracle has a history and a phenomenology of its own. In antiquity, miracle was *contrast*. Modern miracle, on the contrary, is *contact:* the simple conjunction of acts not immediately opposite to each other, which are dramatic and revelatory. Miracle—that is, *event*—is the coming together of things which might have remained isolated from each other.

Consider the essence of the everyday miracle, and you will be able to understand the possibility of a new apologetic, of a new demonstration of the existence of God.

No one can prove that God, or the gods, do not intervene daily in our lives. It is possible, even probable, that God shows himself to us *continually*. But how shall we see him, how shall we *recognize* him? God is not obliged to take a form *we* have accorded him.

People say, "Mystery no longer exists!" because mystery does not reveal itself in the form we are expecting. "Where are the angels?" they ask. But the angels are *not* as we have imagined them. Perhaps they intervene constantly in our lives, but we are expecting to see them in the form our parents imagined them, or else *contrarywise*, that is, at the other extreme. But angels, like all other divine, heavenly beings, have no obligations toward our way of conceiving them, nor toward our skeptical demonstrations nor our enthusiastic apologetics. They are as they are. We give to miracle—that is, to the intervention of the divine into history—a value of pure mystery. But the true agents of miracle are under no obligation whatsoever to accept this valorization.

If our conception of mystery does not coincide with the true substance of mystery, so much the worse for us! No logic in the world can compel the divine to assume the forms and act in the ways we have proposed for it. All demonstrations against the existence of God, against angels (that is, against a celestial hierarchy), and against miracles, are absurd and ridiculous. All these demonstrations start from a false premise: the absence of God from the world, the absence of miracle from history. But this is utterly ridiculous. What absence is meant? The absence of God from the place where *we have expected him*, the absence of miracle *as we have imagined it*. To put it bluntly, that's something else entirely.

Christianity, in making Christ the Son of Man, has raised miracle and charity in humanity to a higher level than before, when the gods were something *other* than men. (That is why one could say—very logicially, very scientifically—that from Christ onward the entire substance of history has been changed.) Now, since Christ is *also* man, miracles are performed under human guise every day. Before Christ, miracle could be thaumaturgical, exceptional, dramatic. Since then it is human—that is, unrecognizable.

Miracle has this single difference from an ordinary deed (that is, from an explainable deed, one produced by natural, biological, or historical forces)—it cannot be *different*. However paradoxical this definition may seem, it is nevertheless very simple. (Think it over and you'll understand it.) The unrecognizable is the perfect form of the divine revelation, because divinity is no longer *manifest*, it is no longer realized through contrast, but it acts directly in humanity through contact, through a coming together.

Event, in the sense of the word proposed at the beginning of these notes, acquires now another value. (Event is taken here neither in the sense of something fatal and predestined, but simply as "deed," something that has happened, that is, something realized.) If miracle is something unrecognizable, an act *to all appearances* ordinary, then all ordinary acts acquire a maximal importance, because in any of them there might be an irrational, divine intervention. The event could then become the "guide" of our existence.

But there is something else of even greater importance. An event signifies a real thing, a thing realized, and our orientation toward events signifies a *realistic* orientation. Thus we have still another paradox of the Christian miracle (that is, of the phenomenology of the miracle after the intervention of Christ in history): the return of realism, to common sense, to the everyday. It is an anti-mystical conception of miracle, because it delimits very strictly the religious experience, that is, experience on the exceptional paths of the miraculous.

God no longer makes himself known only by the path of mystical experience—a grave, obscure path, beset with temptations and obstacles—but he makes himself known above all by the way of unrecognizability. That is to say, as he must and as he has always done. Everyday knowledge of God (in distinction from the other degrees of divine knowledge which are clearer: contemplation, mysticism, ecstasy) is obscure, *involuntary*, natural. It is no longer cognition properly speaking, but recognition, a very obscure participation in the divine. Miracle leads us without our knowing and without our willing.

Concerning the "Unseen God" and Other Fragments (from *Soliloquies*)

Concerning the "unseen God."

Jesus said that no one has ever seen God. It is not a matter of his invisibility, but of his unrecognizability. God is of such a nature that he cannot be *recognized* anywhere; because he said: "I am what I am." This is the metaphysical meaning. With respect to the metaphysical meaning, he is the God of Israel.

Religions, if they were many, would be the *same;* but because they are *one,* they are different. And the unity of "religions" will finally be seen when each man will have his own mode of approaching God, when the Supreme Being will be revealed to each one directly, without the precedent of tradition or collective experience. Only then will there be a real, collective participation in the Supreme. When each one will have his own mode of approach, the ritual and dogma proper to his religious experience, then the unity of religions will become manifest.

The incarnation of God on earth was not intended only for the regeneration of man and his salvation from sin (original or actual). This is done indirectly anyhow, through inspiration, through prophets, lawmakers, spiritual leaders, and certain meaningful historical events. The incarnation of God has a larger, more courageous objective. God incarnated himself in order to invest us with divinity. He took our form in order to prove to us the real possibility of man's taking his form. Popularly, it is said that the incarnation has for its object the salvation of man—that is, the breaking of man's human, vicious, egotistical limitations and his elevation through grace to a divine state. But what is this, if it is not his deification? Not, of course, a heroic, titanic, luciferic divination—a divination by one's own means, by the exertion of magical pressure on the Deity. Not that kind of divination, but a purely religious one—that is, by imitating *"their"* life, that of those who have come from God to earth. The plural pronoun which I underscored does not indicate that these incarnations are saints or prophets, people who participate to the highest degree in the divine nature through grace and the imitation of Christ. But it means that the One God himself has descended into creation, not once but innumerable times, to show men the way, the techniques, and the secret of becoming divine. Of course, deification by this route is a mystic process, but it is effected not so much through grace as through the religious will of the individual, through his total surrender to the Divine, through the global offering of his life, his intelligence, his will—to God.

Does someone say that I ignore the value of Grace? No, for I believe that Grace is exercised not so much individually, for each man separately, as generically, through the simple fact that God has incarnated himself and will do so again in order to disclose to us the techniques of deification.

Only fools and saints never contradict themselves. The latter participate in the Absolute revealed through Grace and love. The former are "monoideaists," that is, strictly logical, constructive-linear-evolving thinkers. Non-contradiction is acceptable in one kind of folly only: love. Love does not admit of change, that is, contradiction, because it is an absolute revelation—*sui generis*, independent. It is folly because it brings about the qualitative identity of two quantities: a = b; this relation neglects perhaps the whole aggregate of other possible numbers. It remains and exists as such, in a special space, ignoring existences in the space outside. Having revealed itself, it exists even after love, *psychologically* (not metaphysically) has disappeared (due to psychic change, weariness of the flesh). This is a consequence of the imperfection of human love which is incarnated, not embodied. But the fact that love passes is no reason for us to doubt its objective, absolute reality. I have seen Himalaya but a single time, yet I do not now doubt its existence. The "spell" of a symphony—why do we call it a spell (a passing enchantment, a self-delusion) because it passes? The passing of great thrills is proof of our human limitations, not of the pettiness of the thrills. It seems to me that man cannot withstand the force of unmediated revelations. He can live marvelously in a milieu in which everything is mediated, translated. Although he sees everything in the light of the sun, he cannot look at the sun directly.

When a virtue or a truth is lost, it is not always replaced with a vice or a falacy (logical, metaphysical, historical), but with a virtue *functionally* mistaken, with a truth *functionally* wrong. Every illusion has its origin and justification in a misunderstood truth. Every vice is the product of an alteration of perspective of a virtue. But with a *functional* illusion of truth, virtue, etc., it is very difficult to find the origin. For example, the virtue of making a serious judgment on an act is, in modern times, functionally displaced. We are serious when we ought to be making fun of something or passing over it quickly. We are serious about illusory problems: political crises, the decadence of the West, the census of the population, the latest book, contemporary philosophy, etc. Yet we are not serious about essential problems: happiness, hope, amusements, cinematography, etc. Cinematography cultivates the most honorable of man's faculties: fantasy, fantastical activity, adventure, the paradoxical rupture of the everyday, and life in a fairy land. Films ought to be discussed, critiqued, promoted, perfected. We ought not to criticize them aesthetically or "spiritually," but we should amplify their fantastical substance. They are the romances and knightly adventure tales of the modern age. They satisfy the craving for the fantastic, for the creation of Don Quixote-like, ideal worlds— without morals and without heroism, perhaps, but no less fertile in suggestions for the fantastic life.

We ought to be more serious about virtues: charity, for instance. We must not ask for the removal of the wretched or the banishment of beggars. They are the daily judges of Christianity, the unwitting messengers or bearers of mercies.

The idea of progress is the only contact with spirituality which inferior people have—those who partake of an inert, materialistic vision of the world. The idea of progress means, for them, evolution toward a greater good. It is, at any rate, a mental construct with an ethical basis. It is, moreover, the soil which can be fecundated by a spiritual message addressed to man as such. By virtue of the fact that the ordinary man accepts progress, he accepts implicitly any message which appeals to his will as man, to his progressive maturation. The idea of progress, the belief in the possibility and reality of a becoming and a perfecting in history, takes the place, in an inferior man, of the essential human function of salvation. That is why only a man who is preoccupied with salvation is able to dispense with faith in human progress.

There is an annoying confusion which is repeated everywhere, between the *roots* of an idea or thing, a superstition, institution, or attitude, and its *origins*. The cause of this confusion might be the historical spirit and the prejudice of evolution, but I am not interested in its cause.

The roots of an idea, of course, are not on the surface and are not to be seen. In order to uncover them, you meet with resistence. A weed is easily uprooted and a superficial prejudice is easily eradicated. but the mind resists, like an old tree, when you start to uncover the roots of an idea held for years—the idea of individual freedom, for example.

The roots are in organic relations, living, and are as irrevocable as the deed which produced them. The origins, on the contrary, have nothing organic in their relationship with the deed. The origins of a truth may be in a happenstance or a stupidity, but its roots are elsewhere. The origins of religions are grotesque, but the roots of the religious sentiment are in God himself, his presence in the soul of man. The origins of the sciences are in the whim of chance, but its roots are themselves a function of the spirit.

A corresponding confusion exists between *implications* and *causes*. A piano implies physical matter, equilibrium, etc., but it does not create music nor generate the musical spirit. A mathematical discovery implies certain historical conditions, but it is not produced by them. Ideas imply objects, but they do not create them nor are they created by them. Religion implies material actions and earthly sentiments, but it is not produced by them, even in their aggregate.

The confusion is multiplied and continued between *accompaniment* and *implication*. For instance, religion is accompanied in its manifestations by certain morbid phenomena, but these are not necessarily implied in the religious experience, for the simple reason that there are truly religious lives which are not morbid. Likewise, religion is accompanied frequently by ethics, social reform, and asceticism or orgiastic behavior, without, however, *necessarily* implying individual or social morality, asceticism or immorality. A religion—that is, a viable experience of the divine—can just as well be *above* anything human, good or evil, as *in* anything human, whether good or evil.

A matter of capital and urgent importance is the perfection of a method of thinking parallel to the body of material gained by observation, which day by day grows in all branches of knowledge. In history and philology you have the impression that the effort to develop and perfect a method of thought is nonexistent. An increasing number of facts are gathered, and they are expressed from an ever-growing number of points of view, but where is their progress in *thinking?* The gathering of observations concerning nature has led to the prefection of scientific thinking. But in history and culture—?

Systems of thought do not disappear through criticism or discussion, but they collapse at the creation of another system of thought. This happens even when the first was logical, coherent, demonstrable. People *saw* perfectly with the former system. If critics confronted it, they were not able to shake it. The history of the sciences teaches us this important fact: that only a new *creation*, a new method, can have results—and not criticism of the old. Men have to *see* in a different way.

Criticisms of the geocentric cosmogony and other "false" theories of antiquity did not lead to anything, precisely because they were coherent and clear-sighted.

A reform of the methodologies of science and modern culture will not be possible by means of criticism, by showing their insufficiency and contradictions. Reform will come about through the creation of a new method, more ample and more justifiable, by means of which men will be able to see and understand more than by existing methods.

When a science is lost, a host of people can be observed practicing it. Thus, in our day, when the incomprehensibility of symbol is patent, when metaphysical and mystic contemplation is well-nigh impossible, when magic is completely lost—one can see a great many theosophists, pseudo-metaphysicians, mystics, and mystagogues. A country can lose a science or an art, but never those who practice it.

If I should have the choice between a truth and a paradox, I should choose the paradox. Truths change, but a paradox is of such a nature that it remains always full, real, and justified. A truth about a thing expresses consistently one point of view. Paradox, on the contrary, is an insurrection against established or imposed "truths." When a truth is changed, it remains a dead thing—inert, empty, and useless. Paradox, however, being an attitude, never loses its elasticity and vitality. For that reason it has a chance of surviving the dogmas against which it rebels.

Inferior Forms of Mysticism
(from *Fragmentarium*)

What a felicitous formula Philippe de Felice has found for the subtitle of his book on "sacred potions and divine drinks": *Essai sur quelques formes inférieures de la mystique!* The tragic thing about the human condition is this eternal return to "inferior forms of mysticism." When it becomes impossible, or it *seems* impossible, for you to "lose yourself in God," you lose yourself in alcohol, opium, peyote, or a collective hysteria.

"Mysticism" remains, because the instinct of man to lose himself, to surrender himself, is just as organic and powerful as the instinct for self-preservation. One needs to go out of himself, in one way or another. And when love can no longer save you, then alcohol, cocaine, or opium will. The rituals remain the same: isolation from the world (the solitary drinker is a true devotee of alcohol), the consecration of the time and place in which you assimilate yourself to the divine drug, etc. The same, too, is the craving to forget yourself, to lose yourself— in an "Absolute" of a toxic essence.

Gods do not die, humanly speaking. They don't die, but they grow old, they become common, they attain the most terrible forms of decrepitude—at least in the consciousness and experience of men. You no longer believe in Dionysos, but you continue to get intoxicated— and this drunkenness is even more sad, even more vulgar, even more desperate than that of the Dionysiac. Some travelers who have returned from Soviet Russia speak about the "mysticism of the tractor" which has taken the place of Orthodox and sectarian mysticisms. It is not a matter, of course, of the need of man for an "ideal," for faith in a myth, a man, an idea, but the need of man to lose himself. And when you can no longer lose yourself in the Holy Trinity, then you lose yourself in the "mysticism of the tractor"! It seems to be the curse of modern man to slip ever lower and to quench his thirst for losing himself in more and more inferior forms of "mysticism." The Luciferism of modern man does not consist in opposing God to his face (speaking in the broadest terms), but in opposing him through the vulgar imitation of his works. Imitation and counterfeiting—these are the true marks of Luciferism. You set yourself against a religion—but you quickly make another religion, inferior to the first. You renounce the mysticism of a St. Theresa—but you accept the inferior mysticism of tractors and opium; you give, you "sacrifice," in order to lose yourself in the ineffable being of the tractor, to make the cult of the tractor victorious. Or in the case of opium, you yield in order to annihilate yourself as an individual, as a separate and suffering being—to discover another reality, the absolute, that "excellent order" of which Thomas de Quincey speaks.

Man's instincts remain intact—this is the simple truth which the "rationalists" forget. And the longing of man for salvation belongs to the natural order of things. Whatever may happen, whatever change may occur, man wishes, hopes, believes that he is saved, that he has found the central meaning of existence, that he has valorized his life.

The longing for salvation—herein lies the meaning of that strange instinct of man to yield himself, to lose himself. So long as this instinct is satisfied naturally, "mystically," religion knows how to channel the human impulses. However, sometimes it happens that the individual no longer believes, or no longer is allowed to believe, in a transcendent order of reality, in religion. This change, far from freeing man, vulgarizes him, allowing him to fall prey to "inferior mysticisms." When you stop believing in Paradise, you start believing in spiritualism.

A Detail from Parsifal (from *Insula lui Euthanasius*)

In the legend of Parsifal there is a very significant episode. It seems that the Fisher King (*le rois péschéor*) fell ill, and no one could cure him. The malady was a curious one, making him impotent, aged, devoid of all virility. We should remember that this Fisher King—around whom so many hypotheses have been constructed—was, in some Medieval texts, the king of the Grail, or at any rate directly related to the Holy Chalice which, according to legend, Joseph of Arimathea had brought to Europe. There is not space here, nor is it my intention in this article, to pursue the symbolic meaning of the denomination "Fisher King." Suffice it to say that the "fish" symbolizes *renewal, rebirth, immortality*. The chalice of the Holy Grail is confused sometimes with the "rich fisherman" (for instance, in *Joseph de Arimathea* by Robert de Boron). On the other hand, Nordic and Celtic elements have intruded into the Grail legend. And this Celtic tradition speaks of a "salmon of wisdom" which can be brought into relationship with the Grail and the "Fisher King" (A. Nutt, *Studies on the Legend of the Holy Grail*, London, 1888, p. 158).

The illness of the Fisher King brought with it the sterility of all life in the vicinity of the castle where the mysterious sovereign suffered. The rivers no longer flowed in their channels, the trees no longer put forth leaves, the earth was no longer fruitful, the flowers no longer blossomed. The legend says that so cruel was this incomprehensible curse that the birds ceased to mate, and pigeons pined alone among the ruins until they dropped, struck down by death's wing. Even the castle fell to ruin. The walls slowly crumbled as though crushed by an unseen force, the wooden bridges rotted, the stones came loose from the parapet and disintegrated, as if centuries had passed like moments. (In order to illuminate the significance of the detail on which I am commenting, I have used, in this description of the desolation of the country and the illness of the king, episodes from two different texts: the first referring to Sir Gawain, the other to Parsifal. The former is Ms. Bibl. Nat. f. Français 12576, cited by Jesse L. Weston, *From Ritual to Romance*, Cambridge, 1920; the latter is from *Percival*, ed. Hucher, p. 466, cited by Weston, p. 13.)

Knights came continually from all corners of the world, drawn by the fame of the Fisher King. But they were so astonished by the decay of the castle and the mysterious illness of the ruler that they forgot they had come to ask about the fate and location of the Holy Grail— and they approached the king in embarrassment, pitying him and consoling him. After each visit of a knight the king's illness worsened and the whole land became more ravaged. The knights who spent the night in the castle were found dead the following morning.

But lo! Parsifal comes riding toward the castle of the Fisher King, not knowing about the king's illness. In passing, it should be said that Crétien de Troyes in his *Perceval* (a novel left unfinished, as is well known) makes his hero actually a fool. Crétien de Troyes, in order to exalt the divine grace which transforms the knight-errant, endeavors to present him to us as a true *Perceval le simple*, or, as Nutt says, a representation of the Great Fool, a well-known type in world folklore (cf. Eugene Amitchof, *Joachim de Flore et le milieu courtois*, Rome, 1931, pp. 308–09). Parsifal's departure is ridiculous: all the knights laugh when they see how he mounts his horse and when they see him passing with *gaverlos*. Then too, what could be more ludicrous for a knight than the fact that he uses a whip, *une roote*, to drive his mount? When he reaches the royal court Parsifal continues to behave comically and to amuse the bystanders with his uncouth deportment. He is not only uncouth, he is even asinine. Crétien de Troyes tells us that once when Parsifal met a girl, he ran up and kissed her, because he had been told that *la courtoisie* required it. (All episodes are cited in the book by Anitchof, pp. 309 ff.)

Does it not seem that this Parsifal—at least as Chrétien de Troyes understands him—is a wonderful prototype for Don Quixote? There are identical episodes, and psychologically they correspond in all respects. For instance, Parsifal's stupid horse and his ridiculous departure (his mother tries to stop him, *to keep him from making the king's court laugh!*). Also the scene when he embraces the girl. But above all, what seems relevant to us is the stupidity of the two knights. Behind their foolishness and their ridiculousness is the activity of Grace (Parsifal) or the Dream (Quixote). What a pity that Unamuno, who read everything, was not acquainted with Chrétien de Troyes' delightful descriptions of Parsifal! The Knight of the Sad Countenance would have found an admirable comrade in this *Perceval le simple,* indifferent toward all rules of knightly conduct, yet bearing the Grace which was to transform Medieval knighthood into a new type of humanity.

Let us return, however, to the castle of the Fisher King where Parsifal has now arrived. On his first visit he does not prove himself to be a "sent one." He leaves, and then is told that *he has to ask the Fisher King about the Grail.* "Se tu eusses demandé quel'en on faisoit, que li rois ton aiol fust gariz de l'enfermetex qu'il a, et fust reveneu en sa juventé" (*Perceval,* ed. Hucher, p. 966; Weston, *op cit.,* p. 13). Indeed, the second time, when he approaches the Fisher King and *asks him the right question,* the *necessary* question—the king recovers as if by miracle, and he becomes young again. "Le rois péschéor estoit gariz et tot muez de sa nature."

In the other parallel legend of Sir Gawain, once the hero has asked the King about the *Lance* with which the Savior was pierced on the cross (hence a substitute or an auxiliary of the chalice of the Grail), "the waters flowed again thro' their channels, and all the woods were turned to verdure" (Weston, *ibid.,* p. 12). Other versions mention the miraculous restoration of the castle and the regeneration of the whole realm through the simple *question* asked by Parsifal.

A single question sufficed to accomplish the miracle. But Parsifal's question *was awaited.* Because no one asked it—because no knight was so imbued with the madness of the Grail Quest that he ignored all rules of good breeding (not to ask questions of a sick man) in order to learn the secret of the holy chalice—the illness of the king was aggravated and the whole cosmic rhythm of life was affected. It was just a simple question—as were all the others which the other knights before him had uttered—but it was the *right question,* the one question which was awaited, the only one which could fructify. The queries of the others were born of astonishment or courtesy. They did not arise out of an urgent need for knowledge of truth and salvation (because this is what the chalice of the Holy Grail symbolized for the Medieval world: truth and salvation). But Parsifal, who had come to the castle in order to learn about the Grail, asks only *one question:* the right question. And you observe that its utterance enlightens not only Parsifal. Even before he receives a reply as to the whereabouts of the Grail, the correct pronunciation of the right question produces a cosmic regeneration on all planes of reality: the waters flow, the forest trees put forth leaves, fertility descends upon the earth, and the vitality and youth of the king are restored.

This episode from the legend of Parsifal seems to me significant for the entire human condition. Perhaps it is our destiny to refuse the *right question*, the necessary and urgent one, the only question which fructifies and the only one that matters. Instead of asking, in Christian terms, "Where is the way, the truth, and the life?" we wander in a labyrinth of questions and preoccupations which may have a certain charm and even a certain value, but which do not make our spiritual lives fruitful.

This episode from Parsifal illustrates excellently the fact that *even before a satisfactory answer is found*, the "right question" regenerates and fertilizes—not only man's being, but also the whole Cosmos. Nothing reflects more precisely the failure of man who refuses to ask about the meaning of his existence than this picture of the whole of nature suffering in anticipation of a question. It seems to us that we are wandering all alone, one by one, because we refuse to ask, "Where is the way, the truth, and the life?" We believe that our salvation or shipwreck is our concern, and ours alone. It seems to us that our predicament, good or bad, involves no one other than ourselves.

But this is not so. There is a solidarity of men in their spiritual destiny, as well as a solidarity on the lower planes of instincts and economic interests. It is difficult for a man who dwells in the midst of society to save himself—if his fellowmen do not even raise the question of salvation. Even a thinker as profound and original as Origen was not prepared to affirm that all men will be saved together, in a unity (*apokathastasis*), rather than one by one. It is hard to say to what extent Origen was right on this point. But it is certain that universalism remains the ideal of every form of Christian life.

Now, if I have interpreted correctly the *Parsifal* episode, we might say that all nature suffers from man's indifference to the central question. Solidarity, then, would extend not only over the entire human community of which we are a part, but even over the life of the Cosmos, animate or apparently inanimate, around us. *Paideuma* suffers and is tainted together with our insignificant human failure. Wasting our time on futilities and frivolous questions, we kill not only ourselves, as did those unwise knights in the legend of the Fisher King, but we kill also, through a slow and sterile death, a particle of the Cosmos. When man forgets to ask in what direction the source of his salvation lies, the fields wither and the birds become sorrowful and infertile. What a wonderful symbol of the solidarity of man with the whole Cosmos!

Then too, in the light of this episode from *Parsifal*, what a tremendous significance they suddenly acquire—all those who do not hesitate to ask and to wonder about truth and life! The questions which trouble the sleep of those men and the dramas which macerate their souls sustain and nourish an entire people. By means of the passions of these few elect individuals the culture of every nation succeeds and becomes fruitful, and makes a place for itself in history. It is not only that men can live in *health* thanks to the questions asked by those few elect ones who, like Parsifal, suffer for our spiritual sloth, but all nature would run down and become barren for lack of intelligence, generosity, and courage on our part. I like to think, as *Parsifal* gives us to understand, that we would suddenly, over night, become sterile and sick—like all life in the castle of the Fisher King—if there did not exist in every country, in every moment in history, certain persons, steadfast and enlightened, who are *asking the right question.* . . .

Notes about Genius
(from *Fragmentarium*)

"Everything that pertains to a genius is sacred." So Ardengo Soffici begins his volume of notes and journals, *Taccuino di Arno Borghi* (Firenze, 1933). "If Dante or Leopardi had, in an obscure moment of their lives of genius, written anything inept or stupid, their ineptitudes and stupidities would not have been worthless literature—but still Dantesque or Leopardian."

In one of my early books, *Isabel şi apele diavolului* (p. 142), I find the following lines which I am no longer happy to own: "A complete genius does not exist, and the most natural thing for us to do is not to imagine that he does exist; otherwise the admirer reads through a veil of adoration and he lauds the latest scribblings of his idol, while innumerable other good books by other writers remain hidden from him. In a word, the only thing which deserves to be praised is superiority—wherever and in whomever it may be found."

Of course a complete genius does not exist—fortunately, I might add, for the rest of us mortals! Because the most inspiring spectacle for people on the outside is precisely this spontaneous and intermittant mediocrity of geniuses. Only when confronted with ineptitudes and stupidities signed by a genius (and, thank God, they exist in abundance) do you realize what a tremendous distance there is between you, a mediocre man, and a creator. "How?" you ask yourself in astonishment. "Why, I wouldn't have had the gall to write such a platitude or something so inept—and *he*, the 'genius,' conceived it and signed his name to it!" But despite all these mediocre productions, mental weaknesses, and nonsense, he remains a genius while you are just a decent, ordinary man.

When you begin to grasp this fact, you perceive also the enormous distance which separates you from a genius. Only then do you *realize* the mediocrity of your condition, the nothingness of your mentality— you, who believe in intelligence, originality, profundity, coherence, talent, and innumerable other spiritual values. All at once you discover that a genius can be stupid, mediocre, sometimes ridiculous, sometimes banal, and most of the time commonplace! In other words, all those spiritual virtues which you recognize in an incipient stage in yourself, which you believe are maximized and consummated in a genius, are, from this point of view, *worthless*. It is not a *greater* intelligence, a *greater* originality, etc., or all of these combined, that make a genius.

Genius, like sainthood, enjoys an utter autonomy from the ornaments of mental faculties. It is something else entirely—and this "something else" exasperates, saddens, or delights (according to circumstances) other people who are happy and "normal."

Read the "stupidities" of geniuses, their inferior, banal, uninspired pages, and a terrible sense of despair will come over you. *You* would never be able to write that way, you begin to realize. You, as well as I and others, will have to say interesting, original, profound things always; above all you will have to say them beautifully, or at least correctly. You will try always to be at least *up to par*, if not to succeed in outdoing yourself.

All these things you will do, not because you made up the rules. You do them because all people, all books teach you this: to perfect yourself, never to write foolish things, to be continually conceiving something new, profound, and original.

How do you keep from despairing and being overwhelmed by sadness when you observe that these virtues do not carry you to the heights? You, who have loved Dostoevsky's profundity and have believed that profundity is a sign of genius—have you not shuddered while reading page after page of platitudes and superstitions in his *Journal of a Writer?* In other words, a "profound" genius can be banal and commonplace—without for a moment ceasing to be a genius. A writer of genius like Balzac can write a confused, mediocre, uninteresting piece. A Leopardi can comment on ancient writings as pedantically as a German professor. Baudelaire, genius of paradox and melancholia, can write a reflection which sounds like paragraphs found in textbooks on ethics the world over: "There is given to all men, of all times, two postulates, the one about God, the other about Satan" (*Mon coeur mis à nu*).

Rudolf Otto, speaking about the divine presence, uses the expression, "that which is wholly Other" (*ganze anderes*). The genius, with respect to the human condition, is "wholly other." That is why the fragments which are uninspired, lifeless, and mediocre in the work of a great creator help us to understand better the phenomenon of genius. Because such fragments draw our attention to the paradox of the genius: on the one hand he is "something else entirely," while on the other hand he is just like everyone else (mediocre, inconsistent, commonplace, etc.). This paradox reminds us of the situation of the saint in the world: although he no longer participates in the human condition, the saint continues to remain among men and is *like* them. He eats, sleeps, walks, and talks exactly as other men do. He is intelligent or stupid, talented or untalented, learned or ignorant, handsome or old—precisely like the rest of humankind—although the state of sainthood transcends and annuls all these characteristics of the human condition. The saint *is* and *is not* a man—at one and the same time. The intermittant mediocrity of the genius corresponds to this paradox of the saint. A genius from time to time shows himself to us as "mediocre" or "inferior," just as a saint remains intelligent or stupid.

Moreover, this "rupture of plane" is found in every religious act. Through the magic of ritual, Prajapati, the god of All, is identified with the bricks of the Vedic altar. *Esse* coincides with *non-esse*, the Universe with a fragment, the Spirit with an object. The same paradoxical formula sums up almost the majority of religious acts: the transcendent coincides with the immanent, the absolute with the relative, *esse* with *non-esse*.

In our case, *genius* coincides with *non-genius*, the mediocre, and the insignificant. Meditate on these coincidences; you will find here the religious valorization of genius.

A Great Man
(from *Oceanografie*)

Several years ago I lived for a goodly space of time in proximity to a great man. He was truly a great man: mature, creative, original, renowned. People spoke of him on three continents. His scientific work was fully accepted and prized everywhere. He had almost ceased to encounter the resistence and controversy which characterize a living man.

And this great man received daily letters or petitions from all over the world which he read with much enjoyment. Only there was one thing that embarrassed him: people were always speaking about "wasting his time" and appealing to his "kindness," etc. Now, this great and famous man would spend a good share of the day reading detective novels, dozing in his easy chair, or bickering with his wife. I witnessed once a very impressive scene. An American woman, passing through the area, wished to see him and talk with him. I was present. The good woman stayed only about ten minutes during which time she listened reverently to everything the master said. She kept excusing herself for taking up his precious time. She believed—as we all believed—that the master spent all his time reading, writing, or meditating. She left begging a thousand pardons. I escorted her to the door. She had made a forty-day journey to spend ten minutes in conversation with her spiritual master. When I came back to the room, I found him scratching his leg with great satisfaction. He said to me, "What interesting people those Americans are!" Then he returned to his novel—one by Edgard Wallace, inevitably. That evening he went to the movies.

I say all this without irony. That man was and is truly great. Nevertheless, we must not exaggerate: we must not think that such men are non-material, that a genius does not have need of the most ordinary pleasures and the most banal distractions. That is why I have always addressed the great men I have known with some measure of impertinence. I imagine that the time I take from them is not destined for their works of genius but, perhaps, for scratching their leg . . .

And yet, why is it that such great men prefer to scratch themselves or read Edgard Wallace instead of prolonging their conversations with us—young men who come to them regarding them as masters? It's an everyday sort of tragedy, I realize. Perhaps they get tired of having always to be *great*. Perhaps they long for a little humanity, for a little comfortable mediocrity. Geniuses have need of warmth and platitudes more than do we who live in warmth and platitudes all the time.

Nevertheless, let us admit, it is sad. It is rather sad to spend only five minutes in conversation with the man you admire, with whom you get along so well, who might be so helpful to you—and to see, the moment you close the door, an ordinary chap, "a friend," coming to visit the master, in order to jabber stupidities till evening.

The Detective Novel
(from *Oceanografie*)

I am a passionate and inveterate investigator of the psychology of the reading public, both in Romania and elsewhere, and it seems to me that nothing reveals more fully that which an individual *wants to be* than the books he seeks out and reads. And of course, what one wishes to be is more obvious than what he is.

It is curious, therefore, to find a disinterest on the part of a "certain public" for detective novels. A summary inquiry at the bookstore and newsstands will convince you, if you need convincing, that Pittigrilli and Dekobra sell better than Edgard Wallace. The same is true in Italy and France, where the literature of romantic love has always been more appreciated than adventure and crime stories. In our country, the detective novel is savored in the lower division of lycée and in certain milieux of clerks (for instance, those employed by banks). In the upper division, lycée students discover the romantic novel, on which they will dwell for the rest of their lives (I do not speak of the elite). The strata who remain beneath the lycée level feed on serial novels which are nothing, in reality, but an inferior and impure form of the romantic novel.

These facts ought to give us pause. The contempt of the elite for the detective novel is, indeed, a rather serious detail. Because a detective novel, especially when it is written by a good author such as Edgar Wallace, Sapper, or Leroux, is indisputably preferable to a sentimental love story of the sort that incites the enthusiasm of the many. A detective novel is always a stimulating, invigorating, and pure form of reading. Above all, pure: there all the criminals end up being caught, the scoundrels commit suicide, and the detectives get engaged. It is the only species of novel in which moralism does not annoy you, because it is a novel both fantastic and logical—and perhaps you have observed that in the games (illusions) of your mad (that is, perfectly logical) fancies, there exists a paradisically pure moralism. When someone daydreams, he never imagines himself a criminal, a thief, or a satyr—but rather a hero, a benefactor, a detective, a Maecenas. The day dream—when you're walking along the street, when you're resting and smoking a cigarette—is a moment of logic and purity, and must not be confused with the sexual and neurotic miseries of which the Vienna School makes such a case.

The small success which the detective novel enjoys among Romanian readers shows something else: it shows a paucity of serious-mindedness. A man who really believes in something, who is completely absorbed in his work, who is preoccupied all day long with a serious, responsible problem, is unable to read the sort of thing found in the average novel: a sentimental, vulgar, universally romantic literature. He has need of a diversion which is pure, gratuitous, something as frivolous and charming as a conversation between two silly girls. He cannot read a novel with third-rate psychology, with vulgar heroes (in the sense that they *want* to appear to be heroes, when in fact they are nothing but mannequins), with a ridiculous problematics (is the woman to blame?), with poetry and pointless "analyses." This vulgar literature can satisfy a seamstress, a law student, an office clerk—all individuals who work, it is true, but who do not work intensively, stubbornly, with responsibilities and in hope of a great victory; they work only to keep from dying of hunger, and their ideal is to play the truant as much as possible—even if they should be bored to death for hours, doing nothing.

Of course, for such readers, the novel of sentimental love affords all delights: it flatters their taste and effort (that minimum effort which, when past, deceives the reader concerning his intellectual powers—and rewards the author with the title of genius).

But a man who works as he ought, will go in his free hours to a movie or read a detective novel. He asks for neither scholarship nor drama, neither psychological analysis nor poetry. All he asks is that it be a story well told, which will relax him and hold his attention to the end. I have known at least a half-dozen important men, savants of world renown, who read a detective novel almost daily, at the conclusion of their work. And the more simply and directly it is written, the more they savor it. The celebrated British philosopher, McTaggart, has read so many detective stories that he has become an authority on them at Cambridge. He remembers perfectly all the details of the crimes, all the tricks of the detectives, all the intricacies of the dramas. And this is a man who, for his whole lifetime, has studied Hegel's logic—one of the most lucid thinkers of our era.

The reason for the success of the detective novel among Anglo-Saxons is something worth analysing. In England this genre has been perfected to such an extent that true masterpieces sometimes appear. The novel becomes a pure narrative, without excess baggage and without stylistics; with marvelous characters, alive and coherent; with an intrigue unveiled by the hand of a master. Instead of being a tale of heroes and dragons, it is a story of detectives and criminals. But it is the same old struggle between good and evil—that eternal fountain of the fantastic. It is the same long series of adventure—"trials"—from the story of Amor and Psyche, *The Golden Ass*, and *Don Quixote*. After having passed through a sad series of transformations (the post-knightly novel, the mystery novel, the serial novel—exaggerated, prolix, insipid, artificial—the Far-West adventure story, the historical novel, the spiritualistic novel)—behold how the adventure novel has returned again to its original mission: that of narrating the extraordinary and the unexpected without any pretention of moving or amusing the reader other than by means of the plot alone. Here we find ourselves confronted by pure narratives which relax and delight—and the delight is all the greater in that you can forget them once you have laid the book aside.

Now, the preference of Anglo-Saxons for this kind of literature is easily understood. Those men work hard and long and with an ideal. Life for them, if not always a struggle, is at least something which has a meaning and system; something for which the individual is responsible. When such men wish, therefore, to amuse themselves, they do not take a second-rate book or a filthy one. At most, their wives might read such trash. They prefer detective novels—pure, absorbing, and stimulating. They want to dream, to forget their work, their problems, and the reckoning they shall have to give some day. A reader of detective stories is an individual with a moral sense, almost a Puritan.

Thus, the fact that the Romanian public does not patronize detective novels worries me. It is evidence of intellectual sloth, apathy, femininity. I understand why only lycée students read detective novels: it is because they are the only group of persons who have to answer for themselves every day; only they work, or have to work, regularly; only at their age does the dream transcend any normal activity. But I'm afraid to guess why the larger public prefers Pittigrilli and Dekobra to Edgard Wallace.—Because it might be necessary to say that the public at large is lazy, disorganized, devoid of purpose, irresponsible, vacuous and poor in spirit. As for the literature it reads—which it does not read for amusement but because it is *good literature*—it fills the emptiness of their souls with third-rate psychology, idiotic ideas, futile vices, false ideologies, bad poetry, and quack medical theories. Instead of distracting themselves for two hours with a detective story, as the English do, they read four hours and discuss for forty a mediocre book which they take, then, as a guide to both life and art. If they could just forget what they read! But only excellent books and utterly stupid ones are forgotten; a mediocre one, never.

About a Certain "Sacrifice"
(from *Fragmentarium*)

Convinced that "sacrifice is the law of expression" and that "to sacrifice is to live," Eugenio d'Ors every New Year's Eve burns a freshly written page. "One page, a page well-filled, written with care, love, and long hard labor is immolated in a holocaust . . . Out of a pile of papers from a manuscript, one is kindled and set ablaze; the flames and smoke envelop each other in the course of drifting to the window . . ."

What moves me about this testimony is the ceremonial and the grave melancholy of the "sacrifice." This act, of minor consequence in itself, is accorded a religious significance. I should not hesitate to believe that after burning this page at the beginning of a new year Eugenio d'Ors feels stronger, richer, and more reconciled with his own versatility. It is a sacrifice made according to all the canons of religion and the Mediterranean. The victim is not lacking, but neither is there a lack of proportion—the sense of limits and norms.

How many absurd "sacrifices" do we all make, sacrificing to oblivion and sleep so many intentions, so many thoughts, so much generosity! I am not thinking now of "big things"—for instance, our life, which we almost never perfect; or our "youth," which we do not burn down to its last spark but consume gradually, sacrificing to vanity the most pathetic hours of love, despair, contemplation, or melancholia.

I am thinking, rather, of something more modest: of certain thoughts which we do not carry to their conclusion, of certain poems which we do not write. There are days when—how shall I put it?—when I feel the heavens open above me, so clearly that insights into the meaning of the world and of man are shown to me. And yet, those days are consumed like any others. They do not preserve, they do not *define* anything for me or for others. At such times I have a sensation of my plentitude and the certainty that I shall never be in doubt about what I have conquered and what I have unraveled then. But all this passes; it is consumed. I am left with a very few "thoughts"—and very vague ones at that. I have "sacrificed" so many blessed hours to vanity. Instead of *defining*, of specifying, of recording nuances, details, I content myself with a few words, hastly jotted on a notebook leaf—words which in that moment of plentitude seemed sufficient for me to "preserve" the thought, but which, in reality, are inadequate even to recall it to my mind.

Of course, a thought carried through to its conclusion, an analogy or a correspondence discovered, a more or less original "intuition"—all these are not "lost" completely. We rediscover them, sometimes with surprise, after a week, a year, in a conversation, in a reading, in a landscape. But the whole problem is not to "preserve" a thought approximately, but to carry it farther and formulate it more rigorously. Yet, this enlargement and formulation of a thought is not done in neutral hours—but precisely in those plenary intervals when, in the words of the poet Camil Petrescu, "one sees ideas." And the truth is that it is these moments of grace, above all, that we "sacrifice." But this "sacrifice" in no way resembles Eugenio d'Ors's ceremonial. It has no significance. It is involuntary and, in the majority of instances, unconscious.

How many great writers in the world have truly worked in their hours of "Grace"? Aside from a few poets—a Shelley, for instance—the majority of writers have written by fits and starts. Some when they needed money, others when asked by a king or a publisher, and still others under the impulse of ambition, jealousy, or nerves. Nietzsche wrote quite frequently while "inspired"—but that pathetic and confused "inspiration" is something entirely different from the calm, full state of "understanding." I am not saying that their production—provoked by hunger, ambition, need, or neurasthenia—is not worthy of the genius and talent of these great writers. I believe, however, that an enormous number of brilliant pages have been "sacrificed" to nothingness; that a great many books which could have been written have never even been begun. I believe, in a word, that every great writer in the world has "sacrificed" at least one inspired fragment to oblivion—by refusing to formulate a thought or record a poem given in an hour of plentitude.

There is no shame in admitting that writers construct their works haphazardly—depending on the time, the publisher, the public, or caprice. Almost the whole of our literary output (essays, novels, and the like) is written *au hazard*. This does not in any degree diminish its ultimate merits. But it makes us stop and think about the *unwritten* books of great authors.

When, a few years ago, Giovanni Papini confessed in a pathetic letter to me that "I have not written a hundredth part of what I have to say," I believed it was an exaggeration. With time, however, I have begun to see the truth in what he said. I did not write the most beautiful book I could have written at twenty, and it is very probable that I shall not write it at thirty. So it happens with everyone: we "sacrifice" the best that is in us, whether of art or of thought—we sacrifice continually to oblivion. And the only melancholia which this sacrifice gives you is that it has no meaning, it enriches no one, it does not make anything whole or complete. You "sacrifice" because you are not "present" in that hour or those hundreds of hours so full and rich, or else because you think you will always retain the plenitude of that time. You realize what you could have done only after you have passed a certain experience or a certain age. And you are the only one who is aware of that thing you failed to do. Others who observe you exteriorly find it very hard to understand that your work—so "great" and so "vast"— is only an ill-formed fragment of what you could have done. Our own shipwreck is difficult for others to discern. And perhaps this is one of the deepest roots of despair . . .

What a fascinating thing it would be if all of us were to "sacrifice" a written page on New Year's Eve—in order to be able to write all the beautiful and otherwise unknown pages which we sacrifice to the many vanities of the year . . .

Notes

The *Oceanographic Fragments* of Part IV were first published as follows:

"About Miracle and Events," *Oceanografie* (Bucharest, 1934), first appeared in *Vremea*, vol. 7, no. 342 (1934), 342, p. 7.

"Concerning the 'Unseen God' and other Fragments" first appeared in *Soliloquies* (1932).

"Inferior Forms of Mysticism," from *Fragmentarium* (Bucharest, 1939) was first published in *Vremea* 10 (1937), 491, p. 11.

"A Detail from Parsifal," from *Insula lui Euthanasius* (Bucharest, 1943), was originally published in *Revista Fundațiilor Regale* VI (1938), 2, pp. 422–26.

"Notes About Genius" from *Fragmentarium* first appeared in *Vremea* 10 (1937), 511, p. 4.

"The Detective Novel," from *Oceanografie*, was first published in *Vremea* 5 (1932) 251, p. 7.

"About a Certain 'Sacrifice' " was first published in *Vremea* 10 (1937), 513, p. 9.

Contributors

Douglas Allen, Associate Professor of Philosophy at the University of Maine, Orono, holds the M.A. and Ph.D. degrees from Vanderbilt University. He has also studied at Yale and Benares Hindu Universities, and has taught at Southern Illinois, Vanderbilt, and Central Connecticut Universities. In addition to scholarly articles, he has published *Structure and Creativity in Religion: Hermeneutics in Mircea Eliade's Phenomenology and New Directions* (Mouton, 1977) and *Mircea Eliade's Phenomenology of Religion* (Payot, 1978). With Dennis Doeing, he co-edited *Mircea Eliade: An Annotated Bibliography* (Garland, 1980).

Seymour Cain studied philosophy and religion at the University of Chicago, where he received his Ph.D. in the history of religions in 1956. He has taught philosophy and religion at the University of Chicago, Tri-College University, Western Michigan University, Kalamazoo College, and Indiana University of Pennsylvania. He was senior editor for religion and philosophy at the *Encyclopaedia Britannica* 1967–73, and received a National Endowment for the Humanities Fellowship 1979–80 for a scholarly study on Mircea Eliade. Among his published works are *Gabriel Marcel* (1963, 1979), *Religion and Theology* (1961), and *Imaginative Literature* (2 volumes, 1961, 1962). Among numerous articles and reviews on the work of Mircea Eliade, his periodical writings also include short fiction, poetry, reportage, and other scholarly essays.

Matei Calinescu is Professor of Comparative Literature and West European Studies at Indiana University. His latest book is *Faces of Modernity: Avant-Garde, Decadence, Kitsch* (Bloomington and London: Indiana University Press, 1977). He is currently working on a study of postmodernism and on a book about Mircea Eliade's fiction.

Norman J. Girardot, Associate Professor and Chairman of the Religion Studies Department at Lehigh University, did his graduate work in the history of religions under Mircea Eliade at the University of Chicago. While at Chicago, he worked as Professor Eliade's secretary for several years and also served as the editorial assistant for the journal, *History of Religions.* He is the author of articles in Chinese religion and mythology, comparative folklore, and methodology in the history of religions. He is also the author of the forthcoming *Myth and Meaning in Early Taoism* (University of California Press, 1982) and has edited, or co-edited, several books and symposia. In 1978 he was the organizer and chairman of a conference devoted to the scholarly and literary work of Mircea Eliade held at the University of Notre Dame.

Adrian Marino, resident of Cluj, Romania, is a Doctor of Literature and docent of the University of Bucharest and a member of the Romanian Writers Union. Considered one of the leading literary critics of Romania, he is the author of eleven books, mostly on literary theory and methodology of literary criticism. Most recently his volume on Eliade's hermeneutics appeared in French translation (*L'herméneutique de Mircea Eliade,* Gallimard, 1981). Between 1973 and 1980 he was director of the predominantly French language journal, *Cahiers roumains d'études littéraires.*

Mac Linscott Ricketts, Professor and Chairman of the Department of Philosophy and of Religion at Louisburg College in North Carolina, studied the history of religions under Mircea Eliade at the University of Chicago, from which he has the M.A. and Ph.D. degrees. He has also taught at Millikin and Duke Universities. The author of several articles on the thought of Mircea Eliade, he is co-translator, with Mary Park Stevenson, of Eliade's novel, *The Forbidden Forest* (University of Notre Dame Press, 1978) and translator of Eliade's *Autobiography, Volume I: 1907–1937. Journey East, Journey West* (Harper & Row, 1981). He is the recipient of a Fulbright research grant for 1981, for study in Romania of Eliade's early writings.

Eugen Simion received his Ph.D. from the University of Bucharest and taught at the Sorbonne from 1970 to 1973. He is currently a professor of the history of Romanian literature at the University of Bucharest. A recipient of several awards from the Romanian Academy and the Romanian Writers' Union, Prof. Simion has published widely on modern Romanian literature including works on Eminescu, Lovinescu, and Eliade.

Index

Accident, 2, 4
Accompaniment, and implication, 187
Aesthetics, 56–63
Alchemy, 113–14
Alchimia Asiatică, 115
Alienation of modern man, 10
Altizer, Thomas J. J., 70, 77, 90
Analysis, 36, 39, 50
Animals, man's friendship with, 11–13
Apocalips, 106, 122
Aquatic symbolism, 35, 42
Archaic-religious universe,
  hermeneutics, 20
Archetypes, 39–40, 45, 54, 136
  in literature, 57–58, 60–61
Aristotle, 95–96, 99
Artistic symbols, 57
Authoritarian bias, in philosophy, 157
Autobiographical writings, Eliade's,
  87–100, 141
  "Autobiographical Fragment," 6,
    98, 100, 113–27, 140
"Aventura spirituală," 123

Bachelard, Gaston, 94, 141, 147–48
Balzac, Honoré de, 59, 135, 197
Barthes, Roland, 23
Baudelaire, Charles, 197
Bednarski, Jules, 77
Birth and Rebirth, 32
Blaga, Lucian, 117
Bodkin, Maud, 59
Bronowski, Jacob, 98, 139

Caiete de Dor, 104
Călinescu, Gheorghe, 118
Calinescu, Matei, 87, 100
Causes, and implications, 187
Chamanisme, Le, see Shamanism
Christianity

miracles, 180
  symbolism, 49
Chute dans l'Histoire, La, 124
Cinematography, 186
Civilization, 21
Collective unconscious, 39
Comarnescu, Petru, 126
Comentarii la legenda Meșterului
  Manole, 58, 122–23
Comparativism, 47
Coomaraswamy, Ananda K., 57
Cosmologie și alchimie babiloniană, 115
Cosmos and History, 106
  see also Myth of the Eternal Return, The
  Creative hermeneutics, 3
Crétien de Troyes, 192–193
Criticism, and reform, 188
Culture, 8–9, 21

Death, mythology of, 152–53
Demythologization, 156
Depth psychology, 47
Detective novels, 201–4
Dialectic of the sacred, 78–79
Dilthey, Wilhelm, 3–4
Documents, in hermeneutics, 31, 35–36,
  43–44, 48
Domnișoara Christina, 123
Don Quixote, 192–93
dos Passos, John, 134
Dostoyevsky, Fyodor, 197
Dragnea, Radu, 126
Durand, Gilbert, 40, 132

Eleusis, mysteries of, 27
Empirical universal, 73
Ensayos luso-romenos, 122
Essence, as source of reality, 2–4
Ethnology, 98, 114–16
Etymon, 45

Event, miracle and, 181–83
Evola, J. 57
Exegesis, 37, 57
Exile, theme of, 150–51
Experience, 2–5, 8–9, 12–13, 72

"Fact, The" (from *Fragmentarium*), 82–83
Fall into History, 124
Fantastic literature, 136, 139, 142, 147–50
Faulkner, William, 134
Felice, Philippe de, 189
Fictional works, Eliade's, 1–2, 7–9, 12,
  87, 89–96, 100, 119–27
  myth as a source of, 131–37
  reconciliation with scientific and
    philosophical work, 113, 121, 123,
    133, 139
  short fiction, 138–58
  see also names of specific works
Flight symbolism, 71
Folklore, 61, 98, 114–18
  as instrument of knowledge, 50
Folk-religious universe, hermeneutics, 20
Forbidden Forest, The (*Noaptea de
  Sânziene*), 91–92, 100, 104–11, 124, 133,
  135, 137, 140, 146–47
Forgotten meanings, 25
Foucault, Michael, 25
Fragmentarium
  "About a Certain 'Sacrifice,' " 205–7
  "The Fact," 82–83
  "Inferior Forms of Mysticism," 189–90
  "Notes about Genius,"
    196–98
Fragments d'un journal, 47, 87–88, 91–92,
  98, 104, 131, 133–34, 138
Frazer, James George, 93
Free variation, 73–74
Freud, Sigmund, 156
Frye, Northrop, 2, 99

Gardner, John, 12
Gaudeamus, 121, 124
Geertz, Clifford, 5
Genius, 196–98, 200
Gide, André, 118, 134
God, 181–84
Goethe, Johann Wolfgang von, 3–6, 59,
  62, 92–93, 99, 141
"Good-bye!," 9, 162–78
Gothic fiction, 142
Grace, 185
Grass, Günter, 135
Greene, Graham, 135

Hermeneutical archeology, 25, 53
Hermeneutical imagination, 51, 55

Hermeneutic circle, 32, 34, 63
Hermeneutics, 6, 19–63
  and aesthetics and literary criticism,
    56–63
  analysis and synthesis, 36–37, 55
  archetypes, 39–40
  barriers, 24–25
  comparativism, 47
  creative, 3
  documents, 35
  global, universal, 22
  and history, 55–56
  intuition, 34–35, 45
  and meaning, 23–27
  meanings of, 21
  methodology, 30–56
  part-whole relation, 49–50
  past-present relation, 52–55
  primordial origin, 27
  of the sacred, 20
  sacred and profane meanings, 37–38
  schematicization and typology, 46–48
  of suspicion, 156–57
  symbol, 40–46
  totalization, 48, 50–52
  of trust, 12, 156
  understanding as the goal of, 28–30
  validity of, 28, 33
Hierophanies, 20, 27, 32–33, 44, 54, 78, 124
*Histoire des croyances et des idées
  religieuses*, 21, 25
History and historiography, 3, 6, 8–9
  intervention in hermeneutical
    process, 55–56
History of religions, 4–6, 9, 13, 55,
  96–98, 116, 121–22
  fragmenting, 50
  generalizations, 51–52
  objectivity, 28, 35–36
  synthesis, 37
History of Religious Ideas, 4, 97, 111
Homoligization, 47–48, 54–55
  in art and literature, 62
Hooligans, The, see Huliganii
"How I Found the Philosopher's
  Stone," 119, 124
Huliganii, 122, 124–25, 142, 147
Husserl, Edmund, 73, 77

Idealism, 3
Ideal religious structure, 76, 79
Ideological meanings, 29
Ierunca, Virgil, 104
Images et symboles, 124
Imagination, 2–3, 6, 10, 12, 139, 151
  hermeneutical, 51, 55
  literary, 89

in scholarly and scientific work, 89, 97–99
Implication
and accompaniment, 187
and causes, 187
Incarnation, 184–185
Indian art and architecture, 57, 62
Indian studies and novels, Eliade's, 114–15, 117, 121–22, 141–42
Induction, 74–78
Initiation trials, 151
Insula lui Euthanasius
"Detail from Parsifal," 191–95
Interpretation, 6–9, 25–28, 32, 34, 52–53, 55, 57
archetypes, 39
symbol, 40, 43
theme of, in *Mântuleasa Street*, 156
totalization, 50–51
Întoarcerea din Rai (Return from Paradise), 121, 124, 126, 142, 147
Intuition, 34–35, 45, 63
in phenomenological method, 72–73, 77
Ionescu, Nae, 125
"Iphigenia," 123
Isabel și apele diavolului, 105, 121–22, 124, 141, 196

"Journey of the Five Junebugs in the Land of the Red Ants, The," 119
Joyce, James, 95, 134
Jung, C. G., 39
Junger, Ernst, 88

Kafka, Franz, 95

Labyrinthe, Le, 123
Langer, Susanne K., 57
Language
modern, symbolic capacity, 43
world as, 7, 22
Leopardi, Giacomo, 197
Leví-Strauss, Claude, 4, 136
Literary destiny, 125
"Literary Imagination and Religious Structure," 88
Literature, 12
creation, 6–8, 12–13, 89, 99, 123
criticism, 56–63, 89, 95, 97
detective novels, 201–4
and myths, 131–37, 148, 152
as redeeming force, 136
Love, 185
Lumina ce se stinge, 108, 121, 127, 134

McTaggart, John, 202–3

Mademoiselle Christina, 142
Maitreyi, 87, 108, 115, 124–25, 127, 141–42
Mandragore, La, 122
Mantuleasa Street, see Pe strada Mântuleasa
Marcel, Gabriel, 100
Marriage in Heaven, see Nunta în Cer
Marx, Karl, 156
Meaning, 4, 6–9, 12
archetypal, 39–40
degrading of, 24–25
deposit of meanings in spiritual life of humanity, 22
and documents, 36
key idea of, 23–27
in modern life, 10
ontological principle of, 27
penetration of, 25
phenomenological insight, 73, 78
sacred and profane, 37–38
signification, 61
simultaneity of meanings, 24
symbol, 41–43
system of, 44–46
"Memoirs of the Lead Soldier, The," 119–21
"Memories of an Outing," 119
"Men and Stones," 122–23
Mephistopheles and the Androgyne, 43
Merleau-Ponty, Maurice, 5, 76–77
Method of invariance, 73
Methodology, 4–6, 19–21, 30–56
phenomenological method, 70–79
Miorita, 40
Miracle, 181–83
unrecognizability of, 124, 139–40, 143, 145–46, 182
Mitolugiile morții, 122–23
Model, 46–47
Morphological method, Goethean, 3–4
Music, 120
Mysticism, inferior forms of, 189–90
Myth and Reality, 38, 58
Mythic novel, 132, 137
Myth maker, 89–90
Myth of the Eternal Return, The, 122, 124, 147, 157
Myths and mythology, 4, 8–9, 13, 21–22, 27, 38, 54, 94
and art and literature, 57–58, 60–61, 96, 131–37, 148, 152
camouflage of, 25
exemplarity of, 158
plurality of interpretations, 26
and political power, 153, 155
as sacred event, 132
and short story, 148
and symbolic system, 45

New Criticism, 23–24, 42, 59–61
Nietzsche, Friedrich, 156, 206
"Nights at Serampore," 138, 142
Noaptea de Sânziene, see Forbidden Forest, The
No Souvenirs, 87–88, 139, 148
   see also Fragments d'un journal
Nostalgie du paradis, La, 124
Novel of the Nearsighted Adolescent, The,
   120–21
Novels, Eliade's, *see* Fictional works
Nuit bengali, La, see Maitreyi
Nunta în Cer (Marriage in Heaven),
   124–25, 145–46

"Oameni şi pietre," *see* "Men and Stones"
Oceanografie, 134
   "About Miracle and Event," 181–83
   "The Detective Novel," 201–4
   "A Great Man," 199–200
Oral literature, 61, 96–97
Oriental studies, 47, 114–18
Origen, 28, 194
Origins, and roots, 187
Ors, Eugenio d', 205
Os Romenos, Latinos de Oriente, 122
Otto, Rudolf, 198

Papini, Giovanni, 207
Paradox, 2, 188
Parsifal, a detail from the legend of,
   191–95
Part-whole relation, 49–50
Past-present relation, 52–55, 62
Patterns, 46–47, 98
Patterns in Comparative Religion (Traité
   d'histoire des Religions), 21, 35, 46, 52,
   90, 106, 116, 122–24, 140
Pe strada Mântuleasa, 137, 148, 153–58
Petrescu, Camil, 206
Petru şi Pavel, 121, 124
Pettazoni, Rafaele, 93
Phenomenological method, 70–79
Phenomenology, 4–5
Philological sciences, 36
Philosophical works, Eliade's, 113–17, 122
Platonism, 47
Plutarch, 22
Poetics, Aristotle's, 95–96
"Portugese Journal," 122
Prajapati, 198
Primal meaning, 39
Prometheus, 48
Primordial spiritual experience, 26–29
Profane, 37, 78, 156–57
   see also Sacred-profane dichotomy
Progress, idea of, 186
Propp, v. 4

Psychoanalysis, 135
Psychocriticism, 59
Psychologism, in fiction, 134

Rationalism, 5
Realism, 3
Reality, 2–5, 94–95
Reason, 3
Reductionism, 44, 46, 51, 156
Regressive deduction, 54
Religion, 4, 8–9, 12–13, 78
   central conception, 45
   unity of religions, 184
Religions, history of, *see* History of
   religions
Religious behavior, 29
Religious experience, phenomenological
   approach to, 72–78
Religious meanings, 24
Religious symbolism, 43
Repetition, and meaning, 27
Return from Paradise, The, see Întoarcerea
   din Rai
Revelation, 33
Ricardou, Jean, 135
Ricoeur, Paul, 4–5, 8, 35, 43, 156
Rite and ritual, 8, 45
Rites and Symbols of Initiation, 32
Robbins, Tom, 10
Rocquet, Claude-Henri, 88, 96
Romanian folklore, 116–18
Romanticism, 3
Roots, and origins, 187

Sacralization, 37–38, 78
Sacred, the, 2, 38, 78–79, 143
   camouflage of, 124, 139–40
   hermeneutics of, 20
   and symbol, 41
   unrecognizability of, 9
Sacred and the Profane, The, 37
Sacred event, 132–33
Sacred meanings, 37
Sacred-profane dichotomy, 78–79, 132, 139
   Sacred space, 34
"Sacrifice," of intentions and thoughts,
   205–7
Saints, 198
Salvation, man's longing for, 190
Şantier, see Work in Progress
Şarpele (The Snake), 100, 108, 123–25, 133,
   140, 143–45, 147
Sartre, Jean-Paul, 135–36
Schematicization, 46–48
Scholem, Gershom, 99
Scientific works, Eliade's, 113–15
"Secret of Dr. Honigberger, The" ("Secretul

doctorului Honigberger''), 123, 133, 138, 142
Secularization (desacralization), 9–10, 37–38
  degradation of meaning, 24–25
Sense, 23
Sewell, Elizabeth, 12
Shamanism (Le chamanisme), 98, 105–6, 116, 124
Short stories, Eliade's, *see* Fictional works
Signification, 23–24
  in literature, 61
Simultaneous reading, 47–48, 62
Snake, The, see Şarpele
Snake, symbolism, 72–74, 77, 123, 140
Soffici, Ardengo, 196
Soliloquii, 123, 140
  fragments from 184–88
Solovyov, Vladimir, 149–50
Spaltmann, Gunther, 91–92
Spiritual sense, 23
Spitzer, Leo, 33, 45
Structuralism, 3–5, 46, 59, 135
Suspicion, 156–57
Symbol, 35, 40–46
  in art and literature, 57–58, 60
  camouflage of, 25
  history, 56
  phenomenological approach to, 71–74, 77
  totalization, 48–49
  world as, 7
Symbolic anthropology, 42
"Symbolisms of Ascension and 'Waking Dreams,' " 71
Synthesis, 36–37, 39, 50, 55

Tantrism, 125
Techniques du Yoga, 32
Thought, systems of, 187–88
"Ţigănci, La," *see* "With the Gypsy Girls"
Time, mystery of, 124

Tolerance, 157–58
Tomashevsky, Boris, 149
Total hermeneutics, 51–52
Totalization, 48, 50–52
  literature, 58–60
Tournier, Michel, 132
Traditional sense, 23
Traité d'histoire des Religions, see Patterns in Comparative Religion
Transcendent in History, unrecognizability of, 124
Trust, 156
Truth, 2, 186
  and paradox, 188
"1241," 122
"Twelve Thousand Head of Cattle," 109
Two loves, motif of, 124
Two Tales of the Occult, 138
Typology, 46–48

Understanding, 28–30, 34, 55, 62–63
  archetypes, 39
  symbols, 43
  and totalization, 51
Universe of meaning, 45

Viaţa Nouă, 122, 125
Vierne, Simone, 132
Virtue, 186

Wallace, Edgar, 201
Wilder, Thornton, 134
"With the Gypsy Girls" ("La ţigănci"), 92–93, 95, 133, 137–38, 148, 150–53
Work in Progress (Şantier), 87, 141
World, 7
  as language, 22

Yoga, 47
Yoga, Le, immortalité et liberté, 32, 98, 106, 109, 116–17, 123, 147

Zalmoxis, 51, 115